# Contradictions of Control

**Critical Social Thought**

Series editor: Michael W. Apple
Professor of Curriculum and Instruction and of Educational Policy
Studies, University of Wisconsin-Madison

*Already published*

*Critical Social Psychology* Philip Wexler
*Reading, Writing and Resistance* Robert B. Everhart
*Arguing for Socialism* Andrew Levine
*Between Two Worlds* Lois Weis
*Culture Wars* Ira Shar
*Power and the Promise of School Reform* William J. Reese
*Becoming Clerical Workers* Linda Valli
*Racial Formation in the United States* Michael Omi and Howard
Winant
*The Politics of Hope* Bernard P. Dauenhauer
*The Common Good* Marcus G. Raskin

# Contradictions of Control

School structure and school knowledge

# Linda M. McNeil

**Routledge & Kegan Paul**

New York and London

*First published in 1986 by*

*Routledge & Kegan Paul Inc.*
*in association with Methuen Inc.*
*29 West 35th Street, New York, NY 10001*

*Published in Great Britain by*
*Routledge & Kegan Paul plc*
*11 New Fetter Lane, London EC4P 4EE*

*Set in 10 on 12pt Times*
*and printed in Great Britain*
*by Butler & Tanner Ltd*
*Frome and London*

*Library of Congress Cataloging in Publication Data*

*British Library CIP Data also available*
*ISBN 0-7102-0246-6*

310772

To Ken

# Contents

# Series editor's introduction

During the past two decades we have made a good deal of progress in showing the connections between curricula, pedagogy and evaluation in our elementary and secondary schools and the unequal structures of the larger society. Even with this growth in sophistication, however, an element has been very clearly missing in many of the studies of the cultural, political and economic role of our formal institutions of education. Here I am speaking of the tendency to ignore – or treat as epiphenomenal – the school's internal workings as an organization. This has been unfortunate.

Schools are not simple places. They are complex organizations that can never easily correspond to theories that claim a mechanistic connection between the ideological and economic requirements of powerful groups and the day-to-day life of the institution. Not only are schools complex, but they are riven with contradictory tensions that have a long history, a history that informs the discussion in this book. Whether these tensions are called the contradictions between accumulation and legitimation, as some analysts have labeled them,[1] the need to support economic stratification and democracy at the same time, as others have argued,[2] or the tensions between educating citizens and providing mechanisms of control, as McNeil calls them here, it is clear that no reductive theory that shows a one-to-one correspondence between the needs of dominant groups and education can ever do justice to what goes on in the day-to-day reality of schools.

Our task is to understand what schools do socially and educationally without reducing them to simple reflections of ideological and economic pressures outside of themselves. Political/economic, cultural and organizational analyses need to be combined if this is to be successful. Any individual study may stress one of these three modes of analysis, but it is in demonstrating the connections among the three that real progress is made.

When we consider the question of what counts as legitimate knowledge in the curriculum and how it is organized and taught, this becomes of even greater import. There have been an increasing number of volumes that have argued that the curriculum in schools has very real connections to the class, gender and race dynamics that create social inequalities.[3] And there has been considerable attention paid to the relationship between curriculum and teaching and the bureaucratic and organizational structure of the school.[4] Unfortunately, these bodies of literature often talk past each other. If these disparate perspectives could be integrated together,[5] then our ability to comprehend how and why schools do what they do would be increased immeasurably. *Contradictions of Control* enables us to take a large step toward such a synthetic view.

McNeil examines four, primarily middle-class, high schools. Each of them attempts to resolve its contradictory requirements in a distinct way. All of the schools are "smooth running." All enjoy reputations (some national) as "good schools." Yet in all but one, it is possible to raise the issue – as the author so clearly does – of whether in the midst of these smoothly operating administrative apparatuses, these schools actually educate in the best sense of that word? Her negative answer may not be one every school reformer, national, state and local school official, and others like; but there is no doubt that it must be taken very seriously if education is to do more than prepare students for an unequal society outside the classroom doors.

At the root of this volume is a seemingly innocent question. How does the administrative context of schools affect the content of the curriculum in the classroom? This innocent query becomes more powerful given the pressures now placed upon school systems, and made so popular by national reports on education such as *A Nation at Risk*, to tighten up controls on students, teaching, curricula, "standards," and so forth.

Part of McNeil's theme is best expressed in words taken from her own preface to this book:

The language of control has become the language of educational reform. ... The irony of these reform efforts is that they perpetuate a basic reality that has created the problems in the first place. We assert the purpose of our schools is to increase learning, but we have organized schools in ways that distort that purpose and even contradict it.

As she goes on to say:

When the school's organization becomes centered on managing and controlling, teachers and students take school less seriously. They fall into a ritual of teaching and learning that tends toward minimal standards and minimum effort. This sets off a vicious cycle. As students disengage from enthusiastic involvement in the learning process, administrators often see the disengagement as a control problem. They then increase their attention to managing students and teachers rather than supporting their instructional purpose.

The effects are what McNeil labels the contradictions of control These contradictions are lived out at the level of what gets taught, how teachers actually do that teaching, and how students respond to these conditions.

I have argued at length elsewhere that the labor of teaching is increasingly being restructured in ways that are very similar to what has happened to other white-, blue and pink-collar employees. The growth of plans for rationalizing and standardizing as many aspects of teaching, curricula and evaluation as possible is creating a situation in which teachers are losing power and, especially, *deskilled*.[6] McNeil goes into considerable detail about this, refining and building on it, and going beyond it when necessary. What is happening to teaching, though, cannot be understood in isolation. It must be linked to changes in the organization of knowledge in schools as well.

School knowledge is a part of, and a product of, the organization of schools. It is *organized* knowledge. This seems almost too trite to say, but it speaks to something of no small moment. We are apt to talk about the organization of school knowledge in particular ways. Within a traditional curricular perspective we speak of disciplinary knowledge in mathematics, science, history, and so on. In a political manner, school knowledge is described as organized around the cultural principles of elite groups. Both of these are significant, and especially the latter when one is concerned about the place of schooling in the reproduction of class, gender and race relations. Yet there is a third way to think this through. Knowledge is also organized around the internal bureaucratic workings of the school, an organization that may stand between and mediate both the disciplinary and political senses of curricular knowledge.

The focus on the relationship between internal organizational processes and the curriculum is a key to McNeil's argument. For her, the *internal* ways that schools operate provide a rationale for and create the conditions that may help serve to prevent students from gaining a critical understanding of their society. "Elite controls" are less necessary than some educational critics have claimed. Pressures from the economy, from dominant groups in society, and so forth make less of an immediate difference than the perceived needs for organizational controls by teachers and administrators. In essence, it is in the "relative autonomy" of the schools from these external forces that the connections between schooling and the larger social order lie.

In many ways, *Contradictions of Control* goes a long way toward specifying in detail some of the more interesting claims made by sociologists such as Pierre Bourdieu and Basil Bernstein that the organization of culture and people in educational institutions follows its own logic and is *not* directly connected to the economy. By following through on its own logic, the educational system is then still able to reproduce some of the cultural conditions "necessary" for the reproduction of inequality.[7]

McNeil's reason for devoting so much of her attention to these internal characteristics is perhaps best stated in her discussion of how this volume fits into the program of critical research on education that has evolved over the past two decades:

> Critical educational scholarship ... needs to trace out the
> contradictions inherent in subordinating teaching and learning
> to institutional controls. The specific linkages and unanticipated
> outcomes within schools need to be clearly documented.
> Variations from traditional patterns need to be examined. If we
> are to understand the impact of further educational reforms
> based on controls, we must describe in detail the legacy of the
> controls from past generations as they shape the school's role
> today. For that reason, [this volume] may appear to be
> internalistic, only slightly cognizant of external economic and
> political factors. It is an attempt to fill in the gap in our

theories of knowledge production and transformation in schools. The close-up detail of classroom processes and administrative policies is not meant to ignore these external forces; it is an attempt to bring into the open those practices in schools which are mistaken for failures of educational planning but are in fact the logical outcomes of that planning as it has subordinated education to control. The research ranged across the entire school, but centered mostly on classrooms, because that is where students encounter the contradictions.

Having said this, the author wants to make it clear that this is not just another study of how schools may operate to reproduce inequality. In fact, she expressly argues against such a reproductive theory in a number of ways.

One of the significant points made by the volume is in fact that schools do not merely reproduce existing cultural content and form. This has been noted by others as well, of course, who have argued that schools play a major role in the *production* of particular kinds of knowledge – for example, technical/administrative knowledge that is necessary for the expansion of markets and products, for cultural control, and so on.[8] *Contradictions of Control* goes beyond even these theories to demonstrate in a very insightful way how schools *transform* official culture. Schools take official culture and change it into small bits of knowledge and "sequences of assignments that are compatible with the internal bureaucratic processes of the school." One of McNeil's most interesting claims is that after official knowledge is "processed through worksheets, list-filled lectures and short answer tests, the cultural content, regardless of whose interests it may have served before, comes to serve only the interests of institutional efficiencies." Control and credentialling become the rationale for the educational experience; substance is lost. The effects of this process on students are profound.

The very fragmentation of the knowledge that is taught, the omission of crucial elements of content and the "mystification" of much that remains, the presentation of overly simplified "facts," these were characteristics of the curricula in the classrooms McNeil studied. All of these were generated out of a strategy of what she calls "defensive teaching" that itself grew out of the histories of the schools and the attempts by teachers to maintain their own "authority and efficiencies." The ultimate effects were the participation of teachers in their own de-skilling and, just as importantly, the creation of a curriculum that was too impersonal to be appropriated by students but whose effects were still damaging and long lasting.

In these schools, however, teachers and students were not just the passive recipients of administrative designs. They are active agents, altering, reappropriating and mediating a whole array of organizational and curricular structures. It is in their accommodation and sometimes resistance to these structures that the contradictory results of schooling are produced.

*Contradictions of Control* is a case study in the trivialization of education, as control wins out over serious educational purposes. Yet it is much more than that. By also focusing on a school that at least partly resolved its contradictory demands in a somewhat more democratic manner, the book shows the very possibility of difference.

It also demonstrates the fragility of the conditions necessary for good teaching and curricula and for more democratic educational practices. In the face of the legislative and bureaucratic attempts further to rationalize and control classroom discourse, it is this very fragility that should concern us. Many of the current attempts to standardize procedures and develop competency tests for students and teachers may actually create more problems than they solve. McNeil's analysis makes this possibility very clear. Thus, by providing a detailed examination of what actually happens in secondary schools, and why, in the United States, the simplistic remedies suggested by the multitude of reform proposals such as *A Nation At Risk* and others are shown to be exactly that – all too simple.

*Contradictions of Control*, then, is a major contribution to two kinds of debate. It continues the tradition of, and raises questions about, the research on the relationship between the curriculum and teaching practices in our schools and the larger society. Even if this was all it did, it would be well worth reading. The fact that the book also illuminates the organizational conditions inside schools and the day-to-day qualities of teachers' and students' lives, and then relates them to the mass of top-down efforts to "reform" our elementary and secondary schools, makes it an even more interesting book. It is the very combination of critically informed scholarship with an insistence on focusing on questions of the quality and reform of curricular and teaching practice that sets McNeil's study apart from other volumes. It is an articulate challenge to perspectives commonly accepted both by leftist critics of education and by more conservative educators who want to make schools more "efficient" and business-like. As such, it is a welcome addition that deserves our serious attention.

Michael W. Apple
The University of Wisconsin-Madison

## Notes

1 See, for example, Apple, Michael W. (1982), *Education and Power*, Boston and London, Routledge & Kegan Paul.
2 Carnoy, Martin, and Levin, Henry (1985), *Schooling and Work in the Democratic State*, Stanford, Stanford University Press.
3 Among them are Apple, Michael W. (1979), *Ideology and Curriculum*, Boston and London, Routledge & Kegan Paul; Apple (1982), *Education and Power* (see note 1 above); Apple, Michael W. (in press), *Teachers and Texts: A Political Economy of Class and Gender Relations in Education*, Boston and London, Routledge & Kegan Paul; and Giroux, Henry (1983), *Theory and Resistance in Education*, South Hadley, Bergin & Garvey.
4 See Fullan, Michael (1982), *The Meaning of Educational Change*, New York, Teachers College Press.
5 This point is similar to Erik Olin Wright's argument that a synthesis of Marxist and Weberian analyses is essential for understanding complex institutions. See Wright, Erik Olin (1978), *Class, Crisis and the State*, London, New Left Books, pp. 181–225.
6 This is discussed in greater detail in Apple (1982), *Education and Power* (see note 1 above) and Apple (in press), *Teachers and Texts* (see note 3 above).
7 Bourdieu, Pierre and Passeron, Jean-Claude (1977), *Reproduction in Education, Society and Culture*, Beverly Hills, Sage; and Bernstein, Basil (1977), *Class, Codes and Control Volume 3*, London and Boston, Routledge & Kegan Paul.
8 Apple (1982), *Education and Power* (see note 1 above), especially Chapter 2.

# Author's preface

Reforming the mediocre ritualization of American high schools has
become a national political crusade. A spate of reform reports
emerging during the past few years has documented the growing
sense that high schools are in trouble. The content of the curriculum has become watered down, students have become increasingly
disengaged from the learning process and the quality of learning
has suffered.

Amid the diverse prescriptions for school improvements, the reforms most likely to be implemented have been those which call
for more centralized management controls over factors shaping the
curriculum: testing, teacher training, course content. The language
of control has become the language of education reform.

The irony of these reform efforts is that they perpetuate a basic
reality that has created the problems in the first place. We assert
the purpose of our schools is to increase learning, but have organized schools in ways that distort that purpose and even contradict
it. We are so accustomed to thinking of school organization as
separate from instruction that we rarely confront the tension between the two. After all, administrators are trained to "manage";
teachers are trained to "teach." Yet the current pressures to reform
schools by strengthening management controls, even to the point
of standardization, are bringing these two traditionally distinct domains into crisis by threatening the professional role of teachers as
educators.

This book explores the contradictions of management controls
in undermining the goal they supposedly seek to achieve - quality
of learning. It focuses on the area where the tensions between
school management and teaching play themselves out - the
classroom. The theme of the analysis is deceptively simple, yet rich

in variations. *When the school's organization becomes centered on managing and controlling, teachers and students take school less seriously.* They fall into a ritual of teaching and learning that tends toward minimal standards and minimum effort. This sets off a vicious cycle. As students disengage from enthusiastic involvement in the learning process, administrators often see the disengagement as a control problem. They then increase their attention to managing students and teachers rather than supporting their instructional purpose.

The management efficiencies implied by centralized controls are tempting for public officials looking for short-term accountability models. Such "improvements," however, ignore years of complex organization research which tells us that top-down controls seldom produce in workers the intended results and in fact often produce unintended consequences. They ignore the common wisdom that measurable outcomes may be the least significant results of learning. They also ignore the fallacy of equating uniformity with quality, especially the failure of uniform minimum standards to address issues of excellence. Most interestingly, the control-based reforms fail to take into account the calls in the reform reports themselves to increase teacher professionalism, to upgrade their educational level, to attract competent people into the teaching profession. Reforms which tighten administrative controls take a much less optimistic view of the potential of teachers to really teach.

A key reason that many recent reforms have missed the significance of the contradictions of control is that little empirical research has been focused on how the administrative context of schools affects the content of the curriculum in the classroom. Historically, advocates of testing have ignored such dynamics by simply introducing certain curricula, then testing to determine the degree of student "learnings" of that content. Within that model of curriculum analysis, the inputs and outputs are more important than the processes in between the two or the effects not predefined as outputs. Until very recently, critical theorists, who have much less tendency to accept the structure of the school as unproblematic, have nevertheless focused on how schools operate as social control agencies for economic and political elites. This focus has had a tendency to obscure what is happening to the student; often there is the assumption that socialization is occurring because the processes of socialization and social control are so entrenched. In addition, this perspective has tended to emphasize the role of schools in shaping what students do after they leave school (labor force stratification, especially) rather than the educational effects within the controlling institution.

There has been a dearth of empirical work on the actual dynamics of classroom learning and how they are affected by the broader organization of schools. Indeed, this author stumbled inadvertently onto the significance of the organizational structure for teaching and learning while engaged in a classroom study of social studies curriculum. That study (McNeil, 1977), begun as an analysis of the nature and sources of economics content in required social studies classes, discovered on the surface a pattern of classroom interaction much like that described by Goodlad (1983) as flattened content, limited teaching techniques and bored students. The treatment of economics topics differed little from the treatment of other social studies content (social and political history, for example) in its simplistic forms of presentation, devoid of complex explanation or controversy; its short-answer-test evaluations; its air of unreality which made "school economics" somehow very different from the economy in which students and their parents live.

The perception of unreality was not that of the observer alone. The students, docile in class, spoke in interviews of feeling very skeptical about the credibility of what they learned at school. The teachers, too, had knowledge of their subject far beyond what they admitted into class discussion. The two met in a boring but polite ritual of "social studies."

According to the logic of the recent reform efforts, one would conclude that these were ill-prepared teachers, or at least not very smart ones, and that their school's administration was weak. The students' achievements would be expected to be low. In fact, the school had a strong administration, well-educated teachers who kept up in their field, and a solid base of community support for education. The school was known for being a "good school," whose students generally performed well above average in their school work and in their admissions to higher education.

The key to the low level of effort in these classes, to the skepticism felt by the students toward the course content, lay in the tension between the teachers' professional roles within the school and the administrative context within which they worked. They felt the administration to be interested only in processing students through required credentials, through requisites for the diploma. So long as the school ran smoothly, no administrative attention was forthcoming. While this gave teachers a great deal of apparent autonomy, their autonomy operated within a narrow range of discretion. Feeling little support for their professional authority and even less provision for efficiencies of time and effort, the teachers set about to create their own authority, their own efficiencies. To do so, they needed to control the students, both to avoid discipline problems and even more to avoid inefficient exchanges which might alter the pace of the lesson or provide students the opportunity to question the teacher's interpretation of history. Their solution was to control the knowledge, the course content, in order to control the students.

The pattern of knowledge control was evident after only a few days of classroom observation. Tracing the source of this control back to the controlling policies of the administration was the result of many interviews, many questions about the history of the school and about the power relations in its present structure. This tracing was guided not by a theory of school organization but by the unavoidable data emerging as teachers described the rationale behind their choices to control content, as they described policy shifts which left them constrained or additionally burdened, but without administrative support or follow-up.

The classroom observations made clear that the school was functioning in a way that attempted to socialize students into consensus history, into passive learner roles. Yet there were no overt community pressures, no external elites insisting the school take on this social control function. The controlling function stemmed from the way the school as an organization worked, not from outside pressures. And the controlling functions were being resisted at several levels. The teachers resisted the administrative controls by watering down course content and reducing their own teaching efforts; the students cooperated patiently in class, while silently negotiating how much course content to believe and remember after they were tested on it. The controlling purposes within the school reduced educational quality, even though they gave the school the reputation of being a "well run school."

Once the link between the school organization and the nature of course content was established, the question arose *whether this pattern was central to other high schools.* A study was designed to compare selected high schools of similar populations and community bases, but with varying structural arrangements between administrators and teachers, in order to see whether all high schools exhibit this tension between the administrative controls and the educational purposes. Searching for variations in organizational form would allow comparison to see whether the tension is always resolved in favor of the management controls and, if not, whether school knowledge is different, more credible to students, in schools where that tension is resolved in favor of instruction.

The analysis which follows gives evidence that reforms based on increased management controls will prove to be wrong-headed and misguided. In those schools where the tension between the controlling functions and the educational purposes were resolved in favor of controls, teachers felt undermined, professionally threatened and, in my analysis, they began unwittingly to participate in their own de skilling. Where teaching and learning were not taken seriously, students recognized the rewards to minimum participation and were perhaps justifiably reluctant to become actively engaged in learning. The one school where the tension was resolved in favor of educational purposes had teachers who put few walls between their personal knowledge and "school knowledge"; they presented their course content as complex and as having few "right" answers. They viewed students more optimistically as potential contributors to the knowledge exchange and they viewed themselves as more than distributors of the official knowledge of school. Their richer content and more meaningful assignment could not have been *produced* by rigid management controls; they were the result of a history of administrative support for academics.

The chapters which follow attempt to trace the links between school organization and classroom knowledge. The first chapter establishes the historical basis for the administrator–teacher split in the dual and contradictory purposes of our public schools. The second chapter lays out the variations in structure among the schools comprising the analysis. Together, these chapters confirm that across the apparent sameness of our high schools, within traditionally organized schools, there are choices.

The second section of the book describes in school-by-school detail the classroom processes within the organizational variations. The tensions between controlling and teaching take on different guises at the individual schools. Here we see teachers and students negotiating out their roles within the reward systems of their particular school setting.

The third section begins with a closer analysis of the instructional strategies by which teachers control students through control of course content. The effects of these strategies on social studies content, and the consonance between the messages of the content and the messages of the instructional techniques is the subject of the next chapter. These strands of comparison and detail allow us in the final chapter to consider the implications of knowledge controls in schools, controls apparently imbedded in the very structure of the institution. The final result of this control of knowledge seems not to be the lowered achievement scores the current publicity decries, but the de-skilling of teachers and the devaluing of content as the institution rewards the splitting of the knowledge we have of our world from the official knowledge of schools.

The decline in educational quality has this split at its center. It cannot be legislated or managed away. If we are going to have meaningful school reforms, we need a theory of curriculum based on an understanding of the tension between the educational purposes of schools and the controlling purposes which have become embodied in the management of educational settings. If our theories of curriculum, of school knowledge, encompass the organizational role of the institutions, we will also understand the contradictions we set in motion when we try to reform pedagogy by strengthening the controlling functions of management.

# Acknowledgments

I am grateful to the US National Institute of Education, for funding this research. Gail MacColl and Frederick Mulhauser went far beyond the requisite guidance through the agency's bureaucratic procedures by their concern for the substance of the study and their work in building networks among researchers of shared interests. The research was conducted under the auspices of the Wisconsin Center for Public Policy, Madison, Wisconsin. The analysis is my own and does not reflect the endorsement or policies of the Center, nor of NIE.

Many of the teachers and students observed and interviewed serve as ample evidence that the mourning of the death of American public schools is, at best, premature. All of the teachers observed were trying to teach, and to teach effectively, within what they perceived to be their personal and institutional limitations. For their cooperation with the study, for the genuine welcome they showed an observer who stayed many months, for their thoughtful interviews, I owe an incredible debt of thanks. Promises of anonymity prevent my thanking them here by name. I am also extremely indebted to the administrators who granted access to their schools and who took time to be interviewed.

The concern for students' access to knowledge presupposes the need to link observed classroom processes to students' views of what is being taught and learned. This component of the research was highly dependent on student interviews. I am grateful to the many students who were willing to discuss their classes and were articulate and informative in doing so. The issue of the *credibility* of school knowledge came first from students, not from the interviewer's prepared questions.

An independent researcher benefits greatly from the insights of colleagues. Mary Metz was helpful early in discussing our mutual concerns for the individuals who live and work in the institutions we study; John Palmer's theoretical insights into social studies curricula and his encouragement to study what goes on in schools have proved invaluable. Fred Newmann's social studies curricula have stood as a model of conceptualizing the relation between knowledge forms and knowledge content. Michael Hartoonian, who knows and serves the schools of his state well, gave wise advice on selecting the schools.

Rice University has provided a high-quality academic environment in which to complete this book; of special importance were Dean Allen Matusow's analytical questions at a key point in the writing, Joe Austin's collegial support, and interchanges with my students. Esther Smith added the careful editing and typing of the manuscript; Carol Vuchetich, the index.

I am grateful to Michael Apple for our lively theoretical exchanges, for seeing this research in the context of the larger issue of the social role of schools, and for his confidence that the findings should have their voice as this book.

Kenneth McNeil shared his wealth of expertise in organizational analysis as well as his confidence in the importance of the research. Kathryn and Carrie McNeil, who love to learn, provided the inspiration.

The Mock Turtle went on:—

"We had the best of educations – in fact, we went to school every day."

*     *     *

"And how many hours a day did you do lessons?" said Alice, in a hurry to change the subject.

"Ten hours the first day," said the Mock Turtle, "nine the next, and so on."

"What a curious plan!" exclaimed Alice.

"That's the reason they're called lessons," the Gryphon remarked; "because they lessen from day to day."

"Then the eleventh day must have been a holiday?"

"Of course it was," said the Mock Turtle.

"And how did you manage on the twelfth?"

From *Alice in Wonderland* by Lewis Carroll

# PART ONE

# Choice and contradictions

# 1
# School structure and classroom knowledge

How is school knowledge shaped by its organizational context? How does the school as an institution set rewards or define learning in ways that make school knowledge seem very removed from the knowledge of our everyday experience?

Our public schools have evolved historically as organizations serving two potentially conflicting purposes: to educate citizens and to process them into roles for economic production. To accomplish the first, schools have the role of supplying students with information and with learning skills. The results can be unpredictable because children's intellects and skills develop in ways that we cannot predetermine. For the second goal, schools process students through stratified steps leading to predictable, marketable credentials for the workplace. The steps, and some of the outcomes, can be managed, controlled. Thus the school is organized to be in conflict with itself.

School knowledge is shaped in the tension between the school's goals of educating and of controlling students. The focus of this analysis is how the tension between goals of educating students and goals of controlling students is played out in schools and how its resolution affects the forms and content of school knowledge.

What is being labeled in reform efforts as a decline in educational quality in our schools is actually the almost inevitable result of translating our rich cultural heritage into forms that can be consumed by the millions of students trying to satisfy diploma requirements. The bureaucratic controls designed to facilitate this credentialing can easily trivialize the course content and thus undermine the educative goals of the institution.

**Historical evolution of the tension between goals**

This split in purpose has its basis in the changing roles public schooling has played in the history of the nation. The Jeffersonian ideal behind our educational purposes affirms the right of every citizen to be informed, to have knowledge that will help control one's destiny and prevent the rise of oppressive forms of government. The ideal of universal education (rather than a universal certifying agency) pervaded the establishment and organization of early schools. The content was often simple literacy and numeracy, at first. When social groups such as landowners, workers, members of religious groups, immigrant minorities and others contested who should attend school or who should control schools, the issues in conflict centered on the educational content of the school (Katz, 1968). Prior to widespread industrialism, students attended school long enough to learn what they needed for personal purposes. While having school-supplied skills (geography, accounting, literacy) might help a young person find an apprenticeship, there was no notion of going to school in order to get a job or be trained for one, or to obtain a certificate of attendance.[1] The school was no more influential in teaching skills and information than the family, workplace and perhaps the church.

The rhetoric of the Jeffersonian ideal of educating all citizens persists in our claim to want to give every child a chance to be educated; it draws teachers into teaching and gives students expectations that school knowledge will have something to teach them. Even though the mandate Jefferson posed for an education critical of government and other institutions rarely finds an articulate voice among school practitioners, the mandate for universal education is still very much with us. Ironically, the idea of universal education in a democracy helped create such large public schools that organizational forms quite different from those imagined by Jefferson began to develop.

The idea that education could free a person to shape his or her own destiny was turned on its head as industrialists around the turn of the century looked to schools to supply them with labor for their expanding factories. Their desire to control schooling went beyond wanting to socialize students into a particular set of values. These industrialists of the late nineteenth and early twentieth centuries wanted schools to help control the labor supply. Several

4

factors converged to bring schools in line with their controlling purposes. First, many more students were choosing to remain in school through high school (Boyer, 1983). Second, industrial expansion in the US combined with international upheavals to bring many immigrants to this country. Industrialists wanted the cheap labor but feared that if immigrants remained in their social groups they would at worst be resistant, contentious workers and at best take inefficient lengths of time to learn English and to become acquainted with the ways of American production. During this period, industrialists and social reformers alike turned to the school as the only universal institution, as the best organization for breaking down the home culture and replacing it with American values. In addition, the schools could train, sort, select and certify able and willing workers.

Several factors internal to schools made them vulnerable to such outside control. First, political corruption in a number of cities had resulted in appointments to school boards, to school administrative positions, and even to classroom teaching positions, according to political favors and contributions. Schools, as parts of city government, tended to have wasteful spending habits and questionable patterns of contract-letting, and in general were quite far from the industrialists' ideals of efficiency and productivity. In addition, growing numbers of secondary school students meant the need for increased school taxes which citizens were reluctant to pay when so many school expenditures produced so few results. From inside, school administrators wanted to emulate the business leaders whose industries were legends of productivity and efficiency. Those appointed to clean up past corruption especially wanted to adopt industry's scientific management techniques in order to neutralize political factions. These same techniques could also equip schools to organize students and content in incremental processes aimed at tracking students into jobs in industry. In the name of efficiency and honesty, they set in motion plans to place schools on cost-accounting models similar to those of industry, while ignoring the fact that industrialists were shifting to taxpayers the costs of sorting, selecting and tracking their future workers. For school administrators seeking adequate tax funds and for business elites wanting less corruption by machine politicians but more public schooling to provide the selection of their industrial workforce, the rise of scientific management in second-

5

ary schools was a welcome, if contested, compromise (Callahan, 1962).

This period of early industrialization is critical to any understanding of the situating of course content within the organization of the schools. It was during this time, when the school was being directly used as an agency of social control, that our present forms of high school organization were being established. These include administrators who function as business managers rather than as educators; curriculum differentiated by track and time according to students' social class and expected job future; and emphasis on testable "outputs" of schooling rather than on longer-term learnings.

The establishment of secondary school administration to function in relation to economic controls in our society did not mean that the roles of schools would be no longer contested. In her book on Chicago school politics during the first half of this century, Julia Wrigley (1982) documents the bitter struggles of the social efficiency, or scientific management, applications in the Chicago schools. In Chicago in the 1920s, business elites wanted public schools to participate actively in producing docile but moderately skilled workers. The children of working-class parents were to be tracked into vocational education as early as possible; the children of the business executives themselves were in private schools and therefore rarely affected. Because the working-class parents worked as union members, they banded together in opposition to the reorganization of schools along lines that would destine their children forever to working-class jobs. Business executives, on the other hand, thought that a highly tracked, organized school for working-class children would help them secure jobs and would help management keep them controlled in jobs. They proposed schools for working-class children that helped children become "concrete-minded, not abstract-minded." Their industrial education should be free of "the slightest touch of sentimentality. Work is real; work is hard."[2]

To accomplish tracked curricula and "unsentimental" instruction, Chicago school managers, especially Superintendent McAndrew, wanted to isolate management decisions from both teachers and politicians. He claimed that schools needed not more money but more efficiency, spending only the absolute minimum on students in each educational track. Toward this goal, the Chicago schools at one time introduced cost-accounting in the schools for working-class children, giving them cheap white paper to write on rather than the copybooks provided to middle-class children. In addition, they were to do spelling lessons from free resources such as newspapers; no spellers were to be purchased for them.

These practices, which threatened to control their children's job futures as well as their time in school, united laborers with teachers in opposition to the view of children as potential laborers rather than as growing children. Laborers saw the growing sophistication of jobs and wanted their children to have skills to deal with new technologies as well as a more general education to understand those new technologies and possibly to help in getting into college. The Chicago story of social efficiency innovations in schools is full of lively and absurd stories – for example, the account of the school official who displayed children as the outputs, or products, of instruction, in a public hall where they could be viewed and quizzed by the taxpayers who paid for their education. It included the quote by Marshall Field (and he was far from the worst offender) that "education should not be excessively intellectual; that would detract from the young's ability to work with concentration and dedication."

The conflict in Chicago over what kind of education children of different social classes should receive, and over who should make such decisions, ranged from shopfloor to state legislature to executive offices. It is a story of high emotions, dramatic power plays, suspenseful reversals and shifting alliances. It is, on the one hand, a unique story of the application of rational school management techniques to school organization and curriculum in a particular city. It is, at the same time, a typical attempt of business leaders and their chosen school administrators to impose management techniques in the name of efficiency, to control students for the benefit of factors beyond pedagogies.

We are shocked by language which depicts students as raw material or outputs and products; we are surprised at the intensity of the struggle to control what happens in schools. These overt tensions have been obscured by the passing of time. Yet the administrative structures and the splitting off of administrative personnel from teaching functions, which occurred in this time period, remain the dominant features of our high school organizational structures to the present.[3]

7

## The crisis of credentialing in a new economic era

The foundations of our school organization are today anachronistic. What is called a decline in quality of education is actually a crisis in the legitimacy of school practices. This includes both the educational and social control practices and their relative imbalance. During the years of secondary school expansion, when increased immigration and expanding industrialization placed on schools the cost of training and sorting workers, the credential provided by schooling came to dominate *school practice*. But more and more students obtained credentials of completed schooling, while a series of recessions resulted in the production of too few new jobs to employ all the credentialed workers. Thus, the credential itself came into crisis. Having displaced and devalued the substance of education in exchange for anticipated economic benefit, the credential became a questionable commodity. Having contributed to the crisis of credibility for school knowledge, the credential itself began to lose credibility.

A part of the loss of the credential's credibility is attributable to events beyond the scope of the school to affect. The economy of the nation is much more interlinked with international markets for labor, production and consumption. Our modes of production have become ever more highly technological; at the same time, our economic and governmental institutions, in the US and abroad, have become more unstable and vulnerable.

Students of the past few years have begun to doubt that there will necessarily be a pay-off for all their years of school. They know the credential will not be sufficient for job entry or college, yet they know that the stiff competition in shrinking labor markets means that it is nevertheless still necessary. This lack of confidence in the value of the credential makes benefits of schooling all the more suspect because of students' increasingly low expectations that school knowledge has much worth. They have long suspected the quality and validity of course content, reduced as it was to forms readily transmitted and evaluated within the reward structure of the school, often trivialized and rendered lifeless by being turned into "school knowledge." Their assessment of course content challenges the success of our meeting the *educational* goals of our school legacy. And their lack of confidence in the school credential calls into question the emphasis our schools have placed on con-

8

trolling and processing students through requirements aimed at obtaining that credential, controlling processes which de-emphasized learning and content in favor of meeting institutional standards of attendance and minimum grades.

This crisis has been developing for decades, ever since the school came to play such a significant role in the production of workers for economic productivity. It has been staved off by decades of incredible economic expansion which seemed to reward the school's priorities favoring credentialling.

Now that world markets, worldwide production and international recessions have made even the credential of schooling problematic, it is no wonder that students feel estrangement and disengagement from school processes. Yet the fact that there is a crisis of legitimacy indicates that the ideal of education, and not mere processing, is still extant among students and among the public so politicized over school reforms.

In the face of this crisis of the legitimacy of school practices, there is a tendency for policymakers to try to bring events under control. They have failed to appreciate the historical context which demonstrates the inadequacy of control models to solve what is wrong with schools. Unless challenged, the legislatures and school boards who see tighter controls as the solutions to educational quality will snuff out the last vestiges of educational expectations that remain with some of our teachers, with some of our instructional practices and especially with some of our students.

As administrators increase controls, they engender resistance from the persons being controlled. Less organized than the Chicago teachers of social efficiency days, teachers today nevertheless accommodate their teaching role to administrative controls. Interestingly, one response is for them not openly to resist administrators but to increase controls on their students. In the instance of the Chicago teachers, they resisted administrative officials directly through individual and collective efforts and through indirect means such as influence of legislative policy and public opinion. As demonstrated in the schools described in later chapters, when the teachers in today's schools see their autonomy threatened by administrative controls, they are more likely to resist this loss by exerting greater control in the classroom. When students see more attention to controls (to teacher-supplied and controlled content, to tight pacing of lectures with minimum student involvement, to

administrative controls on student behavior), they learn that sometimes these controls are more important to the school staff than is
the matter of the students' understanding of the lessons. When
students see this disproportionate attention to controlling functions, they too resist in their own ways.

Paul Willis (1977) described the experiences of resistance among
working-class boys attending a school whose middle-class values of
deportment and curriculum were alien to them. They thought the
mental work of schools to be too sissy for their masculine participation. To resist, they acted as a group to challenge vocally school
orderliness and determined to produce a "laff" or humorous disruption every day. They were reproducing in the classroom the
forms of resistance typical of their fathers' resistance on the shopfloor. The middle-class students in the schools described in the
following chapters resisted in more private and invisible ways.
Because their economic expectations made them see more value in
obtaining the school credential than did Willis' lads, they resisted
silently, combining their minimal efforts on assignments and disengagement from classroom interactions with active negotiation of
how much content to believe. The administrators and teachers saw
this disengagement and minimum effort as a need for more and
tighter controls on students.

The administrator's misperceptions can be the result of the
organizational distance built into the relationship between school
administration and school instruction. This distance is rarely demonstrated so dramatically as in the conflicting purposes in the Chicago
struggle to define public education. Once institutionalized, however, this distance can come to be accepted, over many years, as
"the way schools are." Administrative attention to maintenance, in
the broadest sense, carries the supposition that maintaining orderly
processes promotes (and is necessary for) learning. This rationale
can justify the distance without raising concern for what *other*
conditions are equally necessary for accomplishing educational
goals. The history of school organization includes not only those
"historical" moments in which our institutions are profoundly
changed or created, but also the passing of time in which forms
and purposes change slowly or, more importantly, change in ways
that take them out of sync with each other.

## Theories of curriculum and theories of control

In light of this historical context we can better understand the tension between the two primary purposes embodied in the organization of our schools. Traditional curriculum theory in the United States has failed to appreciate the grounding of school curriculum in this tension between educational and social control purposes of schools, largely because curriculum itself took on the language of rational planning during the social efficiency era. The specific activity analyses of workers' tasks and the highly differentiated curricula (that produced twenty-one curricular tracks in a single city) did not survive the challenge that the economic depression of the 1930s posed to the climate of productivity which had brought scientific management to schools in the first place (Callahan, 1962). Even without a curriculum drawn from labor force activities, the institution had so locked curriculum development into a rational planning mode that the organization of the school persisted in shaping not only the way our schools have designed curricula, but the way researchers have analyzed course content. Within a planning model, goals are set and variables identified and arranged so as to reach those goals. As applied to curriculum, course content was not problematic; it was the result of rational planning based on "scientific" theories of learning and "scientifically" derived models for sequencing the information and skills for each course. The worth of the curriculum planning was demonstrated in the testing of children. If the curriculum failed to produce predicted outcomes, usually described as "achievements," then the process needed fine-tuning. By appropriating the language of management and management's measures of effectiveness (testing), traditional curriculum theory has shed little light on how knowledge comes to be mediated through school processes.

Far more helpful in understanding how school knowledge relates to its organizational setting has been the growing body of analysis provided by several strands of organization theory, sociology of knowledge and critical analysis of culture. Collectively, this body of research situates school knowledge in its cultural, economic and political contexts as well as in the institution of the school. It represents various philosophical perspectives but shares the view that schools play an important role in shaping cultural values and that the curriculum is a vital part of that role.

11

Such a reflective view of the role of school knowledge is impossible from the perspective of traditional curriculum research which takes the planning process for granted. In particular, traditional curriculum developers and researchers have taken the structure of the school as a given and have tried to change, or reform, the educative role of schools by trying to manipulate the controls, to fine-tune the variables in the production of rational outcomes. Rather than appreciating the need to see how organizational tensions devalue educational content, advocates of the rational-planning model for curriculum development[4] saw the curriculum as divorced from the context and changeable through management techniques applied within the domain of school content. By taking the institutional forms as given, they were ignoring a long line of organizational research on the unanticipated consequences of rule-making.[5] They have ironically contributed to the declining quality of instruction by abstracting content from institutional contradictions.

Of special importance is the contribution critical scholarship has made to the language by which we describe the role played by schools in shaping knowledge and ways of knowing encountered by students. The first such contribution is the concept of the school's role in cultural reproduction. In a fairly homogeneous society, the educational institution would be rightly expected to transmit to children the information and styles of learning valued by that society. In pluralistic societies, the values are splintered; dominant groups in society may choose to impose their culture on the broader population so that the inequities may be preserved in their favor.[6] Thus, cultural and economic reproduction are closely linked. Clearly, the business elites, trying to keep working-class children in working-class job tracks so they would not be lost to college and the professions or to job dissatisfaction, demonstrated in the Chicago schools the elites' attempt to reproduce their own culture, their definitions of social "place" and human capital.

More subtle to identify than cultural and economic reproduction is the role of the school in *producing* culture.[7] Apple (1982c) makes this distinction to explain the impact of school practices which reinforce cultural or economic inequities by aiding in the production of technical knowledge required by industrial production as "knowledge capital." Within this conceptualization, schools mediate the broader culture by selectively participating in producing knowledge or knowledge forms whose chief benefit is not for the development of the student but for the modes of economic production to which he or she is ultimately to be subjected or integrated as another factor of production. The controls may be exercised directly, as with Chicago business elites specifying vocational courses for working-class children in order not to "raise their expectations unnecessarily" (Wrigley, 1982). Or the controls may be imbedded in the processes of the organization so that their logic takes on technical dimensions which seem legitimate within the on-going processes of the organization. Such technical controls include the use of testing to measure student progress, though the content of the tests may be too abstract to capture what is really learned. The value of the testing is its easy translation into the quantitative language of accountability by which school administration justifies school practice within standardized, rational planning.

To the notions of cultural production and reproduction in schools, I am adding in a later chapter the idea that schools *transform* culture.[8] That is, they do more than transmit an official culture to students. They take that culture and transform it into pieces of knowledge and units of courses and sequences of assignments that are compatible with the internal bureaucratic processes of the school. After being processed through worksheets, list-filled lectures and short-answer tests, the cultural content, regardless of whose interests it may have served before, comes to serve only the interests of institutional efficiencies. Its forms may have some utility but its substance has been depleted. Its meaning is whatever meaning the assignments have in helping students meet the institutional requirements of their credentialing.

By looking at the way the school transforms cultural content into "school knowledge," we can begin to understand how students relate to course content. On the one hand, theories of cultural reproduction imply a direct correspondence between external controls, like the business elites in Chicago schools in the 1920s, and the internal processes of schools. This correspondence links cultural or economic pressures outside schools to what happens to students in schools by analyzing the ways schools mediate those forces. The implication is that the school is the agent and the student is the passive recipient of these mediating influences. Much of the work done by cultural theorists along this line has begun with societal

13

issues and has attempted to trace societal forces into schools. This analysis has been very instructive in raising the issue of the social role of schools. One result of this research has been the growing understanding that students are not so passively receiving the mediating processes of schools. The Willis research describing working-class boys' resistance to middle-class schooling is a case in point.[9]

In identifying the dominance of external forces and the complexity of student resistance, the literature on cultural reproduction has done a great deal to break through the perception of school curriculum as rational. But this research has been less helpful in explaining how school practices themselves correspond to the larger social forces, especially forces of economic and political domination, or how school practices are manipulated by those forces. Once its own analysis has determined that students are resisting domination, this theoretical perspective must of necessity acknowledge the complexity of internal school factors and the need to document them. Thus, the missing link in understanding school processes of cultural reproduction has been the internal workings of the school. There has been no systematic attempt to trace external pressures on schools through the internal mechanisms by which those pressures have reached students. These linkages must attend to curricular forms and content as well as to the social relations in schools.

There are two possible explanations for this missing link between external forces and the students. The first is that such critical research is forgetting the necessity of a historical dimension to all institutional analysis. The second is the unarticulated but very present assumptions that, because students are stratified and controlled in schools, the administrative controls must be working. In looking for ways they are "working," social theorists have missed the possibility that they are not working, at least not as would be expected from their rational models.

Historically, the lack of "rationality" exists because the institutional structure of high schools was based around two different purposes. One of those, producing workers for early industrialism, no longer corresponds to the realities of the economy, especially advanced industrial or post-industrial capitalism. It is difficult to find direct, mechanistic correspondence between domination on the outside of schools and domination of course content and procedures inside schools because the patterns of domination within schools have their basis in institutional forms which took shape many years ago. That does not mean that domination does not occur, that schools are not agents of cultural and economic reproduction. It does mean that our present high schools were organized, and their reward structures set, at a time when schools were being overtly and deliberately used as agents of economic and social control. Time has blurred those purposes; the present role of schools is much more confused and complicated. There is, in fact, evidence that elites do not feel their interests, economic or political, to be served by public schools. Their advocacy of a voucher system or direct tax credits to shift non-elite children (working- and middle-class and even minority children) into private schools shows their disillusionment with present public school practice. The emergence of business leaders on reform commissions at the national and state levels gives further evidence of this lack of correspondence between current school practice and the forces of domination implied by those practices. Critical research must investigate the possibilities that our institutional forms are historical artifacts rather than direct products of domination; their staying power, their ability to adapt to new external forces or to turn inward to institutional maintenance controls must be made into questions for our critical inquiry.

The second assumption made by critical school scholarship is that the controls are somehow "working." Despite growing research on student resistance (Everhart, 1980; McNeil, 1977 and 1981a; Willis, 1977), common notions of cultural reproduction in schools are still shaped by the assumptions that internal controls produce socialization. To uncover the basis for resistance, as well as the effects (and effectiveness) of controls, we must examine patterns of acquiescence and accommodation. Administrators, teachers and students all calculate their interests within the institutional rewards of the school, and their interests in translating school rewards into external accountabilities or credentials. How they make these calculations is another vital component in understanding the specific mechanisms by which school knowledge results from school mediation of culture.

**Contradictions and choices**

Within the controlling processes, then, there are contradictions. These contradictions do not lend themselves to easy explanation in our present correspondence theories of the social role of schooling; neither are they explainable within traditional analysis of rational planning in schools. They are evident in the lived culture of the schools which will be described in the following chapters, even though originally these contradictions were not expected in the research, or even looked for.

We have talked about our high schools as though they were alike. Certainly, extensive surveys by Goodlad (1983) and others indicate a pervasive and troubling sameness across many of our schools. Yet all of us who have observed in schools, or who remember what it was like to teach in or attend them, know that schools vary. The individuals within them vary; they exert their influence and they make choices. Their choices, like traditional school organization, help shape school knowledge and its credibility for students.

The remaining chapters compare four schools. Their students and neighborhoods were very much alike. They differed in the way their school administration related to curriculum and classrooms. They differed in the way the tension between the control goals and the educative goals played itself out. The tension was not resolved the same way at all four schools and, as a result, school knowledge and students' access to it took on different meanings in the four settings. By examining closely the overt and hidden patterns of control and resistance in these schools, and by documenting the strategies by which administrators and teachers set up patterns of autonomy or control, we can better understand how schools mediate cultural content.

There is no necessity that school knowledge be significantly different in content or texture or credibility from the experimental knowledge of our lived culture. Yet the case studies to follow will demonstrate that, all too often, school knowledge seemed artificial, contrived and subordinated to the controlling purposes in schools. *The contradiction of these controls is the failure of school knowledge in "smooth-running" schools to educate.*

Our schools are at a crossroads as agents of either education or social control. Debates in current public policy indicate that policy changes are tilting toward even greater imbalance between the controlling functions of schools and the Jeffersonian ideal of educating citizens. The task of critical educational research is to raise to awareness the counter-productive nature of emphasizing controls over educational practice in schools. This disproportionate commitment of personnel and resources to control purposes undermines educational quality by devaluing the content and trivializing the instructional role of teachers. The case studies to follow demonstrate that this emphasis only appears to create efficiencies while alienating students and calling the legitimacy of schools themselves into question. The resulting dominance of controls will be shown not, in fact, to produce educational quality; neither will it solve the economic problems which render credentials problematic.

Applying more outdated controls will not only further reduce educational quality but will also undermine the possibilities for individuals to produce, through their individual and collective resistance, challenges to the dominance of controls in schools. The potential for these challenges is present; it is evidenced in the fact that some teachers and some students do feel a tension between the organizational controls of the school and the tradition of an educational ideal. If they did not feel this tension, they would acquiesce to the controls in exchange for short-term rewards (credentials and classroom efficiencies) without such intricate negotiations of their own interests within the institutional limits of the schools. These possibilities for resistance, as we will see in the case studies to follow, will not all be emancipatory. Some will only further entrap the individuals involved and reinforce administrative controls.[10] But without these possibilities for educative roles for schools, their legitimacy is assured of declining still further.

Critical educational scholarship, then, needs to trace out the contradictions inherent in subordinating teaching and learning to institutional controls. The specific linkages and unanticipated outcomes within schools need to be clearly documented. Variations from traditional patterns need to be examined. If we are to understand the impact of further educational reforms based on controls, we must describe in detail the legacy of the controls of past generations as they shape the school's role today. For that reason, the research to be described here may appear to be internalistic, only slightly cognizant of external economic and political factors. It is an attempt to fill in the gap in our theories of knowledge production and transformation in schools. The close-up detail of class-room processes and administrative policies is not meant to ignore those external forces; it is an attempt to bring into the open those practices in schools which are mistaken for failures of educational planning but are in fact the logical outcomes of that planning as it has subordinated education to control. The research ranged across the entire school, but centered mostly on classrooms, because that is where students encounter the contradictions.

# 2
# Structure and choice

Before we can understand how the organizational forms of schooling mediate and transform the knowledge that becomes accessible to students in schools, those organizational forms themselves must be understood. Although the structural tension within schools has historical roots, it does not leave contemporary school personnel without choices regarding school organization. Nor does the tension indicate only one method of resolving the conflict between educative goals and goals of social control. This chapter examines those choices in four typical American schools. The schools were selected for systematic variation in the relation of the administrative structure to curriculum, classrooms and teacher oversight. The four patterns do not exhaust all possible structures for high schools, but do demonstrate the range of choices, depending on the closeness or distance of the administration and the classroom, and the degree of teacher control over classroom course content. Certain organizational features will represent societal interests long since obscured in the accretion of educational practices presently constituting the culture of the school. Still other institutional policies may seem to represent a textbook case of rational school administration.

This chapter gives a profile of each school as it relates to the others in administrative structure. In light of these formal structures, the informal dynamics which contradict or enact the ostensible purposes behind the formal organization will be analyzed in the subsequent case study chapters (Part II). The formal structural descriptions will give some indication of the ways the educative and social control purposes of the school are embodied in the organizational forms and processes. The way that tension is sustained or resolved is the subject of the case study chapters.

19

To examine school knowledge as a part of, and as a product of, the organization of schools, it is necessary to document that knowledge as it is experienced in the organizational setting. That is, one must experience school course content not merely in printed curriculum guides or texts, but in the classroom, as it is encountered by students. The research techniques of the ethnographer are most appropriate for documenting the in-use curriculum because, as anthropological tools, they are capable of capturing the culture and the dynamics of on-going situations and they build in the corrective of the participants' perceptions. Extended non-participant observations in classrooms provided the data on the forms and content of instruction and on relations among teachers and students. Interviews with participants at all levels added the participants' meanings of observed events and provided additional information about school processes not directly observed. This combination of ethnographic methods overcame the traditional divisions between "curriculum research" and "organizational analysis" by allowing the actual interrelations among components of a given school to come to light.[1]

The schools were selected with the help of university professors whose student teachers had taught in the schools or who themselves had visited the schools. In addition, state education agency personnel gave advice on the basis of observation and general reputation for the predominance of administrators or teachers in the school.[2]

The research centered on one key difference among the schools: the relation of their administrative personnel and policies to classroom knowledge. Forest Hills, the site of the original classroom ethnography in this series, represented a school where teachers tightly controlled classroom knowledge in a setting of ostensible administrative *laissez-faire* distance from curriculum. It was the only school in the study to be a part of a large school system. The teachers maintained tight control over course content.

At Maizeville High, students' access to knowledge was more open in the classroom than the students found at Forest Hills, although the administration was known to be equally removed from course content. Freeburg High was chosen for its reputation for limited student access to knowledge resources, with an administration involved in curriculum reform (the latter proved in reality to be less accurate in practice; see Freeburg High, Chapter 4).

Nelson High was reputed among personnel at the state depart-

ment of education, the nearby teacher training colleges, and regional social studies teachers, as the high school in the area with
the most "academic" principle and substantive curriculum. From
these varied schools a picture emerged of the organizational dynamics shaping teachers' decisions of knowledge access and knowledge control.

The variation among the schools was deliberately sought. As
discussed in the Preface, this comparative analysis was prompted
by questions raised when earlier research revealed that the classroom instruction in a single school proved to be of far lower quality
than the school's reputation would have indicated. At that school,
poor instruction resulted when teachers' very tight control of content made the course content suspect for students because they had
no chance to discuss it or compare it to their own information. At
this school, the administration appeared to function at great distance from the classroom; yet the teachers attributed their own
controlling strategies to this distance, which to them indicated the
administrator's devaluing of instruction in favor of procedures and
controls.

This high school, Forest Hills, was a classic American high
school. The formal *distancing* of administration from instruction
was to be expected. The informal effects of that distancing, especially on the teachers' decision to keep tight reins on content, was
not. That is because, in the words of organization theorists, schools
are complex organizations that are said to be "loosely coupled"
(Weick, 1976). Loosely-coupled organizations are made up of domains of professionals who function semi-autonomously from each
other (McNeil, 1977). Unlike strictly hierarchical bureaucracies,
loosely-coupled organizations preserve limited areas in which one
kind of professional can retain authority without affecting or being
wholly affected by the decisions of professionals in a loosely-linked
department. Within this model, the wisdom has been that, although
administrators are teachers' superiors (in hiring and budgeting),
they leave teachers free to govern their own classrooms. In the case
of Forest Hills, this apparently benign distance concealed an active
tension among divergent priorities. Yet the model has descriptive
power because it addresses the historical split between administrative and educative purposes in a way that a strictly hierarchical
model of school organization fails to do. The appropriateness of
the term "loosely-coupled" for describing variations central to

21

selecting schools is greater, as the case studies will demonstrate, than its power to account for the complex tension actually being acted out among instructional and administrative components of schools. The notion of coupling, or formal and deliberate relationship, between administration and classrooms is most helpful, therefore, as a schematic for representing the variations for which the schools were selected, although as an analytical tool it will be only partially explanatory.

Table 2.1 restates this variation among the schools, according to the pattern of administrative coupling to the classroom and the pattern of knowledge access or control within the classroom.

Table 2.1 *Formal context for control over access to knowledge*

| *Degree of coupling between administration and classroom instruction* | *Degree of formal teacher control of knowledge* | |
|---|---|---|
| | *Tighter control* | *More open access* |
| *Involved administration* | Freeburg High | Nelson High |
| *Distant administration* | Forest Hills High | Maizeville High |

Because the schools were selected specifically for variation from the first school studied, they have some marked differences in policy, procedure, reputation, school climate and, to many observers, efficacy. Because they are all from the same general area, they share many attributes as well.

## Commonalities

Before spotlighting the differences, it will be useful to point out commonalities. Three of the schools were similar in size of enrollment and in community size. All four served fairly homogeneous student populations, mainly white, middle-class students. All of the schools had some students from poorer families, including families which received public assistance, and the largest of the schools included families from two federal housing projects. A small number of students at each school was eligible for school lunch assistance. All the districts included some upper middle-class families, with parents who were professionals or wealthy business people. Much of the upper level of income, however, was provided by two-worker families, where neither parent alone earned an extremely high income. The parents in all four districts tended toward government, university, small business or service sector employment. The industrial base of the counties represented tended to fall outside these four high schools' boundaries, except for an assembly plant and locally-owned light industry. Agriculture was a principal employment of many families at Maizeville and Freeburg.

Perhaps most significant for organizational analysis was the common legal base shared by the four schools. All were within the same state, and thus had the same state guidelines for curriculum, graduation requirements, faculty certification, administrator certification and building specifications.

Each faculty was represented by a teacher union, with all having the same constraints on administrative-faculty roles. For example, according to the union contracts, no faculty member had the authority to hire, dismiss or evaluate other faculty members. Administrative personnel did not hold union membership at any of these schools, and department chairs were considered faculty. At each school, rewards and sanctions were spelled out by the unions and were constant across the four schools; transfers, lay-offs and dismissals due to budgetary considerations were to be based on seniority. Probationary teachers were to be evaluated each year, with three years the usual probationary period. Experienced (tenured) teachers were to be evaluated periodically, but there was no merit system of pay. Pay increments depended on years of experience, usually within that school district, and years and degrees of education. Salary was the usual point of contention in contract negotiation, and it was common for teachers to work without a contract while bargaining disputes were being negotiated or sent to mediation or arbitration. Class size, course load and additional duties such as coaching were specified in the contract; any duties above the minimum load (usually four classes per semester plus specified hall or study hall duty) were reimbursed, including sponsorship of extra-curricular activities, attending meetings or serving on committees beyond the regular faculty or departmental meetings.

While these union-based conditions of work appear "normal," it is important to mention them precisely because so many teachers in this country work without any affiliative arrangement or with only affiliations not recognized for collective bargaining, such as the National Education Association (NEA) in many southern states. At the observed schools, unionization of faculty occurred within the professional careers of the present faculty. Within these teachers' tenure the unions had moved from innovative (and in the minds of administrators, often radical) organizations, to more conservative, taken-for-granted agents for narrow tasks such as pay bargaining. Occasionally a dismissal or hiring issue would be brought by the union grievance mechanisms, but at all the schools the primary function was to bargain for pay and seniority issues. This same framework for employee relations took on different characters at the four schools, although the formal contractual relation was remarkably similar.

The schools also shared a lack of serious discipline problems. That the administrative staff was so disproportionately attuned to discipline problems at three of the schools did not appear to be merited by the conduct of students as observed over a semester. The schools had virtually no violence; few, if any, teachers or students felt unsafe. Despite expectations raised by stories in the national press, I saw no unemployed drop-outs roaming the halls extorting lunch money or selling drugs. Students seemed remarkably prompt and well-behaved at the four schools, though administrators at all four talked about tardiness as a major problem. The primary problems were skipping school or selectively skipping classes. Drug usage was a presence at all these schools, though only among very small numbers of students and in less evidence than alcohol. The drug of choice among youth of this brewery state tended to be beer. While teenage drinking and teenage driving were a concern state-wide and student talk was full of drinking stories, most seemed to confine their drinking to after-school hours and weekends. Few students seemed to come to school drunk or stoned, and the kinds of strong-arm tactics and cohorts of spaced-out students that make good press copy were absent or minimal at these schools. At all but Nelson High, carelessness and indifference among students was the prevailing "discipline" problem.

The four schools also shared strong tax bases and a legacy of strong support for education in the state. Their tax bases differed,

24

as will be noted, but the state as a whole supported public education well, not only at the elementary and secondary levels, but in the establishment of a strong network of technical, undergraduate and graduate campuses. A majority of students at each school would enroll in post-high school education and a majority would earn a degree. Most of these would choose to attend a state college or university, with the three smaller schools also sending a good many students to the technical and vocational schools, for either technical certification or preparation for later college work.

The schools were also similar in lack of emphasis on competitiveness, excellence, ability group tracking or other differential programs.[3] The emphasis at all four was on the middle level of students, with the assumption that high achieving students would "make it on their own." Some remedial or drop-out prevention program at each school reached small numbers of lowest achieving students. Unlike elementary school attention to child development, these high school teachers almost without exception discussed students' abilities as static. Student differences were rarely discussed; when they were, the discussion was very general, without reference to individual children. It was usually couched in the assumption that the way a child is at present is the way he or she will always be. At none of the schools was there a systematic or programmatic concern for increasing students' skills, for changing students' habits, for an active, dynamic model of instruction based on development. Individual teachers who belied this generalization will be noted, but the generalization holds at the school and departmental levels. The students' ability levels were held to be their upper limits in many of the courses, rather than minimums from which the teacher was to work with the student to improve skills.

Such minimum standards are more obviously prevalent among behavioral mastery and competency models in vogue in many elementary schools. At all four of these high schools, the teachers thought of themselves as professionals, as teachers in the model of college instructors, with expertise in a subject area. They found behaviorist reduction of content and instructional technique empty and limiting and had successfully avoided this type of de-skilling so prevalent in elementary curricula since the mid-1970s. These secondary teachers had avoided "teacher proof" packaged curricula, which make teachers into classroom managers rather than subject matter professionals.[4] As will be noted, many of them had

25

not avoided the de-skilling that comes with teaching in schools that subordinates educative goals to social control efforts. This will be the subject of the concluding sections of this analysis. It is mentioned here to emphasize that all these schools followed a traditional secondary instructional model of the teacher as subject-matter expert, as contributor and sometimes creator of knowledge. The teachers' methods of teaching stemmed more from the ways they were taught and the evolution of their personal styles than from fads or innovations introduced by university departments of education, commercial producers of materials and tests, or in-service speakers.

One reason these teachers were secure in their methods was that all were experienced teachers. Social studies in these high schools seemed to be a predominantly male domain. There were, in addition to the woman teacher observed, three women teaching social studies at these schools, but their courses or part-time status fell outside the design of the study. These schools had stable faculties because of stabilized or declining enrollments. In the case of this study, the stable group of faculty happened to be mostly men.

The contractual and personal status of the teachers is critical to the discussion of knowledge access and knowledge control because of the broad latitude the teachers in these schools had in designing the curriculum. The state did not prescribe the content which lay behind even required course titles. Three of these districts had no district-wide curricula, and courses were developed mostly by in-dividual teachers, working under departmental guidelines at times, but otherwise free to structure their courses according to their own styles, pacing and content expertise. At the fourth school (Nelson High School, Chapter 6) there was a curriculum within the departmental areas for all to follow, but even there teachers themselves had written the curriculum and saw the unified materials as bases from which to organize their courses rather than limits beyond which they could not deviate. The degree of autonomy these teachers had to develop courses, to create units within their courses and to make decisions regarding texts and supplemental materials is in striking contrast to teachers in many states where texts, curriculum guides, measures of student performance, and even the pacing of the course are the product of state regulations or strict district-wide centralized policies. That the observed teachers did not always take advantage of their greater degree of curricular autonomy makes that autonomy even more significant.

The schools share one other attribute which made them appropriate to the study. The research was designed to find out how school knowledge is shaped in the normal, day-to-day life of a high school. To discover the regularities of knowledge distribution in schools it was necessary to select schools which were not experimental, which were not under a federal or state intervention, which were not piloting new commercial or university-supplied curricula. Most of all, it was desired that the schools be operating within their usual budgets, not supplemented by funds for special programs unavailable to the majority of high schools. All of these schools fit the pattern of schools going about their usual business. Two had some changes deliberately underway in program revision and building construction, and one was undergoing involuntary changes brought on by declining enrollments. But these changes arose from their usual situation and were not imposed or introduced from outside interventions. Studying schools that lack special funds or programs is essential if we are to move from curriculum research which measures the impact of experimental interventions (thus focusing on student achievement measures) to curriculum research which centers on what the school provides for the children. As federal and other outside sources of revenue become more scarce for public schools, it will be even more important to understand what is usual and what is possible given local budgets and resources.

To recapitulate, the schools shared similar teaching staffs (at least in social studies departments), student populations, union contracts, resource bases and a lack of special interventions or innovations. Their differences are then heavily shaped by their histories, by varied structures and by responses of personnel to those structures.

**Structural variations**

Having established the commonalities shared by these schools, we are ready to compare the variations in their structures, particularly the relationship between the administration and the classroom.[5] These profiles will serve as backdrop for the case study analyses of the processing of classroom knowledge within these structures. In

27

each case, the way the organization deals with the two competing goals of schools, education and social control, or the way the organizational structure embodies this tension, will be the key variant among the schools.

## Forest Hills High School

Forest Hills High best embodies the classic administrator–teacher split. The teachers at this school thought of themselves as professionals in their subject fields; to them, the administrators were intellectual lightweights, concerned with keeping order in the halls and with processing students through required credits to graduation. The split was so marked, by the arrangement of the building, by staff patterns of socializing, by the use of time, by the substance of announcements and other communications between the two groups of personnel, that the administration seemed totally divorced from classroom and curricula. Despite these distances, the teachers justified their treatment of students and course content by citing administrative practices and shifts in policy which had significantly altered their institutional context and had undermined their ability to teach. Although the school fits the classic model of single-teacher classrooms, in a school where both the state and the building administrators left content to teacher discretion, the teachers felt that this *laissez-faire* model applied only to their lack of support, not to administrator constraints.

Forest Hills High was the site of the earlier ethnographic study of the treatment of economics information in required social studies classes.[6] The analysis of social studies instruction as an arena in which teachers controlled students by controlling course content has been the subject of previously published writings.[7] The questions raised by these teachers' rationale provided the impetus for the present research, which included a return to the school for analysis of the administrative context. Since the other three high schools were selected for specific ways in which they varied from Forest Hills, Forest Hills will be discussed for itself, and for its typical arrangement with management-oriented administrators and with teachers removed from management but fairly autonomous over their course content and instructional methods. At Forest Hills it was found that the treatment of economics information did not differ significantly from that of other types of historical information, and that economics was formally an area of extensive study. The extensive treatment of the topic, however, was not indicative of its impact on students. The teachers were controlling access to information in order to elicit minimum participation from students; the students, in turn, were suspecting the validity of the information, albeit silently in order to raise no conflicts that could jeopardize their grade in their required course. Both groups were bracketing their personal information and questions in order to preserve their own efficiencies within the institutional setting.

Several questions arose related to the administration. How did the teachers get away with their pattern of instruction (having almost no student reading, writing or discussing) in a school, and in a school system, where the community supported high-quality education and paid for it with high taxes? How much were the teaching strategies grounded, as the teachers claimed, in indifferent and constraining administrative policies? Were there other schools where the pattern of low expectations demonstrated among teachers and students at Forest Hills was alleviated or minimized by a more supportive administrative context? For the answers to the first two questions it was necessary to return to Forest Hills to investigate the administrative context in more detail.

## Forest Hills school and community

Forest Hills High School is an old, established high school, once known as one of the best high schools in the nation. It serves a predominantly white, middle-class neighborhood in a midwestern city. The neighborhood immediately surrounding the school is made up of families, with most of the parents working in white-collar jobs. Small business owners, tradespeople, government employees and retirees also live in the area. Also in the school's boundaries are a housing project for low-income families and some poor working-class neighborhoods. Typical of the midwest, there are less dramatic ranges of wealth and poverty than in many parts of the country, and the casual dress of the students minimizes social class distinctions. The few minority students are black or Asian, with fewer Hispanics and American Indians. School taxes are high and support for education is strong in this neighborhood.

Several years prior to the observations, the school had been changed from a predominantly college-preparatory school to a more comprehensive high school, complete with a vocational wing.

This change had occurred when the city's downtown high school had been closed in a political shuffle that included building a new high school in a wealthy new neighborhood and shifting downtown students to Forest Hills. These downtown students came from an excellent program and demonstrated a range of test scores similar to that of Forest Hills' students. However, because the downtown district included the housing project and other poor and minority areas, the teachers at Forest Hills were sure their school would "never be the same". Nationally, the effects of integration on white and minority children were being debated. Forest Hills got into the debate when the press picked up on the emotional resistance to the boundary shift and when a doctoral student in educational administration used the shift as his dissertation topic. Teachers at Forest Hills, the downtown school and at the feeder junior highs were polled as to their expectations of student performance when the two school populations were mixed. Students were surveyed as well about the differences in ability, family income and student participation levels they anticipated from the students from "the other school." The students anticipated few differences, but the teachers all believed the downtown students would have worse attendance and academic records. The professional decision was to build the vocational wing, with added *caveats* to look into changes needed to accommodate the new student population in regular academic subjects.[8] This was the first of several policy changes made at administrative levels with no input from teachers. (The teachers were surveyed by a graduate student, not their principal.) Despite general anticipations that the new students would have different needs, no administrative help in materials or workshops or other programmatic means made provision for dealing with the new students. Interestingly, no follow-up was done on their progress nor on the effects their presence had on the ways teachers organized their lessons.

To add to the Forest Hills teachers' feelings that their once-great school was changing for the worse, charges of discrimination led the school board to eliminate ability-group tracking of students. This policy directly contradicted the teachers' personal pedagogies and was made over their objections. Many of their feelings that they could no longer affect students came from the re-organization of their classes against their will.

The other significant change in the teachers' minds was the students' perceptions of the changing legitimacy of school practices. Prior to the late 1960s, the staff was held in some esteem and many students valued school experiences which would help them gain admission to good colleges or build resumés for successful jobs. Teachers recalled that students had seen school work as instrumental to their own future good and had entered into learning in a spirit of cooperation and, often, enthusiasm. Protests against the Vietnam war ended that cooperative spirit; teachers saw their authority over content threatened, and students demanded more authority over procedure. The students' efforts finally produced a student bill of rights for the city's schools. Teachers reclaimed their authority in ways we shall see as we examine course proceedings in a later chapter. A part of their frustration was that, even more serious than student protest, there was a failure of the very control-oriented administration to exert discipline controls in support of teachers' efforts during this troubled time.

## Administrative structure

Teachers' autonomy over content derived from a broad framework of legal and bureaucratic requirements almost independent of the school's administration. The teachers' union, of which these teachers were members, negotiated contracts specifying teaching and order-keeping duties, salary, pay for extra activities, and other specific working conditions. These teachers taught four classes per day, usually the same course all day, or maybe two course preparations per year. The state outlined only very broad graduation requirements, and the city and state requirements combined regulated only half the credits a student needed for graduation; the rest were left up to the individual high school and its students.

While their autonomy over *content* would be envied by teachers in the states where content is prescribed, the teachers at Forest Hills felt little autonomy or authority over *procedure*. Their school was heavily administered, with a principal and four grade-level principals, and each had formal authority over some of the subject departments. This authority was rarely actively exercised except in the brief classroom visits to teachers being evaluated. The five principals attended to budgets, discipline, hall order, athletic schedules and other procedural details. They were rarely evident in department meetings, in classrooms, in conversations with students (especially in non-disciplinary conversations), or in instruction. Like two

*Choice and contradictions*

of the other schools, faculty governance was not a part of the life of this school. Directives came from the office; the teachers felt that the administrator spent his time on control details yet would not back them if they tried to exert authority over behavior.

The same feelings of distance and powerlessness characterized many teachers' views of the central administration. The superintendent was known for being a tough negotiator; he was in charge of school policy. He enjoyed the support of the majority of the school board during the years of observations. In the recent past, the system had had subject matter supervisors and four geographic area supervisors as well. Subject matter supervisors were phased out, ostensibly for cost-cutting reasons, as were two of the four geographic area administrators, again for expressed budgetary reasons.

Later, the superintendent, in an interview prior to his retirement, explained that while cost-cutting was the overt reason for re-organization, the real reason was to consolidate power in the hands of the superintendent by eliminating positions susceptible to community pressures and to being identified with a particular subject or area of the city.

The superintendent was not greatly loved by the teachers interviewed. When their opinions were solicited through a questionnaire regarding his potential replacement, one teacher wrote back to the committee that the selection was their job, not hers. The superintendent's interests reflected the business community more than educators. He mirrored the superintendents Callahan (1962) describes, who, during the early days of industrial and school bureaucratization, emulated executives rather than scholars.[9] This superintendent often made news for his business associations and investments, including once for delinquent property taxes. In this system, far more than in the others observed, administrators moved in different social circles from classroom teachers. Part of the reason was salary; in a year when administrative merit raises averaged $2,200, the teachers almost went on strike over an offer of $100 across-the-board raises that the administration justified by claims of austerity.

The superintendent was very political but imposed rational modes on administrative decisions, perhaps to neutralize strong political opposition. He favored closing neighborhood schools with declining enrollments and was accused of closing first those schools

32

that served as centers of neighborhood organizations and political activities. Whether this is a justified accusation, it is clear that he did not respond favorably to teacher- and parent-initiated movements such as the drive for an open classroom school (though a number of elementary schools were finally permitted to pilot open classroom projects if the pilots could be done within existing budgets). Parents, teachers and a few enthusiastic principals contributed time, money and energy to create classroom environments in which an open classroom model of instruction could be tried within existing schools. Later, these schools were among the first closed.

To monitor the activities of principals and area coordinators below him, the superintendent in conjunction with the school board initiated an evaluation program with management by objectives (MBO), for which he became well known in administrator circles throughout the country. He generated teacher hostility by trying to implement teaching by objectives as well, but this was successfully fought by the union as unprofessional and demeaning. The MBO system for administrators had both real and symbolic effects. Symbolically, it made administrators appear to have rationalized goals related to the total school program and gave the impression of helping to improve schools, or at least job performance. The real impact was that the MBOs could be differentially structured to demand less of favored principals, for example, to influence the merit evaluations.

Each administrator would meet with his or her superior at the beginning of the year or over the summer to set the next year's objectives. They would agree, as in a contract. Months later they met to see if the goals had been accomplished. Teachers complained that their views and students' views of the ways principals could help the school were never considered. They suspected that politics weighed heavily on the setting of easy objectives when it suited the superior. At one point in contract negotiations, personnel from the teachers' union estimated that the equivalent of more than one and a half administrator years was spent on formulating and evaluating management objectives in the district each school year.

The principal of Forest Hills had one management objective to create a new student handbook. He solicited ideas from students, staff and parents before compiling the standard handbook of rules, graduation requirements, disciplinary procedures, school colors, map and song. The teachers saw it as a task more suitable to a

33

secretary or committee of students. They chafed that it merited the principal a bonus since, despite outlining the rules and sanctions, he frequently embarrassed teachers in front of students by failing to back them in enforcing those sanctions.

No departmental structure existed to overcome administrative indifference to classroom concerns. The chair was elected, although one teacher told of being asked to accept the chair as an appointment because the principal was "unsure" he could work with the person elected. The teacher declined. The department chair helped distribute textbooks and place orders and arrange the course schedule but otherwise did not function in a leadership role, either to make policy or to bring the department together to do so.

The teachers' main view of the administration was its distance in terms of support, its intrusions in adding constraints and work loads, and its undermining of previous reward structures derived from tracking the classes. In short, the teachers felt themselves to share almost no common definitions of school goals or school practice with the building or district-level administrators. Lacking collective mechanisms in faculty governance or departmental leadership, they were left to create their own base of authority and their own efficiencies within the context of unsupportive administrators. The top-down form of administration typified the historical classic American high school organization. The inherited form of remote administration was bolstered by the superintendent's choice to employ rational modes of control and evaluation with teachers as workers rather than as co-professionals.

## Freeburg High School

The structural distance between administrators and classroom instruction at Forest Hills High School was the direct result of planning, administrative policy choices and strong central leadership which clearly marked the bounds between decision-makers and workers. The relations at Freeburg High School were much less rational, much more random.

The word most often used to describe Freeburg High was "mess." Not everyone used the word to mean the same thing, but "mess" invariably popped up in discussions of the school. When teachers at the other observed schools heard that Freeburg would be a part of the study, they would comment, "I hear they have a

real mess out there," or, "I'd be interested in what you find there
– they've been in a mess for years." Sometimes the referent was the
repeated failure of Freeburg's voters to pass school bond authori-
zations. When social studies teachers in the area said "mess," they
referred specifically to Freeburg's lack of strong social studies credit
requirements for graduation, thus low social studies enrollments.

"Mess" meant something else to me as I entered the building for
the first time. I stepped through large double doors into a wide
hallway strewn with litter, much of it in piles. My first thought was
that I must have entered a service entrance. I discovered that I was
not near the cafeteria or maintenance area, but the auditorium.
This was the school's "front door." I later left by the other main-
door, which led out through the cafeteria/commons area. Lunch
hour over, the janitor was sweeping litter, mostly paper, into two
huge piles, both taller than the large trash receptacles nearby.
Though I never found the auditorium entrance quite so messy on
later visits, the cafeteria scene was a daily occurrence. Moreover,
litter cluttered halls and classrooms and became a dominant
"school problem" topic for several class discussions.

The contrast of the physical setting at Freeburg with the almost
too-clean Nelson High I had observed the previous semester was a
portent of other striking differences. My first day in the teachers'
lounge, a man teacher in his sixties began telling me of the woes
and missteps of the new construction. We had not been introduced,
so perhaps he mistook me for a substitute teacher. At any rate, he
soon filled me in on his complaints about the planning of the new
addition to the building, especially about the failure of the planners
to consult with many teachers and their failure to follow even the
basic needs of those teachers who had informed them of specific
needs in shops and labs.

The litter and spontaneous complaints were visible evidence of
a less visible uneasiness that permeated the staff and students. The
uneasiness is partly traceable to the overcrowded building and
partly to the historical lack of strong community support for the
school. Interviews with teachers and the principal revealed that the
primary source seemed to be the lack of common purpose and
policy between the administration and faculty. The discord between
them had no mechanisms for resolution. It inspired teacher lethargy
or resistance and administrative inconsistency. And it helped engender widespread student disengagement from school practices.

35

*Choice and contradictions*

As at Forest Hills, exceptions to the general pattern of disengagement arose from teacher initiative, with individual teachers taking the risks of time and effort to attempt improvements, outside and apart from otherwise regular procedures. The analysis of Freeburg, then, will begin with those regularities, the structure of daily routines of order-keeping and teaching, and will then take up a reform effort which countered the pattern of unease and low expectations. These details are the subject of Chapter 4.

Freeburg was selected as the school which varied from Forest Hills in that the administration was reputed to be more closely involved with curriculum than at Forest Hills, though the treatment of information in the classroom was similarly tightly controlled by the teachers. The reputation for administrative involvement was based in part on extensive curriculum reform and re-evaluation measures which involved a person from the state department of public instruction, the school's administration, and a curriculum coordinator from the school district's central office. Although this re-evaluation was taking place, and included a revision of graduation requirements during the observation period, it was the exception to a pattern of administrative distance from classroom practice. The more common link between administrators and teachers was that frequently administrative directives on discipline and procedure intruded into teacher time. The reforms, or revisions, in fact were generated by faculty concern and shepherded through heated school board meetings as much by teachers as by the district office staff; the involvement of the building principal was more in the form of quiet support than initiative.

Although the workings of the school did not entirely bear out the reputation which had prompted its inclusion as a representative of the involved administration/tightly controlled knowledge variation, they did add important insights into internal factors in a traditional high school which can mitigate against effective instruction.

Freeburg school and community

Two of the four schools in the same area were of enough note that parents coming into the area frequently moved to one of those communities so that their children could attend them. Freeburg was not one of them. It is located in a small town which has an interesting history of its own, but had become in the past fifteen

36

years more and more of a suburban adjunct to a larger town nearby. Freeburg itself has several light industries but otherwise is characterized by small businesses which serve its residents and surrounding farming areas. Most employment and major shopping are supplied by the larger town. The high school drew its 1,400 students from the town of Freeburg, a smaller town which no longer had a high school of its own, from farm families in the 75 square miles around the school, and from the newly exurban population which had moved to acreages in the country but were otherwise urban in their employment and styles of living.

The school building had been in need of repair and additional space for a number of years, as had the central administration offices, which were housed in a very old elementary school building. Enrollments had been increasing with the increased suburbanization of the community, but not at the rates anticipated by school personnel. In the late 1960s and early 1970s a number of apartment complexes were built, changing the character of the town and raising expectations of quickly rising school enrollments. Quite often the apartment dwellers turned out to be young singles, couples without children, or families who moved into the larger town when their children reached school age. New subdivisions of large, expensive single-family residences and town houses added projections of rapid expansions of school population, but these did not materialize. The houses were so expensive, according to the principal, that they were more affordable to professionals without children, or with grown children, than to families. School enrollments, then, were still increasing but at a very slow rate, in contrast to the rapid growth rate originally expected for Freeburg schools during this period. Many of the people who had chosen to buy residences in Freeburg, but work in the larger town, had done so partly because property taxes, including school taxes, had been lower there than in the larger community. In addition, only one-third of the households had school-aged children. The combination of adults who chose to live in Freeburg for its low tax rates, the elderly whose incomes and family situations hindered their willingness to support rising school costs, and the presence of many young childless adults added to the lack of interest in increased financing for the schools. Bond issues for an addition to the high school, a new administration building and a swimming pool for the city were repeatedly defeated. Only after repairs and additions to the school buildings were separated from the other expenditures were they approved by voters. According to the teachers, tax base differences between the larger town and satellite communities such as Freeburg were narrowing with increased costs of services in these outlying areas. The per pupil expenditures at Freeburg now rivaled those of neighboring towns, though the legacy of past differentials was a gap in the quality of buildings and resources and, at some levels, teacher pay.

The lack of a high priority for money for the schools was further exacerbated by the diversity within the population served by the school. The teachers spoke of a rural–urban (or suburban) split among the students, with the presumption that this extended to their families' interests. Although these differences among students were not visually apparent in observations or student interviews, the teachers explained that the students segregated themselves by "town" and "country" categories in the cafeteria and in some school activities. Similar divisions appeared in the school board, again not so blatantly evident in simplistic dichotomies, but disunified enough to prevent cohesive long-range planning around a consensus or coalition of purpose.

Administrative structure

Like Forest Hills High, Freeburg High was organized in the classic model of American secondary schools, with a building principal and assistant principals, subject matter departments chaired by a faculty member, courses divided by grade level and traditional academic disciplines, taught by teachers in single-teacher classrooms. As at Forest Hills, there had been no ability-based tracking or grouping, except that better students elected to take economics, upper-level science and math courses and foreign languages in greater numbers than low-achieving students. According to the principal, 60 per cent of the graduates attended two- or four-year colleges, and another 15 per cent attended trade and vocational schools after high school. Of the remaining quarter of the students, it is known but not documented that a good many returned to some kind of schooling after working at jobs or in the home for a few years. Most of those who attended college and trade schools remained in the state, and by far the largest numbers attended campuses of the state university system.

Because of the size of the school system, having only one high school, the system was not as top-heavy with administrative staff as some larger systems. The superintendent had been with the system for a number of years; within the past five years a curriculum supervisor had been added. Although this person's role helped in the selection of Freeburg as a school with administrative input into curriculum, the secondary teachers saw him as primarily interested in and responsible for involvement with elementary school curriculum.

The building principal could be characterized as a weak person in a strong role. That is, the school was organized such that the principal had centralized authority over all subject fields, discipline, staff review, budget, building and other traditional principals' duties. By union contract, department chairs could not review and evaluate their peers, nor could they hire or dismiss other teachers. The centralization of authority in the school was, according to the teachers interviewed, of less concern than its haphazard and unpredictable application. The principal was preoccupied with order at the expense of program development, resources, planning and oversight of academic goals. There existed no other mechanisms in the school to deal with these. If indeed order-keeping had been such a problem that it merited predominance, or if in fact the order-keeping policies had been so effective that the teaching staff could devote its time to these other matters, there might have been less impatience with the administration's priorities. In fact, the means of dealing with order and other issues tended to be trial-and-error, with frequent shifts in mid-course, leaving students and teachers with little idea of what to expect next. Order, to the administration, meant controlled behavior. Social control through attention to credentials was of less concern than controlling people by assigning them to specified places in the building.

There was no faculty governance arrangement. Because the union largely confined its bargaining to transfer, lay-off and salary issues, there was no effective faculty voice about other matters of working conditions, program evaluation, student needs or resources. The department chair was appointed; the current social studies chair replaced a man who in his own words had too many differences with the administration to be effective. The current chair was popular within the department and greatly respected by the principal, and since no one else wanted the job, he would serve until he asked to be relieved of it. Departments met monthly or at the discretion of the chair, or at the request of members with pressing concerns. Because the social studies chair was so respected, this department had as effective a voice as any in bringing matters to the principal regarding course changes, teaching assignments and the like. There was less feeling of efficacy in shaping more general policies which affected the overall climate of the school.

During the 1960s the student government had voted itself out of existence. No similar organization had arisen to take its place. To elicit students' perspectives, the principal organized a Student Rap Group, comprised of appointed and elected students from each grade who met with him twice each month to discuss such issues as examination schedules, school rules and the like. They succeeded in getting an exam schedule changed during the semester of observation.

Information within the school tended to flow from the top down. The principal was responsible for overseeing the primary academic subject matter departments. He delegated to assistant principals oversight of the four cooperative-vacational areas (such as business and agriculture), athletics, the arts, physical education and extracurricular activities. In reality, these areas required more administrative involvement because of scheduling buildings and buses and because of added budget and community relations responsibilities. Both the principal and his assistants were to observe and evaluate probationary teachers during each year of their probation. There were few probationary teachers, none in social studies. The experienced teachers were supposed to be observed and evaluated at regular intervals. There was no merit salary or other compensation, so the evaluation was rarely substantive.

While the organizational framework of this school fits thousands of American high schools, with its apparently distant administration and somewhat autonomous teachers, these teachers felt that its particular application in their school undermined many of their efforts to teach. Its superficially neutral, rational structure only thinly disguised a vulnerability to inconsistency and ambiguity. There was seldom doubt among the faculty that the policies of the school emanated from the main office. The uncertainty came in not knowing when and under what circumstances the policies would be changed. There seemed little expectation that the principal or others in administrative capacities would automatically be concerned with educational quality. By far the greatest numbers of communications from the office to the teachers concerned discipline and procedures. This concern for order would have been appreciated if in fact it had succeeded in alleviating litter, class skipping or general disengagement from learning activities. More often, the new directives on discipline would come in the form of announcements brought in by student messengers interrupting class or would come as policy shifts in the middle of the semester. The directives were almost always reactive, hasty responses to immediate problems – clumsy attempts to "put out fires."

To understand the concern for orderly behavior, one must picture the school building. It was a series of additions to a very old brick structure. The cafeteria/commons, auditorium and a wing of classrooms and lecture halls were relatively new additions. The central portion of the building, housing the cramped teachers' lounge and work area, was very old and condemned as unsafe. The office and adjoining classrooms were from a vintage newer than the condemned part but much older than the cafeteria/commons. Parts of the building were never well-lighted. Old sections had been allowed to fall into disrepair while succeeding bond issues were hopefully but vainly put before voters. One of the sources for leverage for new construction came from an accreditation report which noted the overcrowding. The state department of public instruction had revised its per pupil space guidelines to 150 square feet per pupil; Freeburg's building had closer to one-third that amount. Even though part of the new state guidelines were space requirements for vocational, handicapped access and laboratory space, and thus misleading if construed as traditional classroom space (they included, for example, space allocations for girls' physical education equal to that for boys), the overcrowded school building did contribute to several problems. The first of these was simply crowded halls; passing periods between classes were not extended to allow for large numbers of people passing through narrow corridors. Also a problem was teacher space. None of the teachers observed had exclusive use of a classroom. Rather than designate bulletin board space for those teachers using a room, the teachers for the most part tended to ignore the bulletin boards or leave fading announcements or posters up for weeks at a time. Similarly, the bookshelves seemed to be used randomly. Bookshelves for which no one felt fully responsible became filled with litter, pieces of books, unkempt piles of books a teacher brought in for a special

41

lesson but never straightened or took back to storage. Since teachers as a rule did not have their room empty during their planning period, they did not have time in there to arrange displays related to the course, keep things straight (or see that students did the caretaking), or otherwise make the room an attractive or useful resource for their teaching. Impersonal space tended to become neglected space; neglected space fostered further feelings of carelessness, of personal distance from the unattractiveness.

Whether because of crowding or a desire for order, teachers were assigned to patrol the halls and cafeteria during lunch. The lunch hour was staggered, so teachers did not see each other unless they had the same lunch hour and were not on patrol. Those who did not wish to eat in the unruly cafeteria took bag lunches or trays to the faculty lounge, a tiny room upstairs with a sink, table and a few chairs. Teachers patrolling the halls were to prohibit students from leaving the cafeteria when they finished eating. Students could leave only when their lunch hour was over. While this may have kept the halls quiet, it apparently increased the amount of idle time for littering in the cafeteria. (Cynics will see this description as "the way kids are." The cafeteria at Nelson, however, was a pleasant place, free of litter, full of chattering students; a teacher monitor stood by the serving lines, and occasionally a teacher might have to remind a student to throw paper in the trash can, but by and large lunch there was taken as an uncomplicated routine, not a state of siege.)

Academic areas at Freeburg were not free of these preoccupations with order. The library was locked during lunch hours, with students inside. Those students wishing to use the library during one of the lunch hours had to enter as the bell was ringing or be locked out; those inside were to stay inside until the end of the period.

The crowding must have caused some dislocations and needs for extra caution on discipline, but it does not fully explain the lack of caring about the environment which administrative personnel displayed. Two incidents involving windows reveal there was more to the problem. In Mr Lennon's classroom, a long crack slanted across a large window. A sturdy wind or accidental push on the window would have sent shards of glass on the nearest row of desks. Mr Lennon tried over a two-year period to have the window replaced or at least taped. One would think that for insurance liability reasons, if not concern for the students, the maintenance staff would have been instructed to replace the window at once. This did not happen; the rationale, when given, was that the window would be replaced when the new construction began. Windows in parts of the building not being razed would be replaced or caulked for insulation. The window remained a hazard during my entire time in the building.

When the insulating caulking did occur, it brought its own problems. Following the semester of observation, the Freeburg city paper carried a story about a social studies teacher's problem with toxic fumes in his classroom. It seems that Mr Edwards, a teacher I did not observe but who was considered excellent by the principal and the department and who had won a citizen-sponsored teaching award, taught in a room across from Mr Lennon's during the time the windows were being sealed with new insulating material. The fumes became so strong he had to open a window for ventilation over a weekend. When he returned to school, the window had been closed. Later the superintendent visited the room to check on his complaint but did nothing. The room was being used seven of the eight class periods during the day. Two weeks later, Mr Edwards got a note saying that the assistant principal discovered the cause of the fumes; a second builder had looked at the work and said that the caulking compound had been applied too thickly and so would continue to give off toxic fumes. A reporter who found Mr Edwards' letter to the press called the principal and was told all students had been removed from the room the minute a danger was known; in fact, no students or teachers had ever been moved. Mr Edwards' letter had said that students' well-being and safety should be the first priority. Like the broken window, which remained broken during two school years, the improperly sealed window was eventually fixed, but only after being a hazard to the students, a disruptive concern to the teacher, and an example of administrative indifference. Administrative concern for orderliness was weighted toward directing and controlling students rather than toward providing an atmosphere conducive to teaching and learning. This was lost on neither teachers nor students.

Relations between the administration and faculty shifted between *laissez-faire*-distant and adversarial. All the teachers spoke pleasantly about Mr Morton, the principal, as a person, called him "nice" and "gentlemanly," but several stated that he never should have been a principal. They expressed a perception of clear boundaries in the school between teaching responsibilities and administrative functions. Except for periodic meetings on budgets and teaching assignments, it was clear that the work of the department proceeded quite apart from the principal. Several past links between the two levels had been eroded by changing circumstances. Mr Lennon said that in the past the department had been able to help interview prospective new teachers and submit a ranked list of preferences. After the department disagreed over a hiring (it was his theory that a better woman candidate had lost to a man who would do some coaching), teachers were no longer invited to interview candidates. The chair described his role as including having a chance to rank resumés of teaching applicants, as well as sitting in on hiring interviews. Since no new teachers had been hired in several years, except for a temporary replacement during a maternity leave, this staff privilege became moot. In addition, the lack of staff turnover itself meant that these opportunities jointly to review program needs had ceased.

At Forest Hills, the faculty had been physically distant from the principal as well as distant in task. The building was quite large, the grade level principals handled many discipline actions, and the counseling staff took care of student placement in course assignments, attendance and other student-related matters. The principal at Freeburg was physically nearer, with his office near the social studies rooms, and more intrusive in policy. Except for faculty meetings, the teachers at Forest Hills heard from the principal directly only through infrequent memoranda. Routine there was so established that new policy statements during the semester were rare. Since materials and resources were handled at the department level, mainly through the social studies resource centers and the chair, there was little need to solicit the principal's participation.

In contrast, Freeburg never seemed to hit a stride, establish a routine. Both schools had an absence of constructive administrative participation in curriculum development or attention to classroom practice. At Forest Hills, the teachers felt indirect effects as they watched ability grouping be eliminated and as they themselves taught differently in reaction to administrative policy shifts. At Freeburg, reaction against (even adjustment to) administrative policies was more open, more observable, more attributable to the person occupying the principal role maybe than to the structured relationship itself. That Forest Hills teachers saw the social control goals of the school as the administrations' concern for processing students through credentials helps explain why administrative policies there were aimed at routines. The emphasis at Freeburg on social control as behavioral control, especially the control of groups of students, makes the administrative directives more intrusive because they were in response to student behaviors, unpredictable in time and event, rather than to standardizable credentialling functions. At these schools the tension between the social control purposes and the educative purposes reflects differences in teachers' accommodations to routinized or haphazard administrative practices.

## Maizeville High School

The formal structure at Maizeville High School resembled that of Forest Hills and Freeburg, with similar union contracts, an administration concerned with order keeping, and teachers assigned to individual classrooms according to their academic subjects. Despite outward similarities, the school differed from the other two schools in two important ways. First, the administrative distance from classrooms was mitigated by a strong-chairman model of departmental organization, which delegated to the chairman many duties and powers ordinarily retained by administrators. Second, the school's social studies department had a reputation for quality instruction which opened to students a wide variety of topics and learning activities. Maizeville, then, was chosen because it differed from Forest Hills in having a distant administration but openness of content within the classroom. Its strong-chair model demonstrates the potential for variation within traditional school structures to overcome the predominance of social control functions. A number of benefits accrued to the students, and to many of the staff, as a direct result of this arrangement.

### Maizeville school and community

Maizeville is a small farming community which has become a bedroom suburb for two nearby urban areas. Like Freeburg, Maizeville has few jobs to offer its adults and teenagers. There are few restaurants, no movies, few parks or other sources of recreation. Maizeville is a family town. Many who live there came because housing was more affordable and taxes were lower than in the cities

45

where parents worked. Many students said that their mother had returned to work when energy costs rose; in other words, two parents had to commute to the city to work, in order to pay commuting and heating costs. Inflation and the need for a car had sent many of Maizeville's teenagers into the workforce as well. Many worked more than twenty-five hours per week, partly to support the car needed to get to their jobs in the shopping malls and fast-food restaurants of the cities.[10] In addition, a number of farm children helped seasonally on family farms or on large commercial farms that also hired non-farm children during the summers.

The town was settled by north European immigrants, and many students at the high school could trace their roots to the early settlers of the area. New families and new housing appeared to outnumber the old, causing a redefinition of the community over a few short years. Growth in population was causing increased school population, rare in this time of declining enrollments in most schools in this part of the state.

Maizeville High, the district's only high school, served approximately 1,600 students, only slightly more than at Freeburg. Whereas the administration at Freeburg was observed to be less involved with curriculum than indicated by its reputation, the administration at Maizeville actually had a more active policy of teacher evaluation, and a symbolic gesture toward curriculum oversight, than believed when the school was selected for its variation from Forest Hills. For the most part, however, traditional administrative prerogatives in these areas, which at Forest Hills and Freeburg existed but were rarely exercised, were transferred to the strong-chair to the extent possible within the union contract.

The teachers' lounge was filled with complaints about the principal and assistant principals, mostly about the failure to support teachers in discipline matters, about promises not kept or projects not followed through to completion. The low morale among teachers in general at the school was not typical of the social studies teachers. The lack of administrative attention to detail was, however, evident in some school maintenance areas. Only the sidewalk nearest the front door was adequately shoveled in winter; other walks and paths to parking lots often remained precariously icy. New construction, necessitated by increasing enrollments, was plagued with problems. The teaching staff was happier with the planning stages than Freeburg's staff had been about their new

46

addition, and the social studies department looked forward to having adjacent rooms, a spacious office and proximity to the modern library. Though not a construction expert, I was surprised to see how little insulation went into the roof of the new building; the warehouse-type construction made stages of building easy to see. On returning to the school a year later, I was told the heating and cooling unit never worked properly in the new wings and that other rather basic design problems had emerged in this multi-million-dollar expansion project. The social studies rooms were an appreciated improvement, but the problems that cropped up seemed to the teachers too basic to be unavoidable.

The atmosphere of the school was generally cordial and pleasant, lacking in the intensity among the better students at Forest Hills and Nelson, but avoiding the antagonisms found between staff and students at Freeburg. A detention hall each afternoon meted punishments to the tardy or disruptive. During study hall periods, students used the detention hall room for quiet study but could go to the library or other places of business upon request. At all four schools, athletics was one of the few extra-curricular activities that competed successfully with the time demands of student jobs. Maizeville, in addition, had a small but strong music and drama cohort.

The principal anticipated that about half the graduates would enroll in technical or undergraduate schools. Classes were tracked by ability levels, rare among schools in this area during this time. Whereas the faculty at Forest Hills had fought to preserve tracking, but had lost out to central administration shifts toward homogeneous classes to avoid appearances of discrimination, the teachers at Maizeville were committed to altering curriculum and materials to suit several levels of student ability. They felt this could best be done in tracked classes, including basic or lowest level, general level, advanced and, in some subjects, an honors levels. According to the chairman of social studies, the teachers' wishes had influence since the district was small, they had no other high schools in the town to coordinate with, and they had fewer layers of bureaucracy to cut through. The unique feature of Maizeville's tracking system was that students could participate in the decision for placement. Several staff people told me that students tracked themselves. The chairman explained that the initial assignment came from the previous year's teacher in each subject, but that students could elect a higher track if they wished. At the end of a nine-week or semester grading period, if the teacher felt a student could not perform at that level, the placement would be reassessed with the student, the counselor and perhaps the parents. No permission would be granted to elect a lower level unless extreme circumstances warranted it; wanting free time for a job or an "easy senior year" were not accepted as reasons for a lower track placement. In social studies the enthusiasm among the staff for this plan was high; several teachers requested teaching upper-level classes and all taught some middle-level courses. One woman in particular was committed to teaching the lower ability students and developed her materials especially for this group, though other teachers were assigned to that level when needed. Her special expertise with that group prevented the status stratification that can occur within departments when high status accrues to those teaching upper level or honors classes.

Administrative structure
About twelve years prior to the observation, the school organization had shifted from a traditional principal-teacher plan common to schools such as Freeburg to a strong-chairman model of organization. The "strong chairman" was called a department coordinator and given a salary increment higher than that previously paid to department chairs. In addition, these coordinators were given greater responsibilities and, to fill them, more extensive powers. The coordinator, or strong chairman, acted as the administrator in all curriculum areas and in as many departments, those teacher–administrator boundaries were observed more in letter than in spirit. The result was that the administrators, the principal and assistant principals retained their authority over discipline and the signing of personnel evaluations. Authority over the substance of curriculum, the management of departmental budgets and the substance of evaluation and improvement were delegated to the chairman. The principal's distance from classroom concerns and preoccupation with order-keeping was thereby less of a threat, or a source of antagonisms, than that relationship held at Freeburg.

Among the responsibilities delegated to the department coordinator, or strong-chair, were the interviewing of prospective faculty members, observing in classrooms, making recommendations for instructional improvement, ordering of materials, and providing the basic substance of teacher evaluations discussed and signed by the principal. The coordinator could bargain for resource budgets for his department, could participate in encouraging faculty members to resign, could oversee the revision of courses or the development of new ones. In addition, responsibility for developing articulation with junior high curriculum and for tracking decisions lay with the coordinator. These responsibilities implied powers beyond that of the chairman at Freeburg or Forest Hills, where the role remained confined to helping schedule courses and teachers, planning budget allocations within funds set by the principal or central administration, and interacting informally with colleagues regarding course content or teaching styles. Such restraints as not being permitted to contact a publisher directly, as one teacher found at Freeburg, would have been unheard of, even unworkable, under the strong-chair model.

Whereas the teachers at Freeburg would have welcomed such a model as a gift of new privileges, the administration at Maizeville saw their plan as serving their interests even more than those of the faculty. The principal and assistant principal interviewed explained that almost half their time was spent "tracking down truants." When pressed for numbers, they estimated that only 100 students were truancy problems. But "those same kids" took enormous amounts of clerical and administrative energies to locate, process paperwork on, and bring to the attention of their parents. The principal further noted that though school attendance was mandatory under the law, the juvenile courts in this jurisdiction did not support the school in prosecuting truancy. Suspensions for the offense were "a laugh," since they rewarded absence with absence, usually for students whose poor grades would not demonstrably suffer for the loss. The administration position on parents' roles was equally critical; the principal said that most of the truants had family problems or a history of drug usage and that the parents often did not support the school in discipline matters. Often neither parent was home, or even in town, because of jobs in surrounding cities. When they heard of a problem, they tended to blame the school rather than their own inaccessibility. As the principal told it, "The kid does the same thing in the summer but no one sees it. When school starts, he does these things and misses school. Since the parent hasn't heard of the behavior before, he thinks it's the school's problem."

In addition, the administrators felt unqualified to have a more active role in curriculum development and evaluation. They said they could not be an expert in every subject area and so did not want all the responsibility for content. The assistant principal assigned to oversee social studies explained that he had no expertise or experience in the field, but had several relatives who did. He himself enjoyed reading history and had an interest in the subject. He approved of the school's policy of rotating the subject area assignments of the assistant principals every two or three years so that all became acquainted with the various departments. The gain in knowledge of overall program offset the loss in extended oversight of a narrower range of departments.

For the teachers, the delegation of curriculum matters to the coordinator filled an intellectual vacuum in the school. One coordinator stressed that "we have never had intellectual leadership in this school." The school district had an assistant superintendent for curriculum coordination but none of the faculty knew what this person did. Although in the past the job had on occasion served as a stepping-stone to the superintendent's office, or to such a job with another district, several of the teachers did not know where this person's office was located.

The delegation of considerable powers to the coordinator made the department as a whole more cohesive. In social studies, the present coordinator had hired half the present faculty. The arrangement centralized the department's leverage with the administration in the proposing of new courses or budget changes. While those departments whose coordinators chose not to exercise strong leadership did not suffer under this arrangement any more than under a traditional chairmanship, the plan gave wide latitude to those departments or coordinators who did want to be active in building their department's reputation within the school or among similar departments in the state.

According to the principal, some coordinators chose a passive role, perhaps because they accepted the appointment reluctantly, because the department was small, or because they had no interest in expanding their own administrative powers with their accompanying loads of paperwork and decisions. Most coordinators, however, found the freedom to make decisions worth the extra trouble in attention to detail.

The strong-chairman/coordinator model filled a purpose in giving administrators a method of offering rewards and sanctions. As mentioned in the introduction to the case studies, similar union contracts at all four schools specified seniority and workload issues, with rigid pay scales for years of service, degrees of education, and additional responsibilities of activity sponsorship or coaching. Administrative discretion to withhold, decrease, delay, or increase pay or other rewards for merit was absent.

When the assistant principal at Maizeville was describing varying teacher effort and competence, he was asked whether he felt frustrated that there were so few reward and sanction mechanisms by which administrators could affect teacher competence. His answer was more blunt than that of most administrators interviewed on this same topic, but its spirit was typical of their perception of what motivates teachers:

> Most of us just want to do a good job, and you know it, and that's all the reward you really need. In fact, I personally, when I have an evaluation, requested [sic] the principal not to put anything good, ... if something was done wrong, I don't want to know I'm not doing wrong, otherwise how can you improve? But, now that's a little different with teachers, and, it's a little different story, now as far as incentive, you know I don't think that they're discriminated against because you can't give them money, or we don't get any bonus ... Monetarily you can't reward a teacher and that's a shame, you know, and that budgetary things are getting more and more critical each year with the cost controls, there's just no doubt about that. But you know the only way you can really do it is verbally, and *throw a medal once in a while and sign it or if they do something outstanding, ah, write up a special letter and thank them for it* and so forth. Or verbal appreciation ... If you think of incentive systems, there's a variety of ways, you know you are talking about time, you're talking about money, you're talking about letters of thanks or verbal thanks. *And I really can't think of anything else.* (emphasis added)

He felt that salary bonuses for extra hours, for added attention to students needing extra help, for creative course development would not be the reward for which teachers were taking on extra tasks. These rewards would backfire by causing dissention among teachers not receiving such bonuses. When asked whether rewards for

51

taking on extra projects, or enriching standard courses, or meeting with students needing individual help might take the form of aides, added course budgets, small class sizes or other "working condition" adjustments, the assistant principal said that verbal thanks was the only way he could think of to thank teachers for their efforts.

The restrictions on negative evaluations were not so limited by imagination as by bureaucratic and union formal guidelines. For a *negative* evaluation to result in the teacher's reassignment to a different task or removal from the payroll, the requirements were bound up in legalities which administrators found time-consuming and vulnerable to law suits. Any misconduct, failure to perform classroom duties, or other serious inadequacy could be dealt with only after being carefully documented as to time, place, nature of offense, witnesses, effects on students and relation to school policy. To say that a teacher was not "a good teacher" or "did not conduct his class effectively" was not reason for taking procedures against that teacher. The teacher had to be absent from class frequently, fail to grade papers and give them back to students, or otherwise shirk assigned duties in observable, concrete ways.

Rather than undertake these procedures, which are costly in administrator time, unfavorable publicity and staff ill-will, the administrators said that they occasionally would use the *threat* of the formal procedures as leverage for pressuring teachers to improve. Because teacher improvement was so closely tied to course content, the administrators were pleased to delegate the applying of pressure on teachers to the departmental coordinators who did share the teachers' subject matter expertise.

Retained by the administrators were the formal, paper evaluations of each non-probationary teacher. Within broad course outlines developed within the department, the teacher submitted periodic lesson plans to the office for filing. The principal then used these for the two-fold purpose of providing a framework for substitute teachers to follow and of guiding the administrators' annual visit to the classroom. The use made of the guide was somewhat symbolic: the principal said that before visiting a classroom an administrator would pull the folder to see what the teacher listed as the subject of the day. He said, "If you go in there and the teacher is showing them a movie on the Civil War and [the lesson plan says they are] in the Revolution, you know that something is wrong." More subtle evaluative judgments are left to the department coordinators.

For the administrators, the strong-chair/coordinator model relieved them of the direct impact of one set of pressures. They could not, however, avoid the pressures of feeling ineffectual in controlling student attendance. The assistant principal described the students as "having no fear." With good-paying jobs, more discretionary income than many of their teachers, and an adult sensibility that came from commuting to the city of work after school hours, or a false adulthood provided by drink or drugs, the students were not easily manipulated by disciplinary threats at school:

> The kids don't have a sense of fear anymore. They're not
> afraid of anybody. They're not afraid of the police; they're not
> afraid of local authorities, they're not afraid of their parents,
> they are not afraid of courts. There's no fear. And in the past,
> you know, you used to be afraid of . . . the threatening would
> scare them; they were a little bit afraid. They're not afraid.
> They want to act like adults but they don't want to assume the
> responsibility of adults.

If intractable students challenged the administrative control efforts, disinterested teachers challenged the educational goals. In the assistant principal's mind, this disinterest extended to teachers' refusal to handle discipline, including staying after school, thus the need for a detention hall. The disinterest also surfaced in their inability or unwillingness to explain lessons enough times for all students to understand. To provide attention to students of all abilities, without expensive resource personnel, the school retained ability tracking. To deal with instruction and classroom competency more closely but in ways that did not intrude on administrator time or reveal administrator inadequacies, the strong-chair/coordinator model was established. This helped overcome what the assistant principal saw as teaching's primary problem:

> I guess probably the biggest problem that I've seen in
> education, whether it's here or other high schools I've been in,
> there's a kind of indifference. You know – I'll do my job, but
> that's it, I'll leave. I don't think that it's hard to really pinpoint
> what it is, but there isn't [sic] an awful lot of devoted people.
> That's my personal feeling.

*Choice and contradictions*

The structural arrangement by which the Maizeville school staff adapted traditional school organization to its own purposes was unique among the schools studied. It shares with the more typical administrative/teacher split of Forest Hills the fact that both arrangements are the result of deliberate choice. The uneasy relationship between the teachers and administration at Freeburg was based on shifts in policy and subordination of instruction to the control of behavior, never a routinized task. The strong administrator model at Forest Hills and the strong-chair model at Maizeville demonstrate that school structure, even within the limits of traditional American school forms, has deliberate as well as historical bases. The fourth school not only gives further evidence of the power of choice in shaping school structure but demonstrates the potential for emphasizing educational purposes over social control goals.


Nelson High School

Nelson High was known among social studies teachers, neighboring communities and regional educators as the school with the "academic" principals. It was chosen for its variation from Forest Hills in the closeness with which administrative personnel worked with teachers in support of instruction and with the openness of course content to students. While the structures at Maizeville and Freeburg differed somewhat from their reputations, the Nelson High organization bore out its image of a collegial place for teachers and administrators to work together. During the observation period, the curriculum and staff organization reflected many years of working toward this goal; in the year following the field work, declining enrollments and potential faculty lay-offs clouded this otherwise constructive relationship.

Nelson school and community
Nelson Heights and Blackhawk were small suburban communities which also served some rural families. Nelson High served both communities, drawing from elementary and junior high schools in the separate towns. Nelson Heights was characterized by residential areas and small businesses, and Blackhawk by residential areas of working-class and middle-class families. There was no significant industry in the towns, and many parents drove to nearby cities to

work in high technology, government and service industries. A number of parents of Nelson High students owned their own businesses in Nelson Heights or the nearest city. Large numbers of the students held jobs outside of school hours in retailing, fast food places and clerical or mechanical work.

The two communities had had the option during the 1950s of sending their children to schools in the nearest big city. They chose instead to risk higher taxes in order to keep their children out of the more bureaucratic school system and nearer to home in schools the community could influence and watch over. They did not want their children to become "lost" in a bigger, more impersonal school system; they wanted schools that served the needs of Nelson Heights children. From the beginning, then, the Nelson Heights schools reflected community support, conscious attempts to work out an educational philosophy compatible with the varied population within the district, and a sense of responsibility among citizens for the welfare of the school. There had been no divisive battles over bond issues, as in Freeburg, just to guarantee safe, functional buildings. In fact, the science chairman told me that the building constructed for the high school was the least expensive per square foot of any high school in the state; it was not as elegant as the schools built in the 1920s nor as shiny modern as many contemporary schools, but its physical layout was planned with instructional needs in mind and its economy reflected careful budgeting. A man was hired to be the principal-superintendent in those early years; he and a few staff members worked during the year of building construction on a philosophy for the school system, starting with the community's desire for an education that would be strong in skills and in human values about how to live in the world. The teachers hired to open the school were given forewarning of this philosophy and their obligation to work within it.

Administrative structure
The history of principals was a key to the establishing of a school beneficial to the students and the community. Nelson High was known in the region as the only high school with a history of "academic" principals, principals whose beginnings as classroom teachers had not been rationalized into bureaucratic modes by their advanced degrees in educational administration, principals who could discuss subject matter and instruction with teachers with

informed and involved concern. Best known was Mr Shepherd, who had served as principal longest. At the time of the field work, Mr Shepherd had just been promoted to assistant superintendent in charge of instruction. He still came by the school to chat with teachers over lunch or discuss business with the new principal. There were no social class or status walls (like those at Forest Hills) separating Mr Shepherd from the teachers; they were friends, proud of the school they had built together. With a new principal interested in carrying out Mr Shepherd's model of organization but less strong in several academic areas, the teachers still sought out Mr Shepherd for consultations over program improvement.

The program Mr Shepherd helped build was a unified curriculum within broad subject fields. In the early 1960s the faculty and administrators had held workshops to determine the future curriculum and organization of the school. By the mid-1960s they had put in place a curriculum in which narrow specializations within broad subject fields were interwoven into courses developed along complex interdisciplinary themes. Teachers were hired who were willing to teach in coordination with others in their departments, who were willing to develop their own curriculum and share in developing curriculum with their colleagues, who would not seek the privacy and efficiency of single-teacher isolated classrooms. Teachers unwilling to participate in this collegiality were pressured by the comprehensiveness of the plan to seek employment in a school where they could find their autonomous classrooms. Those hired were the ones who demonstrated expertise in broad fields. For example, science was not divided into specialities such as biology, geology and chemistry. These separate fields were meshed in a four-year sequence built around topics on ecology, energy, scientific investigation and so on. A physics teacher who knew little biology or who did not want to teach chemistry would not be a successful job candidate at this school.

In exchange for teachers' yielding some autonomy over their classroom content, the administration provided many supports for collegial curriculum building. Each department was given an office for meeting students, exchanging ideas or storing materials; the chairman had an office in the departmental office area. The resource center for each was, where possible, positioned between the departmental offices and the rest of the library holdings. Each department received a part-time aide and a secretary. Over the years, as teaching jobs became scarce, the aide was often an otherwise unemployed teacher qualified to help students in the resource center, help in materials development or otherwise contribute to more than the paperwork of the department. Very special to the social studies chairman and the teacher he teamed with was the secretary, who could take their rough diagrams for learning models and turn them into attractive, clear teaching instruments because she understood the content and purpose as well as the typing or layout procedures.

The role of the chair was something between the Freeburg–Forest Hills model of keeper of department schedules and records, liaison between the department and the administration, and the Maizeville model of delegated administrative authority. The chairman at Nelson High saw his role in the social studies department as helper to the teachers, as their representative to the principal, as coordinator of schedules and overseer of programs. He had good rapport with the teachers in his department and did not presume to evaluate his colleagues or visit their classes for purposes of personnel evaluations. Like the strong chair at Maizeville, the Nelson chairman of social studies spent a great deal of non-paid time on department work, on developing his own teaching materials, and on professional meetings and other activities designed to help him keep up in the field.

The considerable energies of the chair and his colleagues in developing materials was supported by the most impressive administrative policy in any school – almost unlimited access to the school's print shop for any materials a teacher would want to develop. As a result, few teachers used adopted texts; they used text allocation funds for reproducing materials from a wide variety of educational and media sources, according to the needs and interests of their students and according to changes in the topic over time. All of the social studies teachers took advantage of this plan. Even though some courses had a text, the resulting remaining funds generated hundreds of handouts for students, most of them informative from scholarly sources, many of them drawn from pertinent news items or excerpted from famous writers whose books in their entirety might not be understandable to students. Very few of them were worksheets or busy work. Many were also the teachers' own writings.

The effect of these supports worked out in cooperation with the past administration was to stimulate teachers to participate in creating classroom knowledge. Without this teacher effort, the unified curriculum would have been very difficult to sustain because of the lack of unified texts in most subject fields. Discipline-centered texts required much supplementing to be of use and drained off funds needed to cover the texts' inadequacies. It was easier for the teachers of a given course to work together to develop a framework for the course, congruent with the goals of the rest of the department, and then to fill in that framework with materials they developed alone or in the group, than to begin with an inadequate text and work around it. The print shop budget was virtually unlimited. Both the chairman and principal told me that they did not keep records on print shop billings by department because they did not want departments competing for funds or measuring their courses by their use of the print shop. That no departmental billings were maintained seemed unbelievable, especially as budget retrenchments threatened the school during the end of the observation time. Unbelievable or not, the fact that both presented this as truth showed either a very creative use of budget powers or a strong desire to avoid any contentions over the use of the funds.

At certain key times, as will be explained in connection with a course taught jointly in the science and social studies fields, summer money supported teacher workshops on planned innovations or program improvement. The paid weeks, usually two or four, were brief compared to summer hours without pay put in by the chair and many of his colleagues. This pattern had been begun under Mr Shepherd's principalship. He was described as having been very much in favor of interdisciplinary programming and highly receptive to staff suggestions. He continued to work with the teachers on long-range goals of better articulation with the junior highs and of more attempts even to cross subject field lines for curriculum development, say with literature and history or math and science linkages.

Other aspects of the structure influenced the teachers' curriculum decisions. One was the lack of disproportionate administrative attention to discipline. There were discipline problems at this school almost identical to those at Maizeville and Freeburg – truancy, tardiness, rudeness, sloppy habits, occasional drugs or, more likely, drinking. The administrative personnel, chiefly the assistant principal and the guidance counselors, dealt with these students, complained about parent disinterest or unavailability and followed some of the same control strategies as those at the other schools. Several important differences emerged in the comparisons. First, the administrative attention to discipline did not noticeably intrude into teachers' time. Secondly, the administrators developed fairly consistent policies and stuck with them, not casting about for emergency relief measures under a state of siege. The overall student body was not punished because of the actions of a few. There was nothing like the library doors being locked with students inside, or stern hall monitoring of all students. Administrators were cordial with students when they saw them in the halls and did not act intimidated by them. Most importantly, their concern for discipline did not overwhelm their concern for and availability to support academic concerns. Teachers were sometimes frustrated by administrative discipline decisions, but all levels of staff lay some blame for these on administrators' narrow range of alternatives given courts' and some parents' unwillingness or inability to support them in cases of repeat disrupters and truants. The numbers of students disciplined by the administration was relatively small, as was true at Maizeville, where the administrative response was far more time-consuming. The teachers felt generally more supported in discipline matters and clearly more supported as professional educators trying to improve instructional quality than teachers at any other observed school. Over the years this support from Mr Shepherd had given teachers – and these were all experienced teachers – much time to develop their courses, to organize coherent programs.

The teachers' union at this school resembled the bargaining organizations of the other three schools. The potential adversarial relations which the union–administration dichotomies gave rise to at the other three schools was somewhat overcome by an *ad hoc* committee formed to bring together people from different staff levels. Originally, according to several high seniority teachers, the union had been an agent to assure teachers professional independence and job security so that they could be free to teach under conditions conducive to their students' learning. Academic freedom and other substantive issues had been of concern. Newer union members had in recent years shifted the bargaining focus away from working conditions and toward pay and seniority issues removed from considerations of quality instruction. As the union

59

role narrowed, several members of the staff had the idea of setting up a new group of teachers and administrators to address these broader issues, ones not amenable to clear-cut bargaining and contractual arrangements. The Concerned Coalition met at regular intervals to discuss issues of importance in the schools. In the Coalition, teachers met with administrators of various levels. Occasionally community members would be asked to present ideas. The group had no formal authority to direct policy, but freed personnel from their hierarchical roles to an extent not possible within the union contract bargaining sessions. Differences often emerged and feelings were not always congenial or productive of clear consensus, but the existence of the group over a seven- or eight-year period provided a valuable forum for non-adversarial discussion.

The Coalition drafted influential but non-binding policy statements articulating the school system's philosophy and the appropriate roles and tasks for administrators and teachers within this philosophy. Willingness to work with other teachers and not claim the right to work in isolation was part of the expectations written for teachers. Teachers had to be willing to develop curriculum. Some newer teachers not on the Coalition were angry that union members would serve on a planning committee with "the enemy" and discuss planning and evaluation with administrators outside a bargaining framework. These faculty members saw the forthcoming declining enrollments and wanted to protect their jobs; they feared that one consequence of the planning of the Coalition would be to introduce merit considerations which would undercut their seniority in lay-offs. Those involved in the Coalition saw the long-range planning as essential to maintaining educational quality in the face of such economic changes. For them, involving administrators in program development was essential so that when retrenchments came, the administrators would look at programs as well as budgets when they began cutting. They were partly informed by the experience of the nearest large city, where school closings were based strictly on pupil enrollments, with programmatic concerns unaddressed until after boundary changes based on populations had been announced. The Coalition seemed one way of sustaining administrator–teacher cooperation in program areas.

The lack of disproportionate administrative concern for discipline and control was reinforced in the school by the failure to subordinate totally the learning process to the earning of credentials. The grading system included achievement grades and effort grades. The parent or student could have a better idea whether the grade reflected problems in studying and learning or in effort and attitudes toward learning. The effort grades, EGs, were averaged into the students' semester grade average along with the achievement grades. Several students who had transferred into the school thought this watered down the evaluation standards. Grade inflation could be caused by effort grades higher than achievement grades. Some of the teachers found the assigning of EGs a bother, as a way of letting students off easier. One teacher liked the EGs because they permitted him to reward students who tried but who rarely had academic successes. Others felt that EGs clarified for the teacher the distance between subjective and objective grading procedures. Since teachers often factored in effort and cooperation anyway, the teachers who favored EGs felt that these subjective considerations were made more open to the teacher and to the student by having them separated from the achievement grade.

Effort grades also complemented the school district's philosophy in offering an education which benefited the whole person, with practical skills for getting along in the world. One social studies teacher said that though the EGs presented some problems; they permitted the possibility for rewarding the students' positive contribution to the learning process. He looked at EGs this way:

> I tell kids they can probably get a high school diploma from
> Nelson High School. They can just sit in the back of the room
> and not bark and . . . Sure, I ask the kids what do we need
> most, more knowledge or better behavior? You know, the
> human race is mid-point in the 20th century [sic]. We stand
> back and look at where we are and where we've come from,
> and what do we need more of? Do we need more decent
> people or do we need more smart people? And you can make a
> good argument that we need more decency. Schools have a
> responsibility.

A science teacher echoed this concern for having a system that rewarded students' efforts toward self-improvement:

> I really believe that it is as important for a person to develop
> in terms of their humanity, their view of themselves and how
> they treat other people. And the way they view their task and

61

their job, in this case that of being a student. That is as important as developing skills and I don't believe a person is born with those abilities. You're not born a good student and you are certainly not born with humanism. I think you are born with a potential for humanism. And when you look at the real world and what the measures of success are, it's, many times, inabilities to succeed are related to inabilities to function as a human being. To get along well with others, and in attitudes towards tasks. So I think we have to help students develop this if we expect individuals to become more effective. Then we have to work at it.

The Concerned Coalition, the EGs, the availability of inexpensive printing, the presence of aides and secretaries, were imaginative responses to problems common to many high schools, certainly all those in this sample. The teachers had input into all of these policies, with the possible exception of the actual budget limits on the print shop. They were participants in the formation of policy, participants in the development of a district-wide philosophy of education. In turn, the administration participated in the development of curriculum. This administrative participation was not merely indirect or unintended, as at Forest Hills, or antagonistic, as at Freeburg. It resembled more the creation of the strong-chair model at Maizeville in its assertion of new forms to deal with institutional goals. Through hiring, resource gathering, scheduling, and physical setting, the administration tried to support academic goals and maintain the unified curriculum.

## Choice and structure

Evolving from a history of a split between administrative goals of social control and educative purposes in schools, these high schools reflect significant variations in the structural manifestations of those purposes. They also demonstrate the potential for conscious shaping of institutional relations or for reactive responses to institutional interests. Each school is in some way a product of its community and of the individuals who have filled administrative and faculty roles. We have seen that the variations in structure among these schools grow out of historical factors, individual and collective commitments and expectations of what school organization can be. We have seen the nature of the social control purposes at each school and the way structure relates to credentialing and behavioral controls. One school has emerged which does not base structure on social control purposes but on support for learning.

At all but Nelson, the two purposes of schools are in overt tension, with the social control purposes intruding on the educational pursuits, according to the teachers and many of the students. At Nelson the dominance is reversed, yet some tension remains because of the school's role as a legal institution and as a step in preparing students for future jobs and schooling. The case study chapters which follow trace out the effects the tension between these purposes has as teachers and students meet in classrooms. Again, there will be predictable patterns; but also, as in the organization of the overall school, there will be evidence of choices exercised, initiatives as well as reactive responses taken. This range of possibilities within the school structure will have a resulting variety of influences on students' access to knowledge in these classrooms.

# PART TWO
# Four high schools

# 3
# Forest Hills High School

Forest Hills High[1] was the classic American high school. Within its imposing brick structure, long halls with high ceilings were lined with single-teacher classrooms. Offices, cafeteria, auditorium and other service facilities had their place inside the rectangle of academic corridors. Typical of its early twentieth-century origins, there was no student parking lot, no football stadium. The visual impression was one of business, of serious purpose, tradition and stability.

This impression carried over from architecture to the organization of the school. Like the building, the organization was traditional. The principal was the business manager; the teachers were organized by departments but taught as individuals in their own classrooms. The students were classified by grade. The principal and his assistants kept the school running smoothly; the teachers met their classes; the students earned the required credits. Routine was the key to Forest Hills High School.

If there were no surprises in the organizational structure of Forest Hills, the surprise came in the unexpected ways in which this traditional organizational pattern affected course content and teaching methods. Although the administrative and teaching domains appeared to function almost entirely separately, a strong tension between the two lay just beneath the surface of the smooth routine.

The tension had some basis in a lack of trust and greater grounding in a lack of common goals. The teachers articulated an academic ideal and guarded their notion that the purpose of the school was to convey course content to students. Because of past experiences with administrative policy shifts, they did not trust the administration to affirm their priority either by having teachers participate in policy decisions nor in setting policy which subordinated procedural concerns to instructional ones. They could, however, trust the administration to pursue its own purposes. (While this seems self-evident, the faculty at Freeburg High will be described in a later chapter as distrusting of the administration's erratic policies and priorities.) At Forest Hills, those administrative purposes dealt mostly with preserving routine and processing students through the credentialing system. Disciplinary controls were less overtly a part of administrative concern, at least in their application across aggregates of students, than the maintenance of general order in programs as well as of behavior.

For many years the separation between faculty and administrative domains had yielded felicitous autonomy to the teachers; they would not have chosen any greater administrative involvement with instruction. That autonomy was undermined, however, when the administrative policies to shift school boundaries and to eliminate ability tracking suddenly took away what the teachers viewed as the conditions, and the rewards, needed to sustain their academic ideal. For the administration, long accustomed to top-down decision-making, the new policies were not abrupt shifts in institutional reward structures but continuations of their concern for routine. With a potentially wider range of students entering the school as a result of boundary shifts, de-tracking the classes gave the teachers rather than the administrators responsibility for working out any discontinuities of program needed to deal with the diversity. The administrative effort was in adding the vocational wing and its new classes. Within the regular academic program, having to design and implement new kinds and levels of courses would be avoided if all students met in heterogeneous classes. What was taught in the classes, and how classes were instructed, would then fall into the domain of the teachers.

The tension between the administrative purposes and the instructional purposes of the school came, then, not just from the traditional split between professional domains of teachers and administrators, but from the assumptions behind administrative exercise of authority within their domain (setting up the schedule of courses and students) which ignored the purposes of the teachers' domain (the quality of instruction).

Forest Hills is appropriate as the school to begin this analysis of organizational impact on school knowledge for two reasons. First its structure represents what must be the most typical form of high school organization in America. It is like the school Cusick (1973) describes when he says, "A reader who knows anything at all about secondary schools will recognize the school . . ."

Even more important, at this school the tension between the administrative purposes of control (here, controlling routines) and educational goals was not anticipated in advance of the field work. As was explained in the preface, classroom observations began at this school in an attempt to describe the content and the shape of discourse in economics instruction in social studies classes. The focus was so clearly on content and forms of content that at first even classroom interactions were bracketed from the researcher's concern. The negotiating of the content, and of the forms of content, by the exchanges between teachers and students made analysis of that negotiation, of those exchanges, unavoidable in trying to understand where school knowledge comes from and how it affects students. Only after the students and, especially, the teachers framed their explanations of those exchanges in terms of the school's organizational rewards and incentives did the organization of the school become a component of the analysis of the course content. Those incentives, those exchanges, took place in an organization in which the teachers felt at cross purposes with the goals of those who maintained it. They felt themselves, therefore, to be in an uneven exchange with those who set school policy. The lack of power to place educational concerns on the policy agenda made teachers look for an arena in which their own power, or authority, was not entirely undermined by these school-wide policies. That arena became their classrooms.

The other schools to be discussed in this analysis were chosen for their specific variations in structure from Forest Hills. Therefore, the organizational questions shaped the observations and interviews at those schools from the beginning. Only at Forest Hills was the curriculum content the first focus of analysis. For that reason, description of the tensions at this school which shaped class content must be seen as having been arrived at strictly inductively through long-term field work at the school. They were not sought, pre-specified or even anticipated. The researcher was as conditioned as other education professionals to think of school administration and school curriculum as separate domains. Linking the two came only after teachers' rationale for their shaping of content made the administrative/organizational component an unavoidable consideration. The situating of the course content at Forest Hills within the organizational structure will proceed, then, from describing the courses and that content, not, as in the other cases, from the school structure itself, so that the logic leading to those structures, and their variations, can be appreciated.

## Order in the classrooms

The teachers observed for the original study were attempting to teach American history to juniors in a way that minimized frustrations to themselves and elicited at least minimum cooperation from their students. Historical events to which the teachers were reacting were only vaguely known, and not understood for their impact, when the original observations were begun. This was not to be a study of organization processes or of classroom interactions, already too abundant and too inconclusive in explaining determinants of school knowledge. It was to be an analysis of curriculum content and curriculum materials, an investigation into the curriculum as lived by the students and the teacher in the classroom.

An ethnographic research strategy proved productive for studying in-use curriculum, but led inevitably to inclusion of the impact teacher–student interactions had on the content, and the reciprocal impact of the content on the patterns of interaction. With the focus on economics content, and the hypothesis that economics information would be treated differently from other kinds of historical information, the observations began with two social studies classes and later expanded to a third teacher's class. One teacher was chosen for his expertise in economics; he taught history, plus the school's economics elective. During the planning of the research, it was expected that noting all talk during the classes would be extremely difficult, because inquiry-based social studies had become widespread since the 1960s. This method of involving students in materials and issues would not lend itself to tidy observations because many students would be working in groups or out of the room in the library or community. Such a fear of inadequate observation staff or technology proved to be unfounded. In fact, all course content emanated from teacher lectures or teacher-supplied films. In one class, only a dozen student comments were heard all semester. The reasons for this pattern of centralized content were not apparent until the interviews with students and teachers were completed near the end of the term and the effects of the historical events, such as the anti-war protests, made clear by the teachers. What was apparent from the beginning was that students had little input into the course content. Also clear was that economics information along with other content was restricted because of teacher decisions to control student behavior through control of content.

Two classes of Contemporary United States History in this school of 2,500 students were observed daily for an eighteen-week semester.[2] The third class was observed for ten weeks. The teachers were told the study was to document the kinds of information about the economy students were being exposed to. All these teachers had a keen interest in economics, and access to the school arose from the interest of the economics teacher, who helped recruit the other two teachers. The three teachers spent a great deal of their course (the third in a three-semester history sequence required in high schools throughout the district) on the economy, especially on the Depression and the New Deal. Their course outlines gave the impression of extensive economics study. Their treatment of economics, however, was shaped by the limits they placed on all course content.

The hypothesis of the study was that economics information would be more fragmented, superficial, incoherent or absent than would the study of social, political and biographical topics during the same historical period. The study was to compare the treatment of economics information with the treatment of these other areas. The comparison did not materialize, however, because economics received the same treatment as the other topics. That treatment was the presentation through lectures of facts, lists, abbreviated explanations, unelaborated abstract slogans and other disjointed pieces of information. While the teachers distributed a token book report list of very interesting and varied titles, the students were not expected to read, write, generate or compare information, look up information on their own, raise questions or add information in class. One teacher, Mr Schmidt, a coach, lectured every day from an outline printed on transparencies projected by overhead projector onto a screen in front of the room. His tests were open-notebook, factual, short-answer tests, with unclear directions and non-negotiable answers, even to the point of disallowing synonyms for words from the transparencies. When two good students' parents complained about the testing procedure, he reminded the class that he was a "professional historian," not a "jock," and turned the complaint into an *ad hominem* argument.

This teacher had nine sections on his course outline, five of which dealt with economics topics. An examination of the outline would have given the impression of extensive economics study. Closer inspection would have revealed that even extended topics such as the Depression, on which he spent several weeks, were reduced to lists of causes, names and dates, unelaborated jargon from professional economists. Only the film *The Grapes of Wrath* joined the fragments of information into a meaningful composite, but only if students individually made the connections; they viewed the film with little introduction and no discussion afterward. This teacher did not require students to read and often did not give out books at the beginning of the semester. He rewarded attendance with open-notebook tests; most test scores ranged between 35–55 per cent, so a curve was necessary to assure a reasonable number of passing grades.

The other two teachers used much less extreme methods, but had equally tight control of course content. The woman teacher, Miss Langer, taught a strict chronology organized around presidential administrations and congressional responses to presidential policies. She used witty put-downs to squelch student comment, though she did require a few pages of reading each night and called on students to answer questions from the reading. She had carefully planned her lectures and asides and set such a tone of efficiency and "cover the material" speed that students learned very early that even an enlightened comment would risk being labeled "disruptive" or mark the student as one who wasted class time.

The third teacher, Mr Harris, was an economics teacher who also taught the history course. He was much more casual, much less paced toward covering an exact amount of material each day. But he too restricted content fairly tightly. He lectured on a chronology of major events or topics – the Depression, the Good Neighbor Policy, the Korean War. Like the others, he rarely asked students to add ideas, and often rejected what few student contributions made. Students could talk and joke in his class or answer leading questions, but they could not greatly affect course content. While Miss Langer viewed history as "the story" and her job as being to convey that story efficiently to students, Mr Harris stopped to give extended descriptions, to mention issues as well as facts and, in doing so, gave more three-dimensional portrayals of events through his lectures. Both were conscientiously trying to share large amounts of material with their classes.

Whereas their different teaching styles suggest slightly different patterns of interaction, the resulting course content was less varied. All taught chronologically; all omitted content which was controversial, which was complicated enough to require in-depth treatment, or which was current. They saw "current events" as events which happened during their adult lifetime, even though events five years before had occurred when their students had been in elementary school. They further viewed current news as a waste of time, since no consensus interpretation had yet emerged. They did feel that past events could be explained through a consensus interpretation, "the story," conveyed as representing what "we Americans" know about the subject.

In addition to eliminating current and controversial topics, they frequently reduced complicated topics to items in a list. This flattening or fragmenting of information happened when the information was reducible to facts. Some topics were more complex; the teacher might want the student to know about a certain event or institution but be unable or unwilling to explain it. Instead, he or she might "mystify" the topic (see Chapter 7), mentioning its importance but explaining that it was unknowable or inappropriate for consideration at that time. Thus such topics as the Federal Reserve or the banking system would be mentioned as being very important but remote from the student, remaining a mystery, though listed in the notebook.

Whether mystified or omitted, matters of controversy were rarely dealt with as issues, as matters having more than one interpretation that should be explored. Instead, the teachers used the editorial "we" as in "During the Depression, we Americans ..." or "We are all Progressives now." If a student intimated that there was less than consensus, two of the teachers would ascribe the alternative interpretation to "cynicism."

These patterns of control, and the passive role they necessitated for students, were among the first unanticipated findings of the research. Equally unanticipated was the degree to which the teachers were aware of what they were doing. Until interviews with teachers and students began, the classroom observations seemed to point to passive students being socialized into consensus social studies information by conservative, moderately-educated teachers typical of social studies sterotypes. From the perspective of cultural reproduction, it would seem that the knowledge admissible to these classrooms, favoring consensus models of historical interpretation and loyalty to American institutions without reflection or analysis, derived inevitably from ideologies imbedded in the capitalist system and its schools. This generalized analysis was contradicted by the search for contrasts and counter-examples as validity checks. This search turned up other teachers in the same social system, indeed in the same school system, who set very different limits on the information and student roles permitted in their classrooms. At two other high schools in this district, the teachers set students to looking up information in libraries, attending public meetings, interviewing citizens of the community and otherwise participating in generating and evaluating information. Their tests often asked students to take positions and defend them, with grades based on the thoroughness of the defense rather than the degree of concurrence with the teacher's position. These differences prompted investigation into the factors which shaped the particular patterns of knowledge control at Forest Hills.

From interviews and research into the history of the school, it became apparent that the teachers at Forest Hills felt their teaching styles to be their best accommodation to their institutional setting. All had been in the school prior to the turmoils of the late 1960s. Two had previously derived their status from teaching upper track students and sharing in the light of those students' scholarships and awards. They had objected to the de-tracking policy and had been the last high school in the city to comply with this district ruling. Most stratification analysis by social class (Keddie, 1971; Sharp and Green, 1971; and others) has documented that teachers will often sacrifice their least able students for their highest level students; the majority of teacher time and attention will be directed toward those students perceived as brightest or as having a future most compatible with the teacher's, whether students of varied ability levels are in the same classes or tracked into different classes. This had clearly been the picture at Forest Hills, according to the teachers' recollections, prior to de-tracking. Miss Langer remembered how she had assigned panel discussions, papers and projects to the class of "super bright" students. With the next level of students she was able to require some reading and writing. With the third level, what she called "the masses – 90 to 120 IQ," school knowledge had to be "spoonfed," with teacher lectures in the appropriate format, otherwise, if "you sent them to the library, they'd just copy from an encyclopedia." The least bright group had been scheduled with the coach; for their credit in United States history they read the morning newspaper together.

After de-tracking, the traditional patterns of differential treatment that might be expected within mixed-ability classes did not hold at this school. These teachers had decided to impose their previous level III ("the masses") pattern of control (lectures, objective tests, no reading, no writing) onto all their classes. Thus even the brightests students were sacrificed to the teacher's efficiencies of having no diverse assignments to create or grade. The redrawing of the school's boundary to include the poorer neighborhood and the building of the vocational wing added to their justifications for these instructional strategies, down-grading instruction.

In addition, the anti-war protests had threatened teachers in two ways. First, class had been less efficient when students spoke up, especially when they wanted to debate a point to its resolution. More important was the threat to the teacher's authority as a source of valid knowledge. One teacher reflected that during this time the "really sharp kids" were "writing terrific papers," but they were becoming "self-indoctrinated." He went on to say that the students had put more faith in the information they gained through reading and research than in that heard in class lectures. He decided that they were too impressionable to read so extensively in controversial areas, and so preferred they write no papers rather than have students "misled" by their independent searches.

No doubt there were other factors such as their age, training and personal backgrounds which shaped these teachers' decisions regarding knowledge forms and content in their classes. They had been trained under college lecture methods which they emulated. Middle age caused one teacher to limit long assignments so he would, as he expressed, have energy for other things. He preferred to pour his limited energies into preparing lectures rather than reading student papers. These other factors, however, seemed of secondary importance in the teachers' interpretations of their reasons for their methods.

Being alienated from their former sources of authority was far more critical to their present instructional modes. The de-tracking and the Vietnam war protests had sharpened their feelings of distance from an indifferent administration. In the de-tracking policy, that indifference took the form of unwelcome intrusion. The teachers felt it undercut their ability to deal with student differences. They received no added materials, no added time to work out revised courses or to evaluate course offerings and assignments in light of the incoming students from lower income families. They saw no school-wide or administrative attention to the switch to mixed-ability classes. They were sure that these changes would erode their ability to teach, but received no supports for altering or adapting their ways. Instead, they chose to fashion their own efficiencies within the new constraints. They chose to reduce their expectations of all their students and of their teaching and to confine course content to a narrow set of lists and summaries.

Of special interest in light of this decision was the contrast between classroom content and the teachers' own knowledge of their subject. Despite Joint Council on Economic Education policies to the contrary,[3] these teachers did not need more training or materials in order to deal with the economy in a more complex manner. In interviews, they revealed very complex knowledge of controversy, of future economic dislocations, of imperfect institutions, of complicated topics. They said in these interviews that to deal with these realities might make students cynical, as students had been during the Vietnam war protests. Time and the teachers' own energies did not allow for adequate discussion of the controversial, complicated and sometimes unpleasant realities of American and world economics and politics. So they decided it was better to present a factual overview and let students discover the realities after they left school. The teachers, then, were bracketing their personal knowledge in order to get through the "official" knowledge of the course. In the concluding analysis, we will discuss this strategy as a kind of de-skilling, reducing the worker to a mechanism rather than a whole being whose self is participating in the creative work process. At this school, the teachers were choosing de-skilling in exchange for the preservation of efficiencies and authority they saw as threatened by the administrative context.

Before going on to that context, it must be noted that the student interviews revealed a similar bracketing of personal information, including questions and opinions, upon entering the classroom. One of Miss Langer's students told me that at the first class of the semester he held the expectation that social studies meant discussion, so he had ventured comments and questions. Soon he was the object of her witty put-downs and wry comments; to preserve his "class participation" grade, he decided to remain silent. The silence appeared to be acquiescence when observed in the classroom. Only the interviews revealed that the students found the controlled knowledge suspect. This was not true of a small minority; about one-fourth of them did see history as knowledge the teacher had that they lacked. The remainder of the students, however, questioned the methods of instruction and the validity of the information. Approximately one-third of the students in the observed classes were interviewed regarding their views of current economic topics in the news, study of economic-related subjects in previous years, their jobs, their opinions regarding predictions of resource scarcities, and their understanding of such economics jargon used in their classes as "free enterprise" and "productivity." Unsolicited but frequent comments emerged during the interviews about the students' dissatisfaction with the course format which prevented discussion and the presentation of multiple perspectives. In class, most of the students sat passively, sometimes busy copying lecture and blackboard notes into notebooks (especially in the class where exact words from the transparencies were required for test answers), offering little challenge, few questions, few informal contributions. Most student participation took the form of banter in Mr Harris' class, or answers to leading recitation questions in Miss Langer's class. Occasionally, a student would ask a procedural question such as the date of a test, the length of a book report, or the requirements for taking notes on a film. Otherwise, the teachers were remarkably proficient at keeping so much adolescent energy in acquiescence for forty-five minute class periods each day.

The complex responses to interview questions were not foreshadowed by student behaviors in class. Very few of these students were political, despite teacher admonitions that they quit wanting "to tear the system down." They had been young children during most of the American involvement in Vietnam and had only older people's stories to tell them of the protests in their own school during that time. They had no first-hand knowledge of the detracking or of the shift to a comprehensive high school. Therefore, they did not share the teachers' perceptions of the nature of the student body and of the needs for limited access to resources or discussion. They did, however, have their own way of interpreting the situation.

The students who questioned the validity of the tightly-controlled content did so silently, many not aware that other students also held the course content suspect. Unlike the "lads" in Willis' (1977) Hammertown, whose working-class resistance to their school's socializing influences was collective, visible and filled with humorous flaunting of school rules, Forest Hills' middle-class students individually and unobtrusively carried out their own resistance. Many were actively deciding how much teacher-supplied information to accept, how much to reject, how much to question or hold in suspension until some unspecified "later" time. Those who had politically active or informed parents, those who read, those who watched television news – all these found themselves rejecting teacher information when a personal source of information contradicted it. An extended analysis of this negotiation of classroom efficiencies, "Negotiating classroom knowledge: beyond achievement and socialization" (McNeil, 1981a), describes in detail several students who deliberately and thoughtfully made decisions about when to speak out especially in disagreement, and when to comply passively in order to get the course credit. These decisions were active, conscious and in keeping with the students' understanding of their own interests. Many had appropriated the administrative concern for credentials and credits at the expense of knowledge and skills; they saw the short-term pay-off of earning a high grade by avoiding being called "disruptive." They did not often see the long-term costs of losing this chance to interact with abundant materials and trained teachers. They pointed to a "later" time, after graduation, when they would be able to "find out for themselves" what they needed to know. These questions about the credibility of school knowledge *cut across achievement levels, across the social class distinctions* perceived by the teachers, *across gender lines* and other categories education researchers use to characterize student differences.

The effects of this pattern of negotiating their efficiencies were two-fold. One, it created a client mentality among the students. Unaware of the opportunity cost, of having to sit through so many hours of school without benefiting from the lessons, these students not only did not trust teachers' information; they had just as little confidence in their own abilities to learn things on their own. When discussing ecology, job futures, inflation and other personal economic concerns, they expressed the vague hopes that "someday" "they will tell us" "what we need to know."

A second effect was the impact on the teachers' perceptions of their own sense of efficacy. Already feeling constrained by the administration, the teachers saw the students' passivity as evidence of their worst fears regarding the decline of the school as a result of de-tracking and boundary shifts. They had no sense of the student suspicions of course content. Instead, they saw minimal student efforts as evidence of limits of student abilities. They viewed these limits as liabilities to their own effectiveness as teachers, as the upper limits to which students could reach. These limits of attention span, intelligence or experience were not the beginning point from which the teacher would work to add to skills and information; they were the restrictions within which teachers chose to operate in preparing and conducting their classes. When they observed that a student had trouble reading history, they decided not that they needed to work more on their students' skills, on the methods of reading historical material, but that they could no longer assign reading. They felt compelled, then, to lecture more.

An interview with a student who had been present the year of the de-tracking shed some light on the relationship between that policy change and student participation. Whereas the teachers saw the mixing of intelligence levels as diluting all student abilities, this former student recalled that it was peer pressure that had brought about reduced discussions: "The bright kids didn't want the 'dumb kids' to have the answers. The 'dumb kids' didn't want their friends to know they were dumb." So neither group spoke up. Just as the teacher accommodations to administrative policies were hidden from the administrators, the student responses to knowledge restrictions and de-tracking had been misunderstood by the teachers. Likewise, the students had little idea that teachers were reacting to events in the history of the school several years prior to their own junior class.

The structure of the school, with isolated single-teacher classes, individual achievement modes for student evaluation, and an administration emphasizing credits and order, kept the ironies of this cycle of lowering expectations from coming to light. The vulnerabilities in the cycle became apparent to an outside observer, but were invisible to the participants. The teachers' fears of student disruption made them tighten control of knowledge at the expense of engaging students in the learning process. This oversimplification of topics made the students, in turn, cynical about learning and lowered their expectations that anything substantive was to be gained from the course. Their minimal responses sent signals to the teachers which seemed to confirm the teachers' low expectations of "today's students." The very autonomy which gave teachers their sense of professionalism and control over their courses prevented collective review of the program and its impact on the students, either at the departmental or administrative levels.

## The administrative context

It is doubtful that the principal of this school, or the assistant principal charged with oversight of social studies, knew what went on in these classes beyond the simple fact that Mr Schmidt used an overhead projector, or that Mr Harris was jovial and fairly well-informed, or that Miss Langer was efficient. Yet the existence of these administrators and their policies helped shape decisions made both by students and teachers in these classes just as though the administrators had formally intervened in the selection of instructional methods or curriculum resources.

Analysis of the administrative context will reveal how its structure reinforced this pattern of negotiating minimum efficiencies. Forest Hills was the only high school studied that was a part of a bureaucratic school system having more than one high school and strong central office directives. The powerful superintendent was supported by the board and rarely challenged by principals. His consolidation of power in eliminating geographic area supervisors was primarily a political move. His previous elimination of subject matter supervisors showed low priority for academics. Several of the city-wide programs in place during the study bore the mark of the planning of these subject matter supervisors, including social studies, and their phase-out created a void in academic advocacy in many subject areas. The superintendent's very political nature made him an imposing adversary for the teachers' union; and adversary was the appropriate term for their relationship. His dominant purpose seemed to be to cut financial corners on staff and materials rather than on administration. Not even the rhetoric of academics, of educational purposes, characterized his treatment of school district policies. His office proudly published figures showing that almost all students and almost all schools in the district scored "above average" in national achievement tests. This statistic was probably more a product of city demographics than of school policy. It also implied that one point above average was a worthy goal, which contributed to community wisdom that, under this superintendent, "planned mediocrity" was official policy. It is perhaps ironic that his strong personality and dominance of school policy produced no innovation, built in effect few programs, but was limited to maintaining a smooth *status quo*.

Principals, having little say in district policy, were chosen and rewarded for modeling the superintendent's authority and concern for stability within their school while not challenging it in the district. They were not encouraged to innovate or emphasize unique programs.

To teachers, though, principals or "the administration" seemed to hold all the power to affect programs. Teachers felt slighted by the changes such as de-tracking which originated at administrative levels without adequate recognition of new demands made on teachers to change or re-evaluate programs. De-tracking was the most prominent because it was fought by the teachers, and the concerns raised very vocally during the debate were never addressed. De-tracking was based on the assumption of meeting individual student needs rather than labeling students by broad ability categories. Teachers complained that having these differences together hurt their teaching. They then failed to acknowledge those differences or deal with them in assignments or explanations after de-tracking was in place. They tended to take students' lower limits (where they were at that point) as their upper limits, as static rather than developmental characteristics, and therefore as brakes on teacher influences. Unaware of peer relations influencing students' passivity, and uninformed on what were, in many cases, specific differences among their students, they were convinced that de-tracking diluted their ability to teach. The formal rationale of dealing with individual differences was the administrative justification for avoiding charges of racism and discrimination inherent in the tracking system. Yet neither the formal nor the informal rationale prompted administrators to review the heterogeneous grouping after a year or two of the new plan to assess the impact on students of different races, incomes or abilities. The teachers resented this attention to *pro forma* policies that ignored the classroom realities created by them. The only accommodation to the de-tracking made by the administration was to make sure that three levels of texts were available to the teachers, levels already in the school because of previous tracking. The US history outline series adopted for weaker students was actually harder to understand than narrative history and was more frequently used by bright students reviewing for tests. The middle-level text was dull and, according to Miss Langer, devoid of factual depth. The upper-level book was an old Oscar Handlin college text, published when the students were babies and covering only the first two-thirds of the course outline.

Such a plan for accommodating to student differences and academic goals was a far cry from the teachers' ideal of teaching. Their ideal derived in part from the model of college lecturing they followed. Even more, it derived from nostalgia. Their ideal of teaching came from their memory of how they used to teach their top track classes. An educator who graduated from Forest Hills during the time the classes had been tracked commented on the school's reputation and on this description of the teachers' feelings of loss: "It was a good school in those years, but only for about the top 100 students." He recalled that of over 2,000 students, about 100 (those in the very top track) profited from "real teaching." It was this ideal of the school's "better days," when they could "really teach," that gave Miss Langer and Mr Harris their sense that administrative attention to routine, to a flattening of diversities, had taken away their incentives to open up their personal knowledge and their expectations of student participation to genuine exchanges of knowledge. That their ideal derives from so small a student population challenges its worth but does not diminish its importance in shaping their notion of what teaching should and could be. Miss Langer in fact had explained in an interview that prior to de-tracking, she had drawn her greatest satisfaction from teaching the brightest students, giving them responsibility for searching out presenting and comparing information. She and other teachers had taken pride in watching good students become interested in history, in seeing them excel and go on to good universities. Two attorneys who graduated fifteen years prior to the study reflected on the fierce competition, the lively assignments, the feeling that they and their classmates would go out to become successes at the universities and in their professions. They recalled that that cohort of students was not totally impressed with all instruction at the school, but they questioned its legitimacy less than present students because they could see the school's rewards as instrumental to their futures. In turn, their energies and efforts rewarded teacher effort. Their descriptions of the activity and energy generated by their teachers and fellow students in instructional projects bore no relation to the passive classes observed. After hearing the intense questioning of school policies and content during the Vietnam era, teachers saw their own authority over information eroded, further so after these Nixon supporters had faced students knowledgeable about Watergate. Mr Harris reacted more to this decline in authority over content; Miss Langer to the loss of a chance for excellence in instruction. They responded by eliminating Vietnam and Watergate from the chronologies of contemporary United States history. With each retrenchment, some of the former student-teacher interaction was lost.

During those protest days, administrative attention to order at the expense of academics gained strong reinforcement. (It must be restated that the students observed in the field study were not the protesting students, nor did they have memory of them.) The assistant principal shed some light on how administrators had responded to these shifts in teacher and student effort. Mr Burger, a very traditional man much like the principal and superintendent, spoke in numbers, in drop-out percentages. He talked about *amounts* of effort rather than ways of teaching, philosophies of student learning or program developments. He said that he met with each department under his jurisdiction three or four times per year then retracted, saying that that was the ideal but that the actual meetings were rare because of the number in the social studies department that had coaching or evening course (driver's education and the like) responsibilities.

The formal evaluation procedures centered on the teacher and corresponding assistant principal. The two met in the fall for a preparatory conference reviewing the teacher's goals for the year. These were not strictly management (or teacher) objectives, but areas of general concern such as discipline, preparation and so on. The assistant principal said these talks ranged from thirty seconds to thirty minutes. Then the assistant principal was to visit the teacher's class three or four times during the year. At an ending

83

evaluation conference, the administrator would present the teacher with his evaluations of teaching ability, professional knowledge of and interest in the subject, clarity of assignments, control of pupils (note the word control rather than a word more respectful of students as participants and not objects), and "daily preparation and continuity." The teacher would sign a concurrence or write out an objection or amending statement and sign that for the personnel file.

Mr Harris explained how the procedures worked in reality. One of the assistant principals had visited his class two or three times during the year, only once for longer than just stepping in for a few minutes. Mr Harris was flattered at first to read his very favorable evaluation and felt that he had been recognized for his good efforts. His pleasure changed to amusement when he read "excellent" beside "use of audio-visual equipment." "As you know, Mrs McNeil, I *never* use A-V equipment," he laughed. "I have no idea where that came from." Perhaps it was another teacher's evaluation, or the ritual evaluation based on the assistant principal's assumptions of what a conscientious, pleasant teacher would be doing.

The same assistant principal who wrote this evaluation differed from the dominant managerial mode among administrators in the school; he saw himself not as an advocate of bureaucratic rules and credits but of students. His views on minimum expectations among teachers and students came from being a member of a racial minority and from being the parent of children who attended a different high school. He saw shortcomings of the school's curriculum as the product of the impersonality of the school and of the teachers' unwillingness to factor students' personal lives into their expectations of students. When he evaluated teachers, he ordinarily added comments about how he saw teachers interact with students in the halls as well as in their classes. He viewed counselors and other administrative personnel as paper-shufflers, unable to see students in this large high school as individuals. He said sometimes students came by his secretary's office just to have someone say good morning to them or to see how they looked that day. He valued his role as a grade level principal, which included following one class through all four years, as the other assistant principals did, more than his assignment over a group of subject matter areas. As grade level principal, he got to know students, especially those frequently in trouble or having family problems. He tried to become an advocate to the teachers for these students. Although his approach to discipline was caring, he exhibited little carry-over into his evaluation of teaching. He saw no concrete way of improving poor teacher performance or rewarding outstanding teachers, saying, as most of the administrators did, that internal motivation, not school policy, made good teachers: "I've seen a teacher have 40-45 kids and still teach every one of them."

He favored de-tracking for its avoidance of potential discrimination problems, but said that some students might get "lost" in mixed classes. Then he said, though, that perhaps coming to high school was a chance to get lost, a chance for some students to hide, change and start over.

His biggest problems with the school centered in the lack of reality. He said that teachers refused to deal with the effects of peer relations on their courses or with the problem of the large number of students holding outside jobs. He said that the students worked in order to have money to spend, that few saved it for future education, and many had trouble saving for cars and other major purchases because of their large entertainment expenses.[4] His own children and their friends made hundreds of dollars each month and had "nothing to show for it." He felt that teachers' ignorance of such student values prevented them from relating their courses to students in a way that would engage them.

His other concern was with the lack of reality faced by students. He estimated that 80 per cent were born in the state, just as 80 per cent of the teachers had been born and raised in the state. The city's nice neighborhood shopping areas kept people from having to cross town to shop and thus to be forced to meet varieties of people. He thought that neither the students nor the teachers had enough experience with the "real world" to be able to understand it. As he put it, "the kids are working, drinking, playing more, and the teachers are blissfully unaware. They know kids won't do as much homework but think it's because of attitudes rather than lifestyle changes." He was concerned that he could not get teachers interested in what students' lives were like. In this he confirmed the classroom observation; the passive role assigned to students in their courses offered little chance for teachers to know about students as individuals.

In this particular school, he also attributed teachers' minimum efforts to their feelings of intimidation from the high educational level of many parents in the district, not because of direct community pressure, but because the feelings of inadequacy made teachers predisposed not to try anything new. Most tried, in his estimation, to keep a low profile in order to keep parents out of the school. (The irony came in teachers' *wanting* parents to be involved in their child's discipline problems, but *not* wanting them to be involved in the course content.)

His view of teachers echoed that of administrators interviewed at the later schools: "Teachers can do anything in this school. Good kids, good resources. *It's the administrators whose hands are tied.*" For teachers who teach well, he saw "thank you" as reward enough. He said he tried to give good teachers visibility and public praise. He theorized that the ones who burn out "are the ones who don't get the strokes." He claimed to prefer this form of reward for himself. The teachers would have pointed out that as an administrator he had merit raises, promotions and ultimately a principalship as rewards in his career structure, not just verbal thank you's.

As for students' relation to authority structures in schools, he traced their lack of respect for authority in school to their upbringing. Children fight with their parents over who will walk a block to the store for an onion, in his analysis, without a concept of obedience. "In the sixties the parents let kids do their own thing let the rope out. They haven't pulled it back yet, though they have discovered, 'Hey, these kids aren't as smart as we thought they were.'"

This assistant principal demonstrated the possibilities for individualizing one's response to structural forms. He also had management objectives, had formal teacher evaluations, had assignments to take charge of a grade level and oversight of certain academic areas. But for him, the formal aspects of schooling merely provided a framework within which he might advance his career, might help some students overcome the anomie of a large high school, might remind teachers that their students had lives outside of school. His being a member of a minority allowed him certain variations from the very standardized expectations of administrators in this school, and his relative effectiveness with students (as compared with some of the more rules-oriented administrators) helped justify his imposing his own style on his work.

The humane intentions of this one administrator found outlet in one-to-one relations with students with whom he came in contact over discipline or over conflicts with the guidance office regarding schedule change requests or other personal adjustments to the school. On a broader plane, the impersonal structure he saw causing problems for some lonely students also prevented his channeling his concerns into policy. The domain of the teacher was clearly the classroom, the content, the testing and grading. He could work with grade level issues and particular students, but had no means, short of the perfunctory teacher evaluations and classroom visits, to affect instruction. That he did not fully take advantage of those powers delegated to him was evident in his mistaken evaluation of Mr Harris' use of audio-visual equipment. He assigned to non-school origins, such as neighborhood and cultural isolation, or parental laxness or student jobs, problems in motivating students and teachers. He did not view inadequacies in either group as originating within the school, but as reflecting within the school the values dominant in their out-of-school lives

While he, the other assistant principals and the principal had considerable discretion even within the union contract to oversee program development and teacher quality, they chose not to. His story of the principal's view of curriculum as course credits is telling. He explained the chain of command in the developing of new courses, and told of taking to the principal a department's request for a new course. "The principal said it was okay; he had no interest in this subject except to say that '*of course, there won't be any more courses added unless something has been dropped* because of enrollments and budget cuts'" (emphasis added). The assistant principal thus had an expectation that program improvements would originate with the administration, nor that substance rather than numbering credits would be a topic for administration to decide. The passive acquiescence to the fact that some teachers are good and some are bad, voiced by this very frank administrator, has its counterpart in two of the other three schools studied.

Interestingly, though the teachers welcomed administrator distance when it left them autonomous in their classrooms, they rejected this distance when it implied acceptance of a bad situation, as with a failure to support discipline efforts, or when it implied lack of concern for problems, especially those problems caused by administrative fiat. This classic split between duties and roles in this school is typical of many high schools. It does not always have to mean minimum expectations all round. At this particular school, the historical events which led to administrative policy changes were events which simultaneously eroded teacher authority and expectations. Prior to that, the teachers recalled, and this has been somewhat verified by talking with a small number of their former students, there was a time when there was less of a wall between personal knowledge and the official knowledge of the classroom. They recalled a time when they demanded more of themselves and of their students of all levels but especially of the upper ability groups. They reminisced about when they had felt efficacy as teachers, as having the ability to add to student skills and knowledge, with the students' participation. In short, the faculty members interviewed remembered a time of higher expectations. In their mind, the lower expectations they and their students were bringing to the classroom stemmed not from the "times," or from changing job and family patterns, but from administrative unconcern for that teaching function. Like the assistant principal who turned teacher evaluations into innocuous ritual, the teachers did not take full advantage of their autonomy. A prime example is the failure to select a new text book just because there was no interest in taking the requisite human relations course needed to sensitize convenors of the text selection committee to potential gender and racial biases in textbooks. The text selection process was seen as a necessary chore to some, but without great hopes that an adequate text for high school students would be available on contemporary history, and as a needless chore to another. (This failure to exercise autonomy is especially regrettable given the lack of choice teachers have in states where texts are adopted or approved at the state level.)

No one such decision was determinative enough in changing their situation to merit extraordinary effort. Their greater task was to carve out, between student indifference and administrative distance, their own efficiencies, their own means of maintaining authority in the classroom. In their goal of sustaining an educative function in a school where credentials were more the order of official policy, they chose to concentrate on building their lectures. Ironically, the lecture methods chosen often turned into defensive teaching (see Chapter 7), or into watered down topics or assignments in order to elicit student compliance. By controlling knowledge in order to control student behavior, they engendered student resistance that they had not expected and in some cases were not yet aware of. The student cynicism toward learning and toward American institutions which teachers had hoped to avoid by eliminating reading and discussing were more widespread perhaps than during the days of small groups of vocal protesters, but this resistance was silent, evidence of students' awareness of the predominance of course credits over learning.

What emerged from going back to Forest Hills to look at the administrative context is a pattern of negotiation between the various layers of persons in the school. In the hands of administrators concerned with management objectives and course credits, the formally divided structure unwittingly created teacher resistance by constraints imposed without accompanying supports. The teachers, in reducing student requirements to preserve their own efficiencies and authority, gave students the impression that the content was ritualistic at best and unbelievable at worst. The passive response of students, necessary in their eyes to earn required credits, sent misleading signals to teachers about student ability grouping and about their own effectiveness as lecturers able to hold an audience silent for long periods of time. In trying to maintain social control goals, the administrators unknowingly created more alienation, albeit rarely disruptive alienation, and resistance. In trying to sustain their concern for the educative goals, the teachers took their content so very seriously that they forgot their students. There existed within the school no mechanism for working through the tension between these conflicting goals. It fell to the individual staff member, the humane and mildly effectual assistant principal with his attempts at student advocacy or the teacher willing to keep informed on subjects while knowing that personal knowledge would only rarely be admitted into classroom discussion – the individual willing to take on the risks of time and energy to overcome the cycle of lowered expectations among all concerned. For these teachers, they expressed that that time in their lives had passed when they would try single-handedly to develop courses, assign research papers, attempt to involve students of all ability levels. They tried instead to make their lectures interesting, their tests fair (at least two of them did this with some forethought) and their demands on their students simple.

This school in many ways represented a "best case" example. The high tax base, large numbers of able students and interested parents, wealth of social studies resource center materials, lack of

89

major discipline problems, high levels of staff education, all pointed to possibilities for productive student–teacher encounters. If limitations placed upon student access to information were so tight even here, significant questions had to be raised regarding the effects of institutional arrangements on patterns of knowledge access and knowledge control in schools. The additional three schools were selected for their specific variations from Forest Hills' structure in order that these questions might be pursued.

# 4
# Freeburg High School

The routines of Forest Hills, while inhibitive of intense teacher and student engagement in instruction, might have been welcomed at Freeburg High, where preoccupation with controls was not matched by consistency. Attention to academics as an issue of school policy was lost in the pressure to keep students physically corraled and correctly behaved. Administrative policies treated students in the aggregate, announcing policies which affected the movement or activities of all, though most caused no problems. The teachers did not ascribe to these discipline policies and rarely had a part in planning them or in making changes in staff time or placement for their implementation.

This traditional school structure, of an administration attentive to discipline and attendance, with teachers functioning somewhat autonomously in their subject fields in separate classrooms, offers no specific structural contrast to Forest Hills. The contrast comes in the way that administrative structure was used to manage the school. At Forest Hills, routine was rewarded; as a goal, the smooth-running of the school and the processing of children through their course requirements dominated other concerns. Discipline was an issue primarily when it disrupted routine practice; we have seen that teachers' enforcement of discipline rules was not always backed, especially in those instances like clearing students from front doorways, where the enforcement itself could prove disruptive of routine. The separate domains of control and education came into conflict at Forest Hills when teachers felt left out of schoolwide policy decision which affected instruction. De-tracking was the prime example.

The teachers at Freeburg felt the administrative-teacher split much more keenly, not only because they were not involved in making policy decisions affecting content, but because instructional policy seemed not to be made at all. They constantly felt that as individuals they were teaching *despite* administrative policies rather than because of them. Where teachers had enough time, planning space or classroom resources, it was only because they scrounged them – from other teachers' space, from personal time, from free or inexpensive sources. The lack of support for basic instructional goals, and the capricious changing of discipline policies and duties by announcement through student messengers, made teachers feel they constantly had to look over their shoulders. They never seemed to feel secure to let go and teach. The same rule changes from the principal's office and patrolling by teachers gave students that same feeling of being watched, of not being trusted. Interestingly, we shall see that the principal, too, felt very distant from the life of the school and felt himself to be in tension with half-hearted teachers and apathetic or unruly students. The uncertainties of the school day fed the tension between the two levels of staff, and the tension in turn produced new uncertainties with sporadic new attempts to get the school under control. More so than at any other school observed, the tensions between control goals and educational purposes here were overt, were articulated by staff at all levels, and were felt by students. The traditional organization was not indicative of stability but of unease and lack of imagination to adapt structure to educational needs and to do so with some consistency.

The inconsistencies were not always major but ubiquitous. Students wondered what rules were in force at what time and, as will be discussed in the case of Mr Lennon's class, they saw no coherence to policies about behavior. Graduation requirements were also in flux. Teachers built their courses around exam schedules that were often changed without notice. They scheduled their free time not knowing when it would be shifted to accommodate new hall duties. At one point the new assignments provoked a union grievance procedure because they were, in the minds of teachers, unbargained changes in the current contract. And the administration seemed always to be nervously watching what students would do. Just as the Forest Hills teachers kept the memories of anti-war dissent alive in their decision to limit student reading, administrators at Freeburg were on edge because of one incident in the past when students managed to put a Volkswagen on top of the school, and because of an exam period disrupted by noise in the halls. In addition, Senior Skip Day (a day in the spring when all seniors stayed out of school and many had a party at a state park or other site out of town) raised fears discussed by the staff all spring, in almost exact proportion to the anticipation the seniors felt in the weeks before their big day.

Each group seemed to feel very insecure in the face of the anticipated actions of the other. Neither students, faculty, nor administration fully trusted that the others would do their job in ways beneficial to the rest of the school. When I asked Mr Morton, the principal, about the littering, he answered, "That's the way society is. I wish the kids were atypical, but they're not. We'll have a faculty meeting where we discuss student littering in the lunch room, and after the meeting of 100 teachers, it'll look like a dump – as bad as the kids. That's the way our throw-away society is."

He had similarly low expectations of teachers' willingness to teach: "Teachers do not exercise their professional judgment on what kids need to do to learn the subject. They may feel that twenty-five problems are needed to teach a math concept, but the students will only do fifteen, or will gripe, so the teacher assigns only fifteen. When they gripe that's too much, they [students] get the teachers to lower it even further." He was not unaware of the defensive strategies teachers were using to elicit student participation, or to avoid student resistance, but saw no authority on his part to challenge the pattern. He viewed his role as passive, trusting that, because the students' families were interested in education, "they'll make it," or that individual teachers would salvage the students' education: "Yet teachers who are demanding are the ones students give high ratings, mention as the good teacher. They gravitate to the demanding teachers." His passive, some might say cynical, view of the faculty and his use of them as patrols and monitors, but disregard for their needs for books and safe classrooms, did nothing to affirm teachers' professionalism. This passivity in fact contributed to the overall sense that things were out of control.

Mr Morton in some ways had inherited a traditional high school organization, with the role of the principal defined by business duties and by discipline. The distance from curricular concerns was built in, as it was at Forest Hills. In Mr Morton's case, the application of this role for purely institutional maintenance purposes was not entirely comfortable. Yet he did not know how to change the role to pursue what had been, prior to his principalship, his interest in instruction. More than any principal, he articulated the distance he felt from the teaching faculty, but he did not see in the principalship a way to alter this distance. The distance itself had its roots in his personal shift from teacher to administrator.

Mr Morton had been a teacher in another city during the time its teachers unionized. He had been active in building the union and remembered its early days with fondness. He said that the teachers had organized in order to get class sizes reduced, course preparation loads equalized and teacher voices heard in more schoolwide decisions. His memory was that the organizing was based on securing better conditions for the children. To increase his income, he left education for a few years to work in industry, but he found the anti-intellectual atmosphere stifling. At his place of work, even mentioning having watched a Public Broadcast System television special instead of the popular situation comedies on commercial television made one an outcast. He returned to education but went into administration, presumably to have a salary closer to his industry pay.

He said that as an administrator, he "still cared about the same things [issues he had worked for in the union], but suddenly the teachers said, 'no, now you're the enemy. You're on the other side.'" He said it was very hard to be an administrator in the community where one has taught, because the "teachers can't accept the fact that you are the same person." He felt deeply the adversarial relations between his office and the teaching staff. He would probably have been surprised to know that the teachers attributed that conflict to his use of the principal's role rather than to the general split between administrators and union members. Mr Morton was a kind man who seemed to have no imagination for making things work at the school. He willingly talked and listened to the Rap Group, and in fact teachers said that, one-to-one, he was quite personable; but he seemed very detached from the student body, the classrooms and the faculty. In the absence of collegial mechanisms for policy he became more authoritarian, thus even more adversarial in the eyes of teachers, handing down directives without staff discussion of their impact or of other alternatives.

Mr Morton did have praise for individual teachers, especially

Mr Jackson and Mr Reznick (a teacher aspiring to administration and a department chair), but overall he felt no confidence in the teachers. The teachers, in turn, saw the seemingly arbitrary shifts in rules and policies as a lack of confidence in their personal professionalism and as irritants which made students rebel against petty rules or inconsistent enforcement. The very attempts to create (or restore) order were often so disproportionate to the immediate or anticipated offense that they seemed desperate. For example, disorder in the halls during the previous semester exams had prompted new rules which forbade any student being in the building during exams except those hours he or she had a scheduled exam. The eight exam periods were to be crowded into two days, giving some students three or four major exams on one day. Rather than having their unscheduled hours during this time to prepare for the next semester's work, put past files in order or finishing grading exams, teachers not giving exams were to patrol the halls. Through the Student Rap Group's working with the principal, teachers and students managed to have exams extended to the original three days, but many of the patrolling rules stayed in place. Such rules ignored purposes not related strictly to order, such as student needs for extra help in a subject before an exam; students using labs, library or other resources; and teachers needing to use their time in ways they considered more productive and basic to their teaching. Such rules made the teachers and students feel a lack of respect for them as persons and for their purposes. As Mary Metz (1978) observed in *Classrooms and Corridors*, students know when they are being taken seriously, and they will respond accordingly. The rules regarding exam periods did not foster more responsible behavior because they presumed students' inability to assume responsibility.

Metz's analysis also points to the close relationship between behavior in the corridors, or non-classroom areas of schools, and the way students will behave and respond within the classroom. Though the observed teachers did not treat their students as adversaries, there existed in the classroom the same mutually low expectations between the teacher and student groups as found outside the classroom between administrative and faculty personnel and between the administration and the students.

**Social studies at Freeburg**

The teachers of social studies at Freeburg were more diverse personally and politically than those at Forest Hills. And they had far fewer "walls" between their personal knowledge and the knowledge they made accessible in the classroom. They did resemble their Forest Hills counterparts in two important ways. Their reaction to their administrative settings tended to make them teach "defensively," maintaining tight control over classroom knowledge, with more student discussion than at Forest Hills but similar reductions in course substance and in student assignments. And they assumed personal costs in time, energy and effort when they attempted to raise standards above that expected by the regularities of the institution. Interestingly, the similarities of the defensive teaching strategies among teachers at the two schools obscured their differences in politics and philosophy. They also reinforced the low expectations students felt within the school as a whole, and therefore contributed to the disengagement that the teachers, in taking on costs of reforms, were trying to overcome.

Before each classroom and teacher can be considered, the department as a whole needs to be understood for the history of its program. During the 1960s, Freeburg had responded to an educational trend by shifting to a modular schedule. The shift entailed changing both the school timetable, by varying lengths of class periods, and the course schedule. Departments reorganized into a series of electives, or modules, which students could take in varying sequence. When this did not prove to be satisfactory to students and teachers, it was later abandoned. In the return to the more traditional timetable and schedule of course offerings, the social studies department retained the requirement that one course would be required for graduation, with all other social studies courses being elected. The one requirement for several years was a general introduction to the social sciences, based on theories and terminology of psychology, sociology, economics, anthropology, geography and historiography. At the time of this study, the single requirement was a world studies course, a survey of selected countries on each continent, primarily focusing on their cultures, with capsule histories and some map work. Elective courses offered included a two-semester US history sequence, a current problems course, a semester of contemporary US history, a women's history course, western civilization, economics, and consumer economics. Several area studies courses (Asia, Africa, for example) were listed in the departmental syllabus, but seldom offered.

The assumption underlying the single requirement plus electives was that students will elect those areas that interest them. The reality was that most students took as little social studies as possible. Very few students enrolled in four years of social studies classes. Of the 1,400 students, only 900 were enrolled in social studies at any one time, fewer if one remembers that the 900 included several students taking more than one course. One explanation is that offered by Mr Lennon. During the 1960s and early 1970s, young people were flocking to history and social sciences to try to understand race relations, the war in Vietnam, student rights and other political issues. By 1980, students were turning to bread-and-butter courses, such as math and science among the college-bound, and agricultural and business co-ops among those heading for jobs and trade schools. In addition, one half of the juniors and seniors at Freeburg (and at the other high schools observed) held part-time jobs during the school year.[1] Many upper-level students stayed in school only as many hours as needed to fill graduation requirements, then left for jobs, many working over thirty hours per week. Unlike the popular course in science and energy at Nelson High or the popular literature courses at Forest Hills, there seemed to be no social studies course which, by virtue of its subject or teacher, drew large numbers of students. The chair told me that the area studies courses, for example, were among several courses listed but rarely taught, for lack of interest. The lack of interest among students and "state of siege" perpetuated by the administration placed teachers in a precarious middle ground. Their teaching styles combined their resistance and accommodation to administrative priorities, their attempts to overcome student inertia and their personal views of their subject.

Mr Reznick chaired the department of eight men and one woman. His "office" was a desk in a former classroom which also contained the desks of the other social studies teachers and some teachers from home economics, English and foreign languages. The room was so unconducive to productive work that the economics teacher, Mr Lennon, in a pique (or so he tells it), had his desk moved to his classroom. Since another teacher used that room during Mr

Lennon's planning period, he could rarely use his desk productively there, either.

The social studies materials for the library were housed in a social studies resource center, a large room lined with bookshelves and filled with tables and chairs. The room was used as a study hall, with a social studies teacher on "duty," and also as a place for taking make-up tests. Occasionally a teacher would take a class there to use materials, but this was not frequent except in the case of Mr Jackson, who was teaching the unit on research papers. Many bookshelves were empty, though the materials that were in the room were quite good, ranging from easy-to-read school texts to political analysis, historical works and some atlases. When asked who stocked the materials, and why they seemed to reflect 1960s purchase, Mr Lennon explained that "that's what new teachers used to do, in fact I guess I did a lot of ordering and looking for things when I first came." One young woman in particular had devoted a great deal of time to selecting and ordering materials for the resource center. She was described as too energetic and political for the previous administration and, while she was not dismissed, she finally became frustrated enough to leave and find work where her activist model of teaching would be more appreciated. The department or a teacher could request an acquisition, and the librarian would consider it, depending on available budget, but there was no systematic collective procedure for reviewing existing holdings or selecting new ones.

For classroom materials the department worked out a five-year budget plan in conjunction with the principal. According to Mr Reznick, their department's budget had held steady for about five years, although costs and enrollments had increased. A portion of some federal title funds had been used for the one-time purchase of wall maps and other major classroom aids.

Like teachers at most other high schools in the state, these teachers had enviable autonomy in the selection of texts. Unlike the teachers at the other observed schools, the Freeburg staff never seemed to have enough copies of texts for their classes. Mr Lennon observed that although Freeburg's per pupil expenditures were becoming equal to those in surrounding communities, and even exceeded those of some school systems with better reputations, there never seemed to be enough of anything. To him, the most serious shortage was books. His economics students had a few copies of a new edition of the book and more copies of an older edition. Early in the year he had ordered sufficient copies for all the class to have the newer edition. His attempts to secure the additional copies became a running joke during the semester. My notes of his lectures include numerous comments regarding having to make assignments from two texts, trying to reconcile test material between the two texts, and expressing hope that the books "should be in by Friday." At one point he explained to the class that although the faculty had a great deal of say in the selection of texts, the selection and administrative approval was just the beginning. Every order for every copy had to be approved by the building principal, then sent to the central office, then back to the building principal. Especially galling to Mr Lennon was the rule that only office staff could telephone publishers. The office staff frequently did not know all the pertinent information, especially distinctions among varying editions of the same book, and did not share the teacher's urgency over the delays in shipment.

Mr Lennon finally announced one day that the economics books had come in, that students would no longer need to share material found only in the newer edition. He decided to play a joke on the class by opening the box during class and pretending the wrong books had been sent. The large box was brought in and placed on his desk. He opened the books and did a dramatic doubletake. And then a second doubletake. It seems that the publisher really did send the wrong books. Five hardback copies of *Elements of Econometrics*, a college-level economics text arrived; fifteen copies of a paperback, *Elements of Economics*, had been ordered. The semester was drawing to a close and the class remained without sufficient books.

Those books that were in the school were often frayed, in pieces, or in short supply. Unlike the Forest Hills teachers, the staff at Freeburg did occasionally assign text material as homework; more often, it was read during class time. These teachers also spent more time than those at Forest Hills gathering material to add to their teaching files. They used handouts, worksheets, newspaper clippings, magazine articles, public service pamphlets from governmental and industry sources, and reprints from sections from books. They saw themselves as creators, compilers and generators of information, not as mere lecturers or guides to textbooks. But they were not furnished with convenient places to store these materials, budgets for purchasing interesting books and journals, or even adequate numbers of basic texts. Their own personal interest in their subjects tended to overcome the institutional drag on their enthusiasms for collecting things. Where it did not, no procedure (program evaluation, staff evaluation or whatever) stood to monitor the students' interests in or needs for the availability of resources.

Just as the administration left the faculty to its own devices on academic matters, the department functioned as a loose coalition of individuals. Instructional technique was left up to individual teaching style and to the dictates of the particular course content. The new project to require a research paper did have the discussion and backing of the department, and gave a rare opportunity for coordination with certain English teachers. The social studies teachers were a congenial group pursuing very different aims, from politics or coaching to building toward administrative leadership, to in-school concerns. Except for their agreement on increasing the social studies graduation requirements, they rarely dealt with their courses as part of an overall departmental policy.

**Inside the classrooms**

In order to make the investigation of curriculum content parallel among the four schools, the procedure used at Forest Hills in the previous study furnished the core of the research – classroom observation of the economics content of the highest-level-required social studies course. At the other three schools, the highest-level-required course was also the course most pertinent to the study of American institutions, United States history, usually a two- or three-semester sequence. Because the only required course at Freeburg was the world studies course, a different approach was needed in order to document the distribution of economics information through social studies courses. More courses, and thus more teachers, would have to be observed. World studies was observed for half a semester because of its status as a graduation requirement. This course was offered to ninth graders and did not focus on American institutions, so it was observed as necessary but not sufficient to the central research questions. In addition, observations were conducted in United States history (for most of the semester), economics (for a semester), women's studies (for the last few weeks of school), consumer economics (a nine-weeks unit), and current problems (most of a semester). Except for western civilization, these comprise the courses most frequently taken; they include those directly related to the purpose of the research. Except for women's studies, each course was observed long enough to watch the teacher's relations with the students and with the topic developing over time. Each course was taught mainly by the person observed and reflected that person's views of students, course material, resources and learning.

Mr Reznick

Mr Reznick was the chair of the department, a man in his late thirties who was extremely hard-working and conscientious. When asked whether he wished he could reward good teachers or sanction weaker ones, Mr Morton had replied that there was no need to reward teachers: "if given no budget, Eric Reznick could still teach. If all our teachers were like Eric ..."

I observed Mr Reznick's class on consumer economics. It was a nine-week unit in a team-taught rotating series on law, government and practical economics. He assigned a text, which was very simple, but taught mostly from materials he had gathered. The students received handouts from governmental, industrial and public service groups on insurance, credit, landlord–tenant relations, and other personal economic issues. The course dealt with economic theory on only very simple levels and only where directly related to everyday issues such as price and the availability of credit. Speakers from utility companies, consumer groups and businesses were brought in several times during the nine weeks to address the students in the whole sequence. Mr Reznick had a strong interest in his subject and a solid grasp of the issues involved and available resources.

Like the other teachers at Freeburg, he had to expect that the richness of the course would be lost on all but a few students. He tolerated less side chatter than most of the teachers but still did not get all students to participate by listening to the speaker, paying attention to the films or discussing. As will be discussed in a later chapter, the Freeburg teachers engaged in what I have termed "defensive" teaching in order to elicit minimal student compliance. For Mr Reznick, this came less in watering down presentations,

for presumably practical economics is already a step down academically from the regular economics course and draws students
accordingly. His lectures remained organized and substantive, but
the assignments were geared to anticipate low effort on the part of
students. As an independent study project, the students were to
collect news items on an economic topic and comment on them in
a prescribed manner, or tackle other more ambitious projects such
as attending public hearings at regulatory boards, attending a city
council meeting, or meeting with people in the community who
dealt with issues being studied; or graphics presentations could be
made, illustrating topics studied. The levels of difficulty were varied; the common response was to take the least demanding, the
news items, and even then a number of students had to be repeatedly reminded that failure to comply would be failure in the course.
In the face of such apathy, Mr Reznick continued to be cheerful
and hard-working, interested in adding to his course, and in improving the department's offerings and teaching strategies. Where
possible, he took initiatives to buffer the department against the
uncertainties of administrative policy shifts or inertia. In fact, he
was interested in this research project precisely because he felt the
department needed outside leverage to bolster their claims for more
resources and more social studies graduation credits. He and Mr
Jackson led the move for those increased credits, even though it
meant friction with other departments and at first lonely efforts on
their parts.

## Mr Jackson

Mr Jackson exhibited the least frustration with administrative and
student apathy. He had his own agenda for teaching and for program development, and this stemmed from his own career plans as
well as his concern for the students. He was working on a graduate
degree during the observations, while also helping several periods
a day with the drop-out prevention program, serving as an unofficial observer/member of the graduation credits reform committee,
and teaching the required world studies course. He was the only
one able to create an orderly workplace out of the chaos of the
crowded teacher office room, and the only one to receive close to
full compliance on a student assignment.

The world studies course was a survey of other countries and cultures. It combined brief historical sketches with current geography and culture. Textbook-based, the course under Mr Jackson was a straightforward march around the planet. The students were assigned pages in the text, were sometimes tested on them without warning, and were required to turn in answers to questions on worksheets or from the text. The content of the course was largely a series of lists, of place names, political leaders, products and terms from the dominant religions. Mr Jackson's knowledge of some of these countries was thin, scarcely more than the textbook summaries. But he conveyed a sense that the material was there to be mastered and an expectation that students would master it.

Although his familiarity with his subject was not nearly so comprehensive as hers, Mr Jackson's style of conveying information most closely resembled Miss Langer's at Forest Hills. Like her, he responded to institutional disorder by creating his own efficiencies. He responded to student disinterest by keeping a tight rein on content, thus assuring his position as the authority on the subject. He differed from Miss Langer in allowing, even requiring, more student talk, especially in answering leading questions about the previous night's reading assignment. He also was the only teacher at Freeburg for whom the students frequently took notes. (Other teachers lectured as though students were taking notes, but few actually did; often I would be the only person writing.)

A look at one of his lectures gives a fairly accurate picture of Mr Jackson's treatment of the content. He began each class period with a question about the news, took a few comments, then proceeded to pull down a map and lecture. On a February day, Mr Jackson pulled down a map of Europe and began to quiz the students on their reading.

Mr J: We usually leave books open. Today I want them closed. I want to see if you really did read it. Take notes if you want. I haven't made a decision yet regarding a quiz. Today we are going to talk about a section in the text – it gave you just a little tidbit – of many civilizations in the Middle East. Now, an ancient civilization formed where there was enough water – Katy?

Katy: No.

George: No.

Dick: No.

103

> Mr J: Okay, the Mesopotamian civilization. We find this on the shores of a couple of rivers ...
>
> Eva: Tigris and Euphrates.
>
> Mr J: Why near water, Mike?
>
> Mike: Irrigation.
>
> Mr J: Anything else?
>
> David: Transportation.
>
> Mike: Water.
>
> Bart: Good soil for crops.
>
> Mr J: We find many civilizations beginning on rivers. What country?
>
> Molly: Israel?
>
> Pete: Iraq.
>
> Mr J: Any other civilizations founded on a river?
>
> Anne: Egypt, on the Nile. Was the soil as rich as Mesopotamian soil?
>
> Mr J: Mesopotamia had richer soil. That's a shot in the dark. [He means that he is guessing.]
>
> Anne: Doesn't the Nile have jungles?
>
> Mr J: You're thinking of the Amazon [chuckles]. Wrong continent. The Tigris and Euphrates had access to the Persian Gulf. I wish I could give you a good time period for these, but I can't. Egyptian, I suppose, 8,000 BC. A ballpark figure. Mesopotamia, earlier, maybe 12,000 to 10,000 BC. I could be several thousand years off.

The class then proceeded to take up the Hebrew flight from Egypt, with such student questions as how the Red Sea parted, whether it was a matter of tides and whether the redness was created by tiny marine organisms. Then Mr J asked where the Hebrew people "ended up."

> David: I don't know.
>
> Mr J: They were heading for Canaan but ended up in Lebanon and Israel. An empire is established – Israelite/Hebrew/Jewish. Two important kings we should remember, who united all the Hebrews under one king, Solomon and David. The Hebrew empire was 973 BC to when it crumbled in 586 BC, conquered by guess who?

The discussion continued and touched on the meaning of *diaspora*, the Babylonians, the Persians, Alexander the Great, the dates of the Greek empire, and the geographic extent of the Roman empire. The class ended on the discussion of Romans as polytheists. Subsequent class periods did not treat single topics from this veritable catalogue of middle eastern countries in further depth; the next day's class moved onto other subjects.

The worksheet for the day had contained such questions as: What were the two great river valley civilizations? Who are the "chosen people," and what is the "promised land"? Who destroyed the Persian Empire? and Define such terms as "*Kaaba*," "*Koran*," "*Allah*," "*Hegira*," "*caliph*" and so on. Fourteen other terms such as "*Saladin*," "*Tamerlane*," "*Mustafa Kemal*" and "Balfour Declaration" could be defined for extra credit.

The students were accustomed to the whirlwind pace of the lectures. The material was extremely fragmented, almost always presented as lists, occasionally organized in outline form, making the disparate pieces difficult to piece together. The manner of testing, answering with short answers or filling in blanks, made piecing the fragments together unnecessary for success in the course. As in Miss Langer's class at Forest Hills, the lists gave the students certainties about what they would be tested on and gave the teacher an efficient way of conveying a great deal of material in a brief timespan. For many of these ninth graders, it was their first course that included notetaking; many of them found the content interesting because of news events in other countries (such as the American hostages held in Iran) or people they had met from abroad.

As the only required course, this one included a research paper. In combination with the English department, the social studies department had, the year before, developed standards for instruction on researching and writing a formal paper. This was the only extended writing assignment observed in this school and the most formally instructive at any of the schools. As might be expected for a first paper, the instruction was weighted more toward proper footnote form than toward substance, say comparing ideas, evaluating the bias of a source, investigating the value of a source, presenting facts or developing a coherent theme. The resulting papers were more precise than interesting, but were graded for both form and content, an exacting task for which Mr Jackson's natural attention to detail well suited him. Topics of the papers ranged from "The Economy of Switzerland" and "Germany After World War II", to "The Cold War and Containment in Europe" and

105

"The St Lawrence Seaway." The required length was a minimum of three typewritten pages or five to seven handwritten ones, almost more appropriate to an elementary school assignment than high school. Most exceeded the minimum limits by a few pages, though none were as extensive as the very general titles indicated. The papers, like the course, were broad surveys. The paper was essential for satisfying the required credit and compliance was far higher than on any other assignment observed for this study.

Mr Jackson seemed to see the vacuum in administrative leadership as a challenge for his own energies and ideas. He was not always complimentary of administrative policies, but as a rules-oriented person, and one preparing himself for an administrative career, he exhibited less conflict with administrative rule shifts than the other teachers. Since he taught the one required course, he had sufficient texts. He also worked with the assistant principals on the drop-out prevention program, so felt less distance from the administration than teachers not having these constructive contacts. He was in a position, in observing the meetings on graduation requirements and in working with the drop-out prevention program, to see some positive developments. His course would seem to have raised some expectations that social studies requires some reading and writing, that it involves student participation, that it covers specified content. If that is the expectation, it was not evident among students in the upper-level courses.

## Mr Hansen

Compared to the order and routine of outlines and worksheets of Mr Jackson's course, Mr Hansen's current problems course was a loose rap session. The semester course was observed for several weeks because its focus on contemporary issues would presumably touch on economic issues. It rarely did because it was based on such psychological and social-psychological themes as personality, death and dying, and the family. The portion on personality included topics on socialization, intelligence, heredity, and psychological theories of personality. The death and dying unit considered stages of death and grief, suicide, funeral practices, abortion, euthanasia and violence.

The procedure in the class was for Mr Hansen to introduce the topic with brief comments or a handout. Almost all reading took place in class, often with materials that were collected at the end of the class rather than taken home to be studied. Readings ranged from brief selections in issues-oriented paperback texts on the topics to xeroxed copies of very simple magazine articles. For example, the lesson on intelligence included a Mensa intelligence test copied from *Reader's Digest*. A one-page mimeo on Freud was copied from a psychology book. A three-page summary of Erik Erikson's *Eight Stages of Man* had been typed specially for the course, and was cited as taken from a book of psychology readings.

After the topic was introduced, the students would complete the readings, usually in fifteen to thirty minutes during class. A discussion or film would follow. Among the strongest components of the class were films on such subjects as funeral practices in different cultures and medical ethics regarding saving severely handicapped infants. Less successful use was made of videotaped programs from television, the videotape room was a small, dark closet-like room behind the stage, awkward to reach and almost airless. The quality of videotaping was poorer than at Nelson and Maizeville, where teachers made greater use of the process and had better support staffs for equipment usage.

Mr Hansen's discussions were very casual. Few students took notes. Three or four students interested in the topic carried the conversation (and this group varied according to topic, although one or two spoke up whatever topic) along with the teacher. Mr Hansen liked to divide the class into groups to discuss the topics, perhaps to make lists of ideas or respond to lists of questions he provided. Here again, there was no expectation that everyone would contribute. A few students dominated the group discussions, more often those interested in the topic than those prepared by reading. Mr Hansen had no high expectation that students would spend a great deal of time on the course; he at one time had put some effort into gathering the materials used, but taught in a very laid-back manner quite different from Mr Jackson's worksheets and quizzes and Mr Reznick's constant searching for interesting and effective materials. Contemporary social problems was a popular course, frequently elected by middle-level and weaker students. More ambitious students usually signed up for economics or western civilization; more political students perhaps for women's history. Contemporary social problems dealt with personal issues students cared about and enjoyed hearing people discuss. There were interesting moments, and these came often enough for students' attention to be held. In its tone and off-hand manner, the course fitted the general ethos of the school, differing only in that most students felt comfortable in the class; Mr Hansen's pleasant manner moderated the tensions felt in other parts of the building. His lack of serious demands on the students invited their cooperation; he did receive their cooperation (few were as rude as students in other classes) but rarely excited commitment or intense participation. His accommodation to the minimal expectations of the administration was to ask for almost no preparation and minimal participation from his students and within that framework he would provide some interesting films and readings. Many students sat silent the entire semester, while the vocal few carried the discussions. Mr Hansen had structured the content in such a way that equilibrium was reached between casual effort, on his part and on the students' part, and topical interest. Given the climate of the school, he may have succeeded in carrying along more of the students with him than those teachers who tried to demand more but could not engage students in the learning process. His simplifications in this elective course demonstrated one way teachers responded in a school of low expectations.

## Mr Lennon

When Mr Jackson polled his class on their views of war, all but four students and Mr Jackson himself called themselves "doves" rather than "hawks." Mr Lennon was a perfect foil to Mr Jackson's announced political conservatism and his strictly ordered lectures and worksheets. Mr Lennon described himself variously as a Marxist, an anarchist and a social democrat. Most accurately, he should probably be called a progressive or a liberal democrat. For many of his views, he would have been censured in the McCarthy era that swept the state, and indeed the nation, in the 1950s. Now, because of his teaching style, students scarcely recognized the political content of many of his lectures. To them, he was just doing "social studies" like the rest of their teachers. Mr Lennon was interesting for this study, then, not just because he taught the course formally called "economics," but because he gave evidence of the way minimal teaching can reduce even controversial content to indistinguishable ritual.

Mr Lennon and Mr Reznick were among the most knowledgeable of the teachers observed for the study. Of all the teachers, Mr Lennon had the least distance, or "wall," between his personal knowledge and the information he conveyed in the classroom. Even so, he was a very frustrated teacher, frustrated not only by broken windows that no one cared to repair, but by the similar administrative indifference to matters he considered important within the school and by society's unwillingness to pay teachers. He was also frustrated with the point he had reached in his career, a point he saw as far from his original motivations for becoming a teacher.

Mr Lennon reminisced that he had become a teacher because "all respectable radicals in the 1960s went into teaching to save the world." At a point when many of his fellow students decided to stay in graduate school, to remain near the scene of campus activism, he felt it was time to leave and to begin to address issues outside the university setting. He had hoped to teach in a much larger city, where friends of his were involved in community organizing, especially in black neighborhoods. When such a job did not materialize, he applied with smaller school systems and happened to be in the placement office when an administrator from Freeburg came in to fill a teaching position in the then new modular schedule. Having been turned down in the middle of another interview, being told by the interviewer, "I don't think we want you," Mr Lennon found the educational philosophy and student participation goals of the Freeburg modular plan compatible with his interests in academic freedom and education for social change.

At the beginning of his teaching career, he had remained active in political issues, eventually turning his attention away from campus and urban issues toward teachers' union work. He had since seen issues such as academic freedom dissolve into self-censorship by teachers and fights for better working conditions yield to issues of salary and seniority protection. He speculated that much of the shift came through the hiring of certain types of teachers. He spoke of the woman teacher who had helped stock the resource center but later left, with the apparent blessing of the administration who preferred less activist, reformist teachers. He also described a man who was not hired, probably because of his energies and ideas. In response to my question of whether self-censorship was more a matter of who was hired or who was afraid, he replied:

> I think it's both. The guy who is going to give the speech at graduation, Sam Reynolds, I think is the perfect example of the kind of guy who doesn't get a job in teaching. He filled in here when a teacher had an extended illness. Mr Reynolds was a dynamic teacher. I was kind of hopin' (laughs) they didn't hire him just because he made me look bad – uh – I don't know if he would have been able to maintain that level (of energy). I think maybe I had that energy at one point, I don't know – but he just involved kids.

The man was, at the time of the interview, involved in a dispute to help keep open neighborhood schools threatened with closing in the district where he lived. "Anyway, they didn't hire him – even though he was recommended by several members of the department."

Mr Lennon had seen potentially committed, energetic teachers let go or never hired. And he had seen a shift from great student interest in political issues to concentration in math and science, mostly because of job possibilities. But also he said that he saw students as "buying technology." Ironically, just as society was awakening to the dangers and inadequacies of many of our technologies, his students were expressing confidence that technology could solve all social problems. Several students could not understand why the economy was in such turmoil; one had asked, "We have all these models. Why don't we just create an economy? The computers are there."

He noticed what I had noticed in extensive interviews with Forest Hills High students: "When the students say *they*, there seems not to be nearly as much interest in *who* makes decisions, as there was, even among high school kids five, six, ten years ago." At times he tried in class to relate their passive view of democracy to the running of the school, to demonstrate how conflict and power and control can operate. At the end of the first semester, when noise during exams had caused such disruptions, he tried to talk with his own classes about their power relative to the administration's.

> I said then, by the end of the year, there's gonna be people down there watching you (in the commons area), detention, all this stuff. They told me I was crazy. They said, "Who could DO that?" Then one kid says, "If it's gonna happen, it's gonna happen." The idea that perhaps if the students took some

initiative and did some things, you know, some of them
exercised some power, people on the Student Rap Group, say,
just didn't occur to them. I tried to tell them, hey, you have
those privileges, you have some rights because some students
before you fought for them. They went to a lot of trouble so
you would have these things.

As he observed, the control on halls and commons areas were
imposed even earlier than he had predicted, and the students re-
belled only by becoming sloppier or less interested, not by trying
to change the policies.

The contradictions between Mr Lennon's goals for his teaching
and his frustration with administrative and student disinterest were
manifest in his teaching. The *reformist* intentions emerged through
the content of the lectures and readings. The *disillusionment* was
visible in the style of his teaching and the lack of demands he made
on the students. Unfortunately, the effect of the latter was often to
trivialize the former.

Mr Lennon's economics and history lessons were rich and substantive *when he taught*. His lectures were full of controversy,
theory, technical terminology, personal experiences, contrasting
ideas and abundant facts. In economics he would frequently assign
contradictory readings, choosing very conservative and radical
economists to represent their opposing points of view. He dared to
explain such difficult concepts as elasticity, marginal propensities
to consume or save, functions of money, market equilibrium and
social goods. Unlike the teachers at Forest Hills, he did not present
a picture of a simplistic economy that worked perfectly, worthy of
unquestioning trust. He presented a very complicated picture of an
uncertain national and international economic scene and honestly
admitted that experts and citizens disagree among themselves and
with each other about what makes the economy work, what causes
problems and how those problems should be solved. His view of
students and of learning would not have permitted sanitized lectures of perfect, abstract models, say of supply and demand or
credit or price. He drew on examples from the news and from
students' own experiences, with the goal not of hiding his personal
knowledge of the subject but of sharing it and, even more, of
drawing them into concern as well.

If the simplistic, too-perfect descriptions of the world presented by the teachers at Forest Hills made the students skeptical of school-supplied information, Mr Lennon's honesty and his willingness to share personal knowledge should have engaged students in the teaching–learning dialogue, perhaps even to the point of their sharing their personal knowledge as well and incorporating portions of the lecture information into their personal store. But despite his fine content, Mr Lennon's teaching style embodied enough defensive simplifications that the lively student–teacher dialogue rarely emerged.

He did not simplify topics, but he did simplify assignments. He did not hide controversy, but he rarely asked students to take part in weighing the disparate sides rather than just reading about them. The textbook, what few copies existed, took a rather straightforward consensus approach to the content. This was the basis for most tests. While lectures figured into Mr Lennon's view of testable material, he never could convince students to take notes.

He rarely tried to convince students of anything. Class always began quite slowly, with a slow roll call and a chat about the news of the day. Here Mr Lennon was at his best; the students knew he was active in politics, often helping with campaigns and once even having run for office, and they respected his first-hand information on the subject. Those who were interested in following the news paid rapt attention to this portion of the class and drew him out with questions, many of them informed inquiries. The tone shifted when "real class" started. Mr Lennon did not lose his expertise, and often continued to lace the lectures with anecdotes or close-to-home examples. Price theory, for example, might be discussed in terms of the Spanish Club's pizza sales in the commons. But Mr Lennon did not exercise authority over the classroom commensurate with his authority over the material.

Side chatter accompanied almost every lecture. Many times I would note that I was the only person taking notes. Notes on this class are filled with such marginalia as "Six conversations going on around the room," or "three people reading novels, one writing a letter, three talking about the weekend, two half asleep." Ironically, the three boys who paid most attention to the formal lectures (if Mr Lennon could be said to be formal as he leaned against his desk or walked around flipping a piece of chalk) were also the most intent science students. They did not concur with his politics, but they often took copious notes and asked for clarifications and further details, the way Mr Lennon remembered many social studies students doing in years past.

He perhaps helped invite this disengagement by his unexpressed but clear anticipation that students were to get the material on their own. He lectured, provided interesting readings, told stories to illustrate abstract concepts, but he felt no obligation to structure the course in a way that monitored student effort. He would have nothing to do with daily worksheets and quizzes. He explained to me that he felt that, by high school, students are adults: "I can't do the studying for them. I put it out and they can get it or not." When one-third of the class made an F on his exam, it became apparent that many had chosen not to "get it." Or they mistook the casual lecture tone for casual, unimportant content. He contributed to this distance from the learning process by backing off after seeming to make a demand of students. As will be discussed later in Chapter 7, to gain even minimal cooperation, to reduce active student protests to assignments, teachers in varying degrees taught defensively. They presented topics, then drew back when student resistance was felt, perhaps even before it was felt. While his lectures were complicated and full, there was much dead time during the hour, during the beginning and end of the period, during times of silent reading of assignments, during other interruptions. And when he was lecturing, Mr Lennon would frequently announce a very difficult topic, then, before too many groans could be heard, he would assure students that all they would have to do would be to "read Chapter 3 in the new book," or "just look up here for a few minutes while we touch on this."

The effect of this apologetic assigning of work in Mr Lennon's class was to reduce all but his most interesting lectures to "just doing social studies." His politics were a novelty to the students, but meant little to them, either as something to agree with or reject. The excellence of parts of his lectures was undermined by the attitude he conveyed that he really did not expect much student interest or effort.

He was not unaware of this interaction, and reflected on its roots in his stage of life, his feelings that teaching had not resulted in changing the world, and his chafing at low pay and general undervaluing of his efforts by the administration and by society in general. In a setting where he had felt at odds with many institutional purposes and rewards, his early enthusiasm had come from

113

caring about the students. Now that he found so few of them responding that source of reward was disappearing as well. Only his great interest in his subject seemed to offer any compensation.

## Changing the graduation requirements

While life in the classrooms was proceeding, Freeburg High was about to change its graduation requirements, beginning with the following year's ninth grade class. Such a change is not uncommon among high schools and rarely provokes the level of intense debate evident at Freeburg. Perhaps its importance was that like the new building, it was a long time coming. And for this research, it was important in demonstrating the difficulties in opening knowledge access in a climate of low expectations, administrative distance and conflicting purposes.

After the modular schedule was dropped, several academic departments retained low requirements for graduation, based on the assumption that students would fill out their schedule with electives in these areas. Social studies was one area in which most students did not elect to take several extra courses. For years the social studies teachers had wanted to increase the requirements, but they always met with opposition from teachers in other areas who feared lay-offs in their areas if more budget were allocated for social studies positions. Even though the lack of substantial requirements in this area met with criticism from other schools and helped add to Freeburg's reputation as a less-than-excellent school, teachers in other departments were often more protective of what they saw as a threat to their jobs than of the reputation of the school among educators in the area.

Several factors converged to prompt the change. For one, Mr Reznick was joined by Mr Jackson in wanting the change. Mr Jackson was eager for his graduate thesis to trace this reform and he contributed the time to do a survey of teachers, students, community and administrators regarding what courses and skills and areas of knowledge they saw as important. In exchange, he could serve as an observer/member of the committee comprising board members, staff, parents and others appointed to analyze the surveys, the accreditation reports, the staff concerns and to make recommendations to the board. In addition to Mr Jackson's contribution, one woman was described as running for the school board on the single issue of upgrading graduation requirements at the high school. Although the curriculum supervisor was seen as concerned more with elementary schools than high schools, his presence in the district had furthered a review of all programs over a period of just a few years.

Those wanting a reform were bolstered by cites of numerous surveys of school goals such diverse groups as the Gallup polling organization, professional education journals and the regional press. A report circulated by the state department of public instruction showed average graduation requirements in English, social studies, math, science and physical education to be substantially above Freeburg's in three of the four academic areas. Freeburg ranked in the lowest 2 per cent of high schools in the state in social studies requirements.[2] Armed with these statistics, the committee held hearing-like meetings in order to consider the concerns and proposals of citizens and staff.

The surveys of students, staff and citizens proved the most interesting source of data. All groups cited literacy skills as very important and foreign language as unimportant. Students rated every area as less important than it was rated by staff or citizens.[3] (Their ratings were consistent, then, with their generally low level of effort in academic pursuits, a level usually appropriate to the demands made of them.)

At the hearings there was no organized student or citizen presentation, but a dozen faculty attended regularly and gave, as Mr Jackson explained, "more input than the committee had really hoped for." Mr Jackson wrote up the surveys and the meetings for his thesis. He noted in his thesis that there was frequent disagreement, but did not explain which group disagreed over which issues. Perhaps because it was formally drafted and represented many people's ideas over a long period of time, the social studies plan, as it was called, was adopted. Its primary change was to increase social studies requirements from one year to two and one-half years, with one year being specified as United States history, or a combination of government and contemporary United States history, and one semester specified as economics or consumer economics.

It is interesting to note the impetus for these changes came from teachers rather than from the administration's overall plan for the school. The teachers found their most active support from the superintendent and curriculum coordinator, though these had to be willing to hear all sides. Mr Morton was not a prime mover in the reform, though he did approve of the plan. Early in my semester in the school, while the debates were still in progress, a teacher told me that one of the building's assistant principals was in favor of increased requirements because it "would keep students out of the halls and keep them from leaving school early in the day." I held this impression for several weeks until a copy of the detailed proposed plan was made available. It seemed that the administrator's support was premature: the total requirements for graduation would remain the same; the difference lay in the numbers to be specified or to be elected by students. This attitude confirmed my assessment of the administrator's preoccupation with behavior controls, a concern coopted in this case by an academic issue.

The chief opposition came from teachers in areas that would lose specified graduation requirements or lose anticipated student electives. While increased academic credits were subtracted mostly from elective credits, the fine arts requirement was to be reduced from one year to one semester, with vocational and business courses allowed the other semester. Tempers were very hot the night the art teachers brought a university art professor to the committee's hearing to speak against the social studies plan.

The social studies plan was adopted; the department did not then anticipate gains in faculty members at the expense of other departments. Rather, assignments would be sifted to accommodate the new United States history requirement and those in the economic areas. Mr Lennon presented to the board his outline for the economics course; one member was reputed to have said that it was too hard, too much like a college course, and that he did not understand it. The language of the course outline was changed to make it more intelligible to the board.

Except for this incident, Mr Jackson said that none of the discussion by the committee or the board centered on *what the content of the courses in question would be*. The discussion remained on the level of course titles and credits.

The reform, gratefully received by the social studies faculty, reveals the adversarial tone underlying many of Freeburg's policies. The teacher initiatives also demonstrate the cost individual teachers bear when they try to make an improvement against traditional institutional inertia. The coincidence of several teachers' concern,

Mr Jackson's surveys, and a board member's support overcame the resistance for improvement and the conflict avoidance strategies which had determined school policy up to that time. A history of low expectations took great effort to overcome.

## Teaching and control

To summarize Freeburg as an example of administrative–teacher relations, one looks again at individuals who had to go against the grain of their institution in order to teach, to raise standards, to try to engage students. With an administration passive in academic concerns but active in promoting discipline and controls, the teachers had to make individual decisions about how to allocate their time and efforts, how to make do with insufficient materials, how to negotiate their own authority within their limits. Mr Jackson responded with great activity, strict classroom rules, worksheets, and an active role in trying to reform curriculum. In a sense, he by-passed the building administration by cooperating with the larger survey effort at the district level. Mr Reznick reacted by assuming the difficult task of assigning the department's slim resources equitably and by keeping up in his field. Mr Lennon, like Mr Hansen, responded by demanding as little of students as the administration demanded of him, although he personally was inclined to demand more than that of himself.

Their proscribed position gave them little efficacy in overcoming the student attitudes, which were partly caused by ever-changing administrative rules for order. The overall impression of Freeburg was that students did not feel it was "their" place; teachers did not feel it was theirs; and the principal felt the school to be equally distant and out of control.

Freeburg had had a reputation of being this way for so long that it seemed it would never change. As one teacher said of the principal, "Unfortunately, he has no ambition to move on." He was wrong. Several months after the observations, Mr Reznick told me that Mr Morton suddenly resigned just after spring semester ended. The proximal reason was said to be a salary dispute with the board. The teachers felt very bad that Mr Morton resigned without having a new job lined up, but felt that their concerns for the school had not gone unnoticed by the board after all. Especially during the planning of the new building, they had felt left out and overruled.

117

Several told of departmental meetings with architects and planners in which teachers' needs were discussed but later overruled without consultation. This most seriously affected lab areas and shop courses, but contributed to a general faculty feeling that they were consulted only as a formality and that many changes had been arbitrary without basis in teaching needs. They were very surprised to learn that Mr Morton apparently had felt some distance from plans for the new building as well. He left having not ordered furnishings they thought he had ordered for several areas of the building. Two teachers told me of this, perhaps, symbolic protest. Even the one most "in charge" had not felt it was "his" school either.

On paper, the structure of this school resembles that of Forest Hills. At Forest Hills, school routine and school system bureaucracy provided enough regularity that principals and teachers could pursue their own, sometimes contradictory, goals with little upheaval. Regardless of the impact on students, the teachers could salvage their authority over content and their efficiency in the classroom; the administrators could manage the building and public relations. The effects of the administrative priorities were real, as in the case of the decision to eliminate ability-group tracking but they were subtle, almost hidden. At Freeburg, that regularity was absent. The disorder provided more opportunity for individuals like Mr Reznick to exert influence in making changes and improvements, but brought added costs in adversarial relations and in failure to engage students. Whether a new personality within the old administrative framework could overcome the previous adversarial relations remained to be seen. The new principal, whom I met only briefly, was selected for his record of energy and program change. When I went to discuss student employment with him, for a subsequent research project, he pulled an article from his files on the attitudinal rewards students find in work that they do not find in school. He had already given thought to the lives of his students outside school, and he gave the appearance of wanting to be kept informed about broad issues affecting youth and schools. The ambiguity that separated the administrative functions at Freeburg from the teaching roles left room for creative relations to link the two. Or it may again have been filled with arbitrariness and discontinuities. The building crowding would be alleviated for the new principal; teacher pay scales would not. This principal brought an anti-labor reputation that put teachers on their guard, their optimism on at least temporary "hold." A change in personality cannot immediately create new structures or overcome resource limitations. The loose coupling between the teachers and administrators left room for constructive possibilities that proves the former problems not to have been inevitable. Whether the new principal would succeed would depend on his ability to tap the staff resources and reconstitute order-keeping in a way that increased rather than minimized student responsibilities.

# 5
# Maizeville High School

Maizeville High had a great deal in common with Freeburg: agricultural base joined by increasing suburban development; teachers' low expectations of administrative support; lack of administrative expertise or active interest in academics; administrative absorption in disciplining a small number of chronic offenders. The overall school climate and lack of common purpose held the same potential for cynical staff relations and administrative-teacher conflict so visible at Freeburg. At both schools administrative attention to truancy and minor but frequent infractions such as littering or occasionally skipping class grew into a full-time exercise which left little time or staff for supporting the educational purposes of the school. The potentially open conflict between these purposes of order and teaching evident in the lowered efforts and open resistance at Freeburg was diverted at Maizeville by a decision to organize the school in a way that dealt with this split rather than ignored or suppressed it.

In a move which acknowledged administrative default on academics, the administration had delegated many administrative powers of curricular and personnel oversight, including program development and review, to a department coordinator functioning as a strong-chair semi-administrator. Such a structure not only coopted the potential conflictual assertiveness of selected teachers but compensated for administrative limitations of time and academic weakness as well. The strong-chair model was a variation of the traditional principal-teacher role division; the principal by contract could not delegate to a teacher powers of peer review, teacher hiring or firing, or budget authority. However, by formally retaining the legal authority of these powers, the principal was able not only to delegate many administrative responsibilities such as staff assignments and program development, but informally confer responsibility for these other non-delegated areas except for official signature endorsements. In the absence of an assistant principal of instruction, the strong chairs could serve in this capacity for their own departments, reserving to the principal only the letter, if not the spirit, of those responsibilities not allowed by union contracts to be shared with teachers. The structure itself was the result of a conscious decision to alter what was otherwise a very traditional school organization. Because it depended so heavily on informal relations as well as formal job descriptions, the effectiveness of this structural arrangement in supporting instruction was greatly determined by the personalities of the individuals occupying these positions.

In the case of the social studies department, the chair had a strong personality to go with the strong powers of the chair. When the assistant principal had said about teachers that "there isn't [sic] an awful lot of devoted people," he had added one exception: "Sam is devoted."

## Social studies at Maizeville

Sam was Mr Carrico, the Maizeville social studies department chair. To see the strong-chair/coordinator model working at its optimum, one had to see Sam Carrico in action. He and the math coordinator were thought by the administration and faculty to be the teachers who took positive advantage of the strong-chair model, both for their careers and for their departments and students. Mr Carrico combined the broad discretionary powers delegated formally and informally by the administration with a strong entrepreneurial drive of his own. He sought out leadership in professional organizations, in economics education and social studies at the state and national levels. In addition to his teaching and coordinating obligations within the school, he ran a small service business after school hours; as he put it, "that's our Acapulco trips." He created the job (which is too exceptional to describe without revealing his identity) over several years' time, marshalled students and other teachers needing outside income, and developed a business that brought in income. He served on a local governmental board and each summer managed to attend workshops related to social studies issues. A strong, aggressive individual who talked freely about his own energies and forceful approach to his role, Mr Carrico dressed more like a professional or businessman than like a social studies teacher in this part of the state, wearing bright sports jackets and ties, conveying a dynamic quality (and affluent appearance) beyond what most teachers went to the trouble for. He told his students he often came to school at 5:30 in the morning to get work done without sacrificing time with his children.

Mr Carrico's personal and professional pride and his energetic approach to problems prompted him to take full advantage of the authority conveyed to the strong-chair role. Over his twelve years in the job, he had hired half the social studies staff and been instrumental in developing the department's philosophy and course offerings. The administrators took his word on hiring decisions and mostly relied on his judgments for staff evaluation within the department. He said that he frequently visited other teachers' classes and came up with ideas to help them improve. He sought staff ideas about new courses or revisions of current ones. He took the lead in seeking out new materials for his own course and for others in the department and encouraged other teachers to take similar initiatives. As a result of his leadership in searching for good materials and of his aggressive pressing for a role in determining department budgets, the social studies department was extremely well supplied with current simulation games, films, texts, auxiliary books and other instructional materials. He was proud that his own energies seemed contagious, that other teachers responded to his concern for quality with equal concern.

His strong personality and considerable powers over peers could have made Mr Carrico very unpopular. His sense of humor helped alleviate some of his strong will; some on the staff took his ego with a grain of salt. Others were grateful to have more adequate materials than their counterparts at other schools in the region, and they were grateful to Mr Carrico for helping build their department's standing within the school and for helping to put the school "on the map" among other high schools and especially other social studies departments in the state. The school was chosen because state department of public instruction personnel and other teachers insisted that no study of social studies in the state would be complete without Mr Carrico. His colleagues within the school knew that when they bothered to put forth effort, their efforts would be supported and made more productive under Mr Carrico's chairmanship. His active use of his teaching role, his speeches on new ways to explain economics concepts (at professional meetings) and his stepping into positions of leadership within the community, contrasted dramatically with the defensive positions taken by teachers at Freeburg and Forest Hills, who felt underpaid, under-appreciated and safer when unobtrusive than when visible.

His peers tolerated his role in their evaluations because they knew him to be more knowledgeable about their methods and subject matter than the administrative staff. Of the principal, one remarked, "How can *he* know what's going on?" Expectations of administrative interest in course content or instructional method were low but less tension-filled than at Freeburg, where evaluations were more haphazard. Whatever Mr Carrico would say to an administrator about a staff member had probably already been conveyed to that staff member when it became an issue, whether it was a need for improvement or an occasion for praise. Mr Carrico saw his evaluative role in terms of "process evaluation," or improvement rather than summary judgments for or against his peers. The others were not obligated to agree, and would in turn have their own conferences with the administrators, much like those held at Forest Hills. Any demands he made on their time, including out-of-class preparation or extra hours beyond the minimum, Mr Carrico was putting in as well. He tried to hire people who would take their teaching seriously and he had no patience with clock punchers. He actively sought the kind of energetic, activist teachers that Mr Lennon at Freeburg said that that school's administrators had preferred not to hire.

His rewards to teachers could include allowing them to arrange their schedules to suit them, assigning favored courses to teach and in many subtle ways making conditions better for their work. As noted, negative rewards were more varied at the administrative level, and could include numbers of threats and possible dismissal; positive rewards for staff efforts at that level were limited to the administrator's imagination, usually to "thank you." At the level of the department coordinator, the range of positive rewards for hard-working teachers was much broader, especially since it included informal tasks, input into departmental policy, the chance to develop new courses, and other matters directly related to work in the classroom. These rewards had the potential of being continuous throughout the school year rather than concentrated at a single evaluation conference.

By delegating so many matters to the strong chair, the administration demonstrated one method at their disposal for rewarding teachers. Certainly the teacher with the most seniority and years of extra effort was chosen as coordinator in this department. In addition, the tensions between the educative goals and social control goals, very prominent at this school as at Freeburg and Forest Hills, could be resolved productively in many instances. For example, the administration's yielding to the expertise of subjective matter specialists in determining most academic policy avoided the faculty backlash seen in Forest Hills teachers' responses to detracking and the Freeburg teachers' resistance to rule changes made without their consent. The Maizeville faculty could be used more for teaching than for "putting out fires," as at Freeburg. Some standards of evaluation were more clear, as well, including items such as how the teacher dealt with high- and low-ability students. Finally, the administration was able to use the strong-chair model to reward extra effort. Not only were the most competent teachers the ones considered for the chairmanships, but others in the departments were not neglected. The strong-chair advocacy of departmental concerns rewarded those departments willing to hash out cohesive policies and collective requests, whether for budgets, curriculum revisions or staffing. While the similarity between administrators and their concerns at Freeburg and Maizeville make it very unlikely that individual teachers would have fared any better at Maizeville than at Freeburg in having influence, the Maizeville teachers had the added leverage of a central advocate in the strong chair. In the case of the social studies department, this advocate was forceful and respected, so faculty input was considerable. The periodic meeting of the coordinators tended to be more substantive than a regular faculty meeting, many of which consisted of the principal's reading announcements. In the absence of a faculty senate, these meetings provided a forum for faculty to remember the existence of the other departments and to recall their department's place in the overall program, with or without strong agreements or policies emerging from the meetings.

From the responses to the differing parties to certain policies it became evident that the arrangement suited all concerned better than the more fragmented, adversarial roles plaguing the Freeburg teachers. Mr Carrico felt that his attendance at professional meetings provided a service to the school because he came in contact with new ideas and materials long before he would have if the contact had depended on mailed ads, libraries or university course work. He clearly liked giving talks and attending these meetings, but he saw his travel as advantageous to all the staff. To the principal, the trips were the school's way of rewarding Mr Carrico's efforts. The principal indicated that he thought of the permission to attend as a favor granted to Mr Carrico rather than as an assignment for Mr Carrico to represent the school or to search for new materials. This attitude reveals a management approach to teachers or labor (to be managed) very like the paternalistic view the Freeburg principal expressed about his teachers' being "on the other side." At Maizeville this attitude existed but its impact on teachers was lessened by the strong-chair mechanism that allowed at least one teacher, and by extension others in his department, to circumvent many programmatic limitations that attitude implies.

**Inside the classrooms**

Mr Carrico

The real test of the strong-chair model of organization has to be its impact on classrooms. As mentioned, one impact most directly felt was the role of the chair in hiring. Mr Carrico had hired teachers he felt would be hard-working. Some he hired away from other school systems; others came to Maizeville for their first job. Most of the teachers in the department took advantage of the resources Mr Carrico helped assemble and responded by collecting materials on their own. Motivation was high for developing new courses. An ecology course, developed just prior to the observations, was a rare link with another department, in this case science. While I was at the school, plans were being drawn for a psychology course within the social studies department. An active view of the teaching role and an absence of walls between official knowledge and teachers' personal knowledge greatly opened up information and resources to students. When I commented that they seemed to have "adequate" resources, Mr Carrico jumped on the word adequate, saying that they had a *wealth* of resources. Unlike the teachers at Freeburg, who never had enough copies of their books,

Mr Carrico said that their problem at Maizeville was remembering what they had so that they could use it. He said that sometimes storage was such a problem that good materials would be forgotten for awhile before being retrieved and used again. (He thought the new additions of classrooms, office and storage would allow materials to be stored more systematically and accessibly; now every nook in his office and in some classrooms was filled with filmstrip sets, extra books, and printed instructional aids.) An added asset which prompted teacher participation in the development of resources was the access the teachers had to good video-tape recording equipment and staff. An audio-visual staff would set timers to pre-tape television programs for teachers. In addition, the availability of the equipment and videotape players gave teachers incentive to return to school at night to tape documentaries or historical news retrospectives if no staff was available to do it. This added a timeliness absent in the Bob-Hope-narrated Korean War films shown at Forest Hills and an improvement in quality over the stuffy room and poor quality of tapes at Freeburg.

The general pattern, then, of impact on the classroom was of setting a lively tone, of establishing expectations that teaching and learning were still going on, and of providing materials and atmosphere conducive to generating more materials and ideas. The administrative concern for truancy could not impact on classrooms by downgrading the role of content, as at Freeburg, or by its concern for budgets and credits, as at Forest Hills. Though Mr Carrico was known to "fill the room" when he entered, the teachers knew that without the strong-chair model and without his particular leadership, their department would have had a small share of resources and less autonomy in developing interesting courses. Their impatience with his potentially domineering personality was tempered by the fact that his aggressiveness paid off in the community and in the office when he represented them.

Within this broad framework of the strong-chair model, the classroom observations focused on two teachers whose classes present perhaps the extremes of ways teachers can respond to the benefits and drawbacks of this model. The first is Mr Carrico's own class, mainly because he, like Mr Harris at Forest Hills, taught history from the perspective of one trained in economics. The second is Mr Seager, a teacher who resembled Mr Lennon at Freeburg for the inconsistency of his methods and effectiveness.

Mr Carrico's upper level junior history class provided a good insight into his teaching methods and into his use of the working conditions he had helped to provide. It was one of the few classes observed (at any school) in which students were required to discuss, read and write. Interestingly, it also was one of the few classes in which students' names were frequently spoken by the teacher. The class consisted of about twenty juniors and was the second year of a two-year history sequence. In contrast to the defensive position of social studies course requirements at Freeburg, the staff at Maizeville had insisted, under Mr Carrico's leadership, that history be a two-year requirement. Mr Carrico explained that this allowed "post-holing," or going into detail rather than skimming through a survey. Sociology and economics were also required, as one-semester courses. "And that's just setting the table." Electives beyond that three-year sequence included ecology, advanced economics and other traditional social studies electives.

The semester of US history observed dealt with the late nineteenth and early twentieth centuries and covered such economics topics as the rise of industrialization and its effects on the economy and social life of the country, the trust-busting days of Roosevelt, the Gilded Age preceding him and the economic booms and busts that followed. Mr Carrico combined a number of teaching strategies. He assigned readings in a book which contained paired, opposing interpretations of historical issues or events. In addition, he occasionally showed films and assigned book reviews on historical topics. His primary means of conveying information was through lectures and directed discussion. His lectures carried none of the connotations of tightly controlled information evidenced at Forest Hills. He frequently chased asides, stopped to re-explain abstract concepts, interjected personal opinions or related current news items and paced between his desk and the blackboard. The outline for the lesson would be on the board when students entered, or written as he talked. It did not substitute for extended descriptions and analyses as did Freeburg's Mr Schmidt's transparency outlines.

In an interview at the end of the semester, Mr Carrico outlined his goals for the history sequence. As the child of immigrants, he wanted the students to have a strong sense of their own cultural heritage and that of others: "They owe it to Thomas Jefferson, to Abraham Lincoln, even to Nixon, and they owe it to the future generations. You need to know the road you're traveling. You need

127

to know these things weren't heaven-sent. There was a Gilded Age, there were immigrants ..." In addition, he thought students needed economics "purely to function." Without information "you're at the mercy of somebody else." He structured his courses to combine theoretical concepts with "factual" history. His teaching style was as assertive as his dealings with the administration. He actually was one of the few teachers to call students by name when addressing them. He called on students with leading, recitation questions, but also called on them to comment on their work or behavior. He had a store of humorous phrases which punctuated the lectures with opinion and perhaps control. He might stop in mid-sentence to say, "Mary, you're flying over Denver. Come back to class." On more than one occasion, he commented in front of the class on a student's paper: "George, by the way, I have to tell you your book review was very thorough. That's a great improvement over that last test you handed in." He had one or two students he teased, usually over a long period of time so that the running joke provided a theme and variation of humor. He said he carefully picked only those students who could take teasing; clearly, this was one way of keeping the class alert and participating. He made assignments, expected them to be in, graded them with comments as well as letter grades, and at times had students read each other's papers on a topic.

The openness of information in this class, the teacher's lack of boundaries between his personal knowledge and the course content, the greater amount of student contribution in written and oral form, the varied use of resources – all differed markedly from the tight patterns of knowledge access at Forest Hills. The students, however, retained some suspicion of course content. They appreciated his expertise, and many felt his apparent personal affluence gave him more credibility than most poorer social studies teachers would have on economics topics. They felt constrained, however, in presenting their own ideas. They felt, unlike Miss Langer's students, that student talk was valued but in interviews expressed frustration at being unable to disagree with Mr Carrico. Some were intimidated by his strong personality; others felt inadequate to address impromptu a subject on which he was prepared and knowledgeable. Most experienced some suspicion of belief of course content similar to that expressed by Forest Hills students, but those who did said it was more because of their own lack of knowledge rather than because his information directly contradicted other sources they had consulted.

It is interesting that one group of students who did question his opinions were holding outside jobs. Several students at Maizeville, and later at Nelson High, disagreed with their teachers over the benefits and safety of nuclear power. One girl at Maizeville directly disagreed with Mr Carrico's assessment of safe and necessary nuclear power plants. She did not speak up in class, but spoke at length in her interview about her own experiences. Her work at a facility for handicapped children had led to an interest in their parents. Many of the parents' radiology-related occupations placed them at risk for having children with birth defects. While she said she would never be convinced by Mr Carrico's view favoring nuclear power, neither would she have shared her independent information in class. Most students felt less sure of their divergent opinions and felt that even if they were proved to be right, the interchange would damage their persuasiveness because of their lack of expertise as compared with his. Other students, in commenting on which sources of information in this class they learned most from, concluded the lectures were most beneficial, the books valuable only after the explanatory lectures and the teacher open to varied opinions. Mr Carrico's class, then, was contradictory in demanding much more of students and requiring active participation, but being so strongly informational as to intimidate dissent or question. Students in his class were consumers of the teacher-supplied content; they felt less able to be contributors or questioners. He did not set up expectations of students as participants in the development of ideas but did at least expect them to master what content he introduced to them.

A part of the success of Mr Carrico's history class was that these students were high in motivation and achievement. Almost all felt themselves to be college bound. They were reflective students, with many outside interests such as jobs, music and volunteer work. I asked Mr Carrico whether he would be able to expect equal compliance with middle or lower level students. He assured me that he demanded work of all students. He said that the lower level needs satisfaction and successes; he advocated structuring assignments so as to give immediate success, since for some of these low-achieving students the hindrance to learning is the feeling of past failures as much as actual intellectual capacity. He said that he assigned simpler readings to middle level students, not using, for example, the book with paired readings, since even upper level students said it was the hardest to understand of all their assignments. But he did not draw back and make no demands on them, as he felt usually happened in non-tracked classes where the teacher gives up, teaches to the lower middle and loses everyone in the process. Whereas the principal felt very hampered by student and community factors, Mr Carrico felt no constraints on his teaching, from truancy and drugs, to parent attitudes, to resources, to staff relations. "If you can't teach at Maizeville, you can't teach."

## Mr Seager

While most of his colleagues took advantage of the breadth of resources to bring students actively into the learning process, Mr Seager did not. Mr Seager taught sociology and middle level history students. He was as casual as Mr Carrico was intense. His class was very small and could have been an opportunity for individual-ized or seminar-type instruction, with explanations and assign-ments geared to the specific needs of the group. Instead, Mr Seager followed a pattern much like that of Mr Lennon at Freeburg where resources were not so abundant. Mr Seager used the resources at Maizeville to reduce his efforts rather than increase them. His lec-tures were brilliant, when he lectured. He too had been a child of immigrants. He also had been active in teacher unions and in elec-tive politics. When he drew on these experiences, the students listened attentively. They expressed in interviews their respect for his wide range of experience and travel and for his grasp of the real world of politics and economics. Like Mr Lennon's students, they saw that this teacher had a great deal to give.

Partly because of health problems, partly because of indifferent students, and perhaps because of declining interest or confidence in his own ability to affect students, Mr Seager demanded little of them. He assigned readings in class, even using inquiry-based, Socratic materials for silent seatwork. He drew on the extensive film collection to show a film several days per week. To his credit, he went to great trouble to build up the school's file of videotaped television documentaries and televised historical events, which he frequently used.

Mr Seager did not want to limit students' knowledge of the

subject, nor was he interested in consensus models of history and politics. He wanted students to care about his concerns but did not structure the course in a way that pulled students into the learning process. Mr Carrico, who had hired Mr Seager away from another school system many years ago when they had worked together in state social studies organization work, felt that Mr Seager was very bright and informed but unable to teach. His inefficacy in the classroom stemmed, according to Mr Carrico, from his false confidence that knowing the information enables one to teach it effectively.

Mr Seager also had a different view of students. Whereas Mr Carrico felt free to yell at students, cajole them, tease them into cooperation, Mr Seager felt that some students just needed a place in the school where they felt welcome. He had several boys in this small class who were frequently absent. Rather than put them in the hands of the truant-trackers, he would give them chances to make up work or return to class unpenalized. His rationale was that if he pressed them too far, they would drop out of school, that his was the only class some of them felt free to come to. Two of the boys appeared to be on drugs part of the time they were in class. When asked about this pattern, Mr Carrico disagreed strongly with the strategy, saying that failing to demand something of students does not convey a message of liking them. His own response to similar students was to tell them to improve or leave.

With the uneven attendance and student passivity, Mr Seager nevertheless proceeded to teach a great deal of history. He was personally knowledgeable about certain Indian tribes, about behind-the-scenes politics, about labor issues, western geography and farming, and many subjects which came up in the course. When he lectured about these topics, the students paid attention, asked questions and mentally participated. They did not take notes and some did not do classwork assignments, which consisted of answering questions at the end of brief in-class readings. Like Mr Lennon, Mr Seager had not come to terms with institutional demands. At his former school, he had been the Mr Carrico, developing new programs, gathering resources on a slim budget, bringing in good teachers. His role at Maizeville had, with passing years, become less active. Like Mr Carrico, he worked outside of school at a job which provided needed supplementary income; in this second job he was self-employed and dependent on his creative energies to keep the business going. But it did affect his energy levels. He too had community standing beyond the teacher role and took an active interest in affairs around him.

Mr Seager's reduced teaching efforts point to one problem with the strong-chair model; it is no less likely to defer or abdicate responsibility than the traditional administrator is when negative evaluations are called for. Mr Carrico said that he constantly tried to get Mr Seager to prepare his lessons more carefully, to make assignments, to grade student papers more thoroughly. Perhaps this was true. According to Mr Carrico, he always approached Mr Seager on the basis of his expertise, his competence in the subject and his past efforts. These comments were aimed at improvement rather than censure.

Mr Seager may be unfairly singled out here because of his problems during that semester. A return to the school over a year later found him to be somewhat more energetic, more upbeat about his teaching and his students. One of his problems had been that the students did not share his keen interest in history; he had not realized that backing off lecturing did not solve that problem but only made it worse because it was his lectures which students found so informative. In the presence of the lecture their reading problems, poor study habits and short attention spans were temporarily overcome by his spinning of historical lore. His lectures were more like story-telling and students became caught up in them, as they did not in doing seatwork, and even less in out-of-class assignments.

Even if singled out unfairly, it has been necessary to review Mr Seager's situation simply because it points to the fact that the way individuals use and respond to their institutional structures helps determine the impact of those structures in accomplishing their goals. In this case, the strong chair did no more than an administrator would have done in sanctioning the weak pattern of teaching in this class. On the other hand, the strong chair did far more to motivate and reward hard-working teachers than would have been true under a traditional school framework.

The effects of the strong-chair model
One last weakness of the strong-chair model must be noted; it does not necessarily provide for examination of the impact of instruction and of content on the students. At all the schools, teachers had

very limited views of what students could contribute to the learning process. Student talk was considered disruptive at Forest Hills, and student effort was so unexpected at Freeburg that few meaningful assignments were made. The low expectations Mr Seager had of students is not entirely surprising. One example of student requirements that *was* surprising was a mock trial in Mr Carrico's class. He had a fair amount of success in having certain students go to senior citizens to interview them about the town and the memories they had of the Depression. He had less success with the mock trial of Harry Truman for the dropping of the bombs on Hiroshima and Nagasaki. Students were assigned to role play the American and Japanese governmental and scientific leaders; other students were assigned to each side for examining witnesses. Mr Carrico gave the students some advance preparation time but no explanations of role playing or of the basic issues to look for in studying about their character. The trial began with a scientist taking the stand but testifying about himself in the third person. One student was in character, but the person interrogating did not know what to ask. Gradually, Mr Carrico began to interject comments, clarifying characters or raising issues. Finally, though the trial had just begun, the students drifted back to their seats while he took up the topic in lecture. After class he told me, "I knew that would happen."

What became apparent after that experience was that the administrative-teacher structure could have considerable impact on what teachers require of themselves and each other. It was less clear whether the observed structural variations could be used to evaluate the impact of knowledge forms on students, or to examine even the credibility of school knowledge itself. Teachers at Maizeville were more aware of instructional differences because the chair made it a point to know, so there was more interchange about the nature of assignments and forms of testing than at the other schools. Because these issues are so closely associated with academic freedom and personal style, they are rarely broached, even within a close department. For that reason, even a structure like the strong-chair model has greater capacity to influence the accessibility of school knowledge than to consider what impact that knowledge and those ways of knowing are having on students.

Even with these drawbacks, the strong-chair model of organization overcame many of the constraints common to schools where administrations emphasize order and control. While the adminis-trators at Maizeville tracked truants and kept the building running, the social studies department was free to teach, supported by abun-dant materials, tangible and intangible rewards for their extra efforts, and a collegial framework. That they did not always teach well, did not always bring students into the learning process even when they demanded a great deal of themselves, demonstrates the difficulty with a structural mechanism that is designed to circum-vent rather than address directly the lack of common purpose in a school. The general school climate of "getting by" and tracking down missing students so that all would be in place was difficult to overcome by this one structural change, especially since not all department chairs used their delegated powers to build school qual-ity as Mr Carrico tried to do. One serious problem not addressed by this structural variation was the lack of tangible rewards that translated into extra pay for extra work. The full use of discretion in distributing teaching assignments, classroom materials allocation and other working conditions improvements available to the chair did not entirely overcome the staff's sense that their efforts went unrewarded. Experienced teachers faced pay ceilings after a certain number of years with the district, limited after that time to across-the-board cost-of-living adjustments. Mr Carrico and Mr Seager were not alone in supplementing their income during the school year with outside jobs. Mr Carrico managed to limit his to weekends and rarely felt that his business limited his teaching. Mr Seager was more typical in feeling fatigued and stretched by the two endeavors and the result showed in his minimal teaching.

While this problem was on-going, another problem was emerg-ing. As many younger teachers built up experience came the di-lemma of sharing the strong-chair position in turn without losing the momentum and continuity built up by Mr Carrico. In order to keep these teachers, it might become necessary to let them share in the responsibility. Given the intense nature of the coordinator posi-tion, this rotation might prove to be beneficial to those who had held the position as well. Whether this ever became necessary, it was clear that this structure offered the staff many constructive supports in an otherwise adversarial, or at best highly distant, teacher–administrator relationship.

At this school it is interesting to note how the choice to limit administrative controls on teachers, by sharing or delegating some discretion and authority, had the effect of making at least some teachers feel empowered to teach. Because it did not fully address the lack of a reward system for all teachers and because it was not accompanied by a similar shift away from a controlling philosophy with students, the students did not always feel so affirmed by school policy. While they exhibited more interest and somewhat more engagement than their Freeburg counterparts, they nevertheless lacked a spirit of expectation, a sense that there was an overarching purpose beyond putting in time at the school. While these teachers were not so directly affected by the language of control in school policy as the Freeburg teachers had been (in their varying patrol duties), they did confront in their classes students whose dominant impression of the school was affected more by the administrators' dispirit than by the enthusiasm of their most motivated teachers. What the strong-chair model did was to leave less to chance, that those motivated teachers would have the resources they needed, that they would be hired in the first place, and that they would have an advocate should their chair choose to use the coordinator role to its fullest.

# 6
# Nelson High School

At first glance, the organizational roles of Nelson High personnel paralleled those in the other high schools. The principal and his assistants held legal authority over staff (hiring, evaluation, course assignments, dismissal), budgets, discipline and attendance. The administrators had no classroom teaching duties. Union contracts defined collectively bargained pay, benefits and employee rights. Teachers developed and taught their courses, taught and evaluated their students. Subjects were organized by academic departments, coordinated by a teacher serving as chair and having teaching duties, not administrative powers.

These ostensibly traditional divisions of authority were far from traditional in their relationships in this school. Here the structure of the school was developed first to implement a particular pedagogical philosophy. Later, it was adapted to support a specific curriculum – the unified curriculum within each subject field. This adaptation included not only shifts in job descriptions, but in the methods used to assign staff, account for finances, organize building space and warrant curricular programs. Most important, the organization, from the beginning, did not exist primarily for maintaining the institution (keeping it "running smoothly"), processing students through credits and course titles, or providing custodial care to children. The staff was organized from the start to consider the content behind course titles and credits; this consideration belonged to principal and teacher alike, in concert with each other. Curriculum was a visible policy item, a notable contrast to policies of schools like Forest Hills and Freeburg where the visible, articulated issues of the school centered around maintaining order.

Those two schools had personnel who accepted the adversarial or distant administrator role as commonplace. They saw school structure as a traditional given. Within that givenness, and the priorities of control it implied, they made calculations about what they could teach. The Nelson staff worked as a group of professional colleagues in administration and instruction to design a structure that fitted their pedagogy, their ideal. A consciously constructed organization, like those accepted as inevitable by tradition, becomes lived structure as it is shaped by individuals and events. Whether this particular organization around curriculum resolved the tension between goals of order and goals of educating in favor of its explicit educational purposes depended heavily on the ability of individuals to take advantage of its predisposition to academics. As one of the school's strongest departments, the social studies group offers a "best case" scenario for examining the classroom impact of a supportive administration.

### Science as the unifier

Before considering the social studies department's responses to this organizational structure, we must trace the role of the science faculty in the shift from traditionally-bounded subject-matter courses to a unified curriculum. The chairman of science was team-teaching with the chairman of social studies during the semester of classroom observations; he provided invaluable insights into the process by which the departments unified their curricula.

The philosophy of the school was set from the beginning. The unified curricula developed a few years later. Mr Erickson began teaching separate fields of biology, chemistry and physics. Over time he began to be frustrated by overlap in these subjects which had no corresponding overlap in their presentation as single subjects. Over time, he began to wish for a unified science program that would overcome the artificial subject distinctions and give students a general, whole approach to the natural sciences. In casting about the country for a role model, the four science teachers involved found only partial attempts at unification; for example, an eighth grade course in Ohio which taught physics one nine weeks and chemistry the second nine weeks. By the early 1960s it became apparent that if such a program were to be developed, these four teachers at this relatively new high school would have to do it.

Mr Erickson wrote to the Ford Foundation to request funding

for the teachers to work summers to develop their own curriculum. When the Ford Foundation responded that they did not support efforts in single schools, Mr Erikson, as he tells it, asked his wife one evening what the US Office of Education did. Her response led him to write a brief letter of inquiry, addressed "to whom it may concern." By chance it landed on the desk of a man interested in science education and in curriculum reform, who, after some correspondence, explained the process of formal proposals, budget requests, and review. After these protocols were completed, the US Office of Education provided $70,000 over a four-year period for the unified science program. The money was spent for materials development, films, a full-time secretary, production of slides, and, most important, summer salary to pay teachers to work on the curriculum. They had to develop all their own course outlines and materials, not finding any precedent for the scope of their project. The teachers worked for several weeks for each of the next four summers. During the third year of the project they had so many materials to reproduce that the school system purchased an offset press, setting the stage for other departments to begin producing their own materials in the years to come. The science department purchased some class sets of texts and some small sets for reserve in the resource center, but other "texts" became the huge lab manuals the teachers produced for the four-year science sequence. The resource center itself began because the teachers had no place in their classrooms for all the materials they were collecting and developing. As Mr Erickson concluded, "I think it difficult to find $70,000 that the US Office has invested that paid off as many dividends as this did. Because also the unified concept has grown too; now there are about 140 high schools in the US that have it." Mr Erickson's workload in answering inquiries about the program and trying to satisfy requests for sample materials was so heavy that he and some teachers in other parts of the country helped establish a center for unified science materials on a university campus.

The experience of the Nelson High science department spilled over into the other subject fields. Their curriculum development work was so productive that the administration expanded to other basic subjects the concept of departmental aides, secretaries and resource centers. When at first some departments resented the science staff's support system, Mr Erickson could only suggest that they too work to acquire these supports. Eventually even those that did not initiate such innovations received them in varying degrees as the structure of the department became a schoolwide model. Many of the teachers continued to work summers, sometimes with two or three weeks' salary from the district, many times without pay. One board member had been uneasy that unified curricula in all departments might dilute the academic quality; he was a professional with four children to put through college. As the older ones reported from college how well prepared they were for their course work, he became a strong advocate of the program.

## Social studies at Nelson

The social studies department under Mr Guthrie's leadership was one of the earliest departments to adopt the science model of unified curricula. By the time of these observations the teachers said they could not imagine teaching any other way. Their four-year social studies sequence followed a very rough chronology that brought together concepts and methods of inquiry from varied social studies disciplines. Ninth grade focused on world backgrounds up to 1500 AD, emphasizing pre-industrial societies, and drawing on anthropology, sociology, geography and history. The tenth grade course in western ideas covered the years 1500 to 1870, with a focus on the establishment of nation states and revolutions within the western world; the principal conceptual contributors were history and political science. World conflicts in contemporary history from 1870 to the present formed the eleventh grade course, building on economics, history and political science. The senior course was contemporary issues, with the theme that "the complexities associated with the urgency for human understanding in our contemporary world require that each individual develop himself as a thinker, individual, and citizen to the optimum of his capacity." Political science and political economy were emphasized, along with consumer economics, futurology and international relations. "The integrated development of mankind," integrating economic, social, political and ethical aspects of man's life, was the thread that linked the four courses. In addition to the four-year sequence, electives such as economics, and later the science and economics of energy course, were available.

The richness of this four-year social studies sequence at Nelson is more remarkable in light of Freeburg's bitter fight to increase the social studies requirement from one to two credits. The principal courses observed at Nelson included a tenth grade course, because the chairman thought this teacher to be the best "asker of questions" on the staff; the science and economics of energy course, because of its uniqueness and relation to the economics focus; and the senior course, under two teachers, because of its economics unit and treatment of American institutions and world problems. Each provided an example of how staff and students responded to the supportive administrative context.

## Inside the classrooms

### Mr Lancaster

Mr Lancaster taught several sections of the senior course. His room resembled the office of I. F. Stone in the documentary about the later years of the publication of his *Weekly* – papers everywhere, in stacks and piles, and bundles and boxes. Mr Lancaster's curiosity knew no limits; his course content within the framework he and Mr Guthrie had worked out over the years was constantly changing in its particulars. He continually sought new information, read scholarly and news publications, and brought his findings into his classroom. The circle of desks around the large room was itself encircled by rows of overfilled bookshelves, posters, diagrams, interesting quotations tacked up on bulletin boards, maps and boxes of books and magazines. Inside the circle of desks, a pair of large work tables held additional magazines, course handouts and student papers.

Mr Lancaster himself was involved with local history, with conservation of a nature area, and with other numerous civic projects. In his late forties, he had been at the school for all but the first five years of his career. He and Mr Guthrie shared the improbable coincidences of having studied in different years at the same college, under the same mentor professor, and worked on the same summer job together after they were both teachers. Unknown to Mr Guthrie, Mr Lancaster had also frequented Mr Guthrie's business before either became teachers. The summer they worked together, Mr Guthrie offered Mr Lancaster a job interview, which he accepted not because he needed a job but because he had been told never to turn down an interview. He found his philosophy of teaching compatible with plans for Nelson High's department and accepted the job. Mr Guthrie considering his hiring of Mr Lancaster one of his best contributions to the school.

Their teaching styles were not alike; in fact, it would be difficult to imagine another teacher like Mr Lancaster. His personal interests were so wide-ranging and his intellect so alive that he seemed not to notice that the students were not always with him. He tolerated side conversations and rude student retorts with patience and gentle amusement while he lectured on, showed films, or directed the students toward readings he reproduced for them from his own broad reading.

Mr Lancaster's theory of teaching, as articulated in his interview and as demonstrated in his teaching, was to stretch students' minds, whether with their cooperation or against their will.

> I'm happy about what I do, and I'm enthusiastic about what I
> do; I know I'm dragging some of them along, kicking and
> screaming that don't want to do it, but that doesn't bother me.
> I push all the time. I enjoy what I'm doing and that's what
> keeps me going ... I can really get down about poor students
> and their ability to hassle me about one thing or another or
> give me problems, or the ones who talk. I don't think I could
> have been in this business since 1956 if I let those sorts of
> things bother me, so I can forget them overnight. Next day I'm
> right at it again. I can deal with those same students as if I had
> no problem with them the day before. I can do that.

When asked if he ever ran into a student whose curiosities matched his own, he replied yes, but that they would never let the class know it because of peer pressures. Those with a question or comments on the reading would approach him after class if a point really interested them.

Mr Lancaster's strategy of teaching was to give students some tools for optimism. He was very well informed on world problems such as food scarcities, power inequities and energy. He believed that these problems can be solved only if people believe they can. One of his jobs was to show students enough ideas and give them enough skills and acquaintance with information resources that they would see themselves as part of a solution that ultimately would come. His futurology unit topics dealt with technology and institutions, such as the creation of new cities and drastic changes in lifestyle. The theme of the futurology lessons was that "we must not walk backwards into the future." His fear expressed over and over during that unit was that humanity would slip unknowingly into an unwanted future because of defeatist attitudes that the worst was inevitable.

He had students read great philosophers and social theorists, whose works he excerpted for them; for personal economics he used many of the materials and models developed by Mr Guthrie. For political awareness, Mr Lancaster had the national news program "Washington Week in Review" videotaped from public television each Friday evening and shown to his classes the following Tuesday. He admitted that most students were probably resistant to this ritual at first but that over the semester each would find topics of interest or favorite commentators to follow so that their level of awareness of news analysis would be sharper when they left the class.

For involving students in information, Mr Lancaster used an independent study project which was built on the steps preliminary to a research paper. The topic, summarized references and precis of findings would be turned in, but no extended paper would be written. Over several weeks he gave up one or two class periods per week for library work, which varied greatly in quality and efficacy among the students. His tests were like law school hypothetical exams, with extended, convoluted informational material in the questions and complicated analysis or comparisons of course material required in answers. Since few students took notes, the tests were difficult to study for, taking students by great surprise at first. The grades were often low, and the tests were slow to be returned to students because of the incredible work in grading them. Still, they were part of Mr Lancaster's determination to stretch students' interests and capabilities. His Renaissance mind baffled students geared more for the instrumental value of jobs and course credits, but he was convinced that, despite their frequent disengagement, they left his course with more than they realized or intended to.

## Mr Hobbs

Mr Hobbs was added to the sample because the chairman wanted me to observe a teacher who could ask questions. The class was

interesting as background for the other observations since Mr
Hobbs had younger students and was instrumental in setting the
expectations students would bring to upper-level social studies
classes. Like Mr Lancaster, Mr Hobbs had an active, inquiring
mind and wide range of interests. He too read widely and gathered
materials for his classes from many sources. Unlike Mr Lancaster,
he was more organized and demanded more concrete involvement
from his students. His course was centered on textbook assignments, with added lectures and films and considerable class discussion based on Mr Hobbs' Socratic-style questions.

Mr Hobbs had come to the school over fifteen years before, just
after the unified curriculum had been established in social studies.
He felt very comfortable with the arrangement:

> I can't imagine, it is just beyond me, I can't comprehend
> teaching people any other way than teaching all their different
> aspects. When you talk about teaching history, it just seems to
> me that history includes just about everything you can think of
> ... How can you teach ancient Greece without teaching
> political theory? How can you teach it without discussing
> philosophy? How can you teach Greece without studying
> sociology and the role of women and slavery? I mean these are
> all unified areas.

To engage his students in reading and in formulating some ideas
of their own, he had resorted to daily worksheets to accompany
the reading assignments. All of these, with their factual and analytical questions, he had developed along with the handouts that often
supplemented the text. The content was richer and asked for more
varied and complicated answers than usually called for in commer-
cially prepared worksheets. The group was taught as a whole, with
everyone doing the same worksheet. To ease logistics, he wrote
each class's coming three weeks' assignments on the board and
walked up and down the aisles checking worksheets rather than
taking them up. He wanted students to have a "map" of where the
course was going and of how they stood in understanding the
topics. A student teacher the year before had helped organize Mr
Hobbs' huge supply of resource materials into attractive storage
files which were clearly indexed and neatly stored around the room.
From the many quotations and informational posters on the
boards, the array of materials, the organization of assignments,

students could sense that the course was going to demand something of them. The particular students observed were among the better classes Mr Hobbs recalled in recent years for their level of participation and interest.

One of Mr Hobbs' techniques in dealing with student writing and speaking was summarized on a colorful piece of cardboard on the bulletin board: "Don't grunt; elucidate." Rather than criticize in great detail, Mr Hobbs had other means of eliciting student effort:

> If they come up short, I develop little shorthand messages to give them, like "Don't grunt" and things like that ... I find, maybe that is what is working, you know, instead of me preaching at the kids, trying to sit down and say "You have to do more," I can quickly say, "Hey, that's a *grunt!*" My kids can relate to that much better than some kind of lecture ... It's a kind of light-hearted way to tell kids you can say more, you can think more, you can put thoughts together a whole lot better than you did.

He tried to be off center stage, acting as a facilitator to get students to interact with the lesson. Through each course ran complex philosophical themes which prevented the degeneration of the course into nothing but fragmented facts and worksheets. One of these themes was the nature of violence; through many periods of history, he would ask students to come to grips with whether the violence of that period was justified. Another dominant theme was the relation of man to the state. He made the Bill of Rights central to his course on western governments and disagreed with the other teacher of the course who wanted to reduce or eliminate the time spent on these constitutional questions.

In their interviews, the students spoke of resources most beneficial to them. Almost all appreciated the work and usefulness of the handouts provided by the teacher. Their most varied responses were about his questions. Several students were clearly upset by the Socratic style of questioning because they did not know how to deal with questions that did not necessarily have clear answers. For example, after a study of the Bill of Rights, the worksheet had a question on the right of free speech. After much discussion, the class decided there should be no restrictions on free speech. Then one by one Mr Hobbs introduced possible exceptions, such as limits on slandering other people, or perjuring oneself. The consensus dissolved, re-formed with qualification, then dissolved again with his next question. Many students were not accustomed to having to think, and found this pattern troubling. Others found it stimulating and responded with hard questions of their own. Less confident than Mr Lancaster that his teaching was changing his students, or that he would know exactly how he would want to change them if he could, Mr Hobbs clearly benefited from the unified curriculum in being able to mesh his own interests and expertise with the philosophy and format of the rest of the department. He and Mr Lancaster demonstrate the variation possible within this framework, variations stemming from the teachers' individual styles and priorities. Mr Lancaster kept the course topic-centered; Mr Hobbs tried to balance teacher, student and materials; the junior level teachers, according to several students, centered the course on the content and work, with many days of students' working at their desks and bringing finished work to the teachers. (My own observations of these teachers fell on days they lectured or showed films, so that pattern was not evident.) Mr Hobbs found the collegiality of the department and support from the chairman to be consonant with his own view of social studies teaching.

## Mr Guthrie

Mr Guthrie was a man of many projects. He chaired the committee to bring closer articulation among social studies teachers at the elementary, junior and senior high levels. He was active in statewide economics education and social studies organizations, and he served on community boards in Nelson Heights.[1] He thought of himself, in the words of Mr Lancaster, as a great compromiser, and as a chairman who could bring the department's consensus successfully to the administration. He had built an effective department because of this administrative support (especially support for hiring quality instructors), his own energies and his personal concern for his fellow teachers and their students. If his pattern of work and community involvement sound reminiscent of Mr Carrico at Maizeville, it is partly because the two were friends and helped build statewide social studies organizations and programs over many years. He was equally tireless but much less personally aggressive. His own philosophy of schooling was cap-

145

tured by his pet phrase, "practical academics." He was scholarly in his own way, but much more oriented toward practical skills for everyday living than the intellectual exercises central to Mr Hobbs' and Mr Lancaster's courses. His emphasis on practical academics included the best of both worlds, wanting students to have an educated basis for their lives as citizens and consumers. He had been a businessman before entering teaching and was accustomed to a public role and to being productive. He wanted as interesting a life, and more, for his students. For him, practical academics meant preparing students for the responsibilities they would have, for opportunities they might face and for problems inherent in a complex society. Practical academics had little in common with processing students through required credits.

He was well grounded in economic theory as well as microeconomics. His real speciality was in figuring out new ways to explain both facts and relationships. He had compiled a resource book for teachers on economic topics, especially cooperatives, filled with information and models for explanations. He had divided the book into distinct sections which could be used separately or together. For his courses, he worked and re-worked diagrams and charts presenting relationships, concepts, change, tables of fact. His presentations of such topics as insurance, banking and law drew on commercial and academic sources, government agency publications and materials he personally devised.

There was no "wall" between his personal knowledge of a subject and his presentation of it in class, except where time intervened. If he felt a constraint in his teaching, it was time rather than indifferent students or a hostile administration. He based much of his economic content on his personal experience and on his expectations for the students' future. Since most of them were middle-class and perhaps lower middle-class, he assumed that their adult lives would follow at least a pattern of trade school or university, steady jobs and modest investments. In his economic units he combined printed handouts, in abundance, with speakers from the community. These included someone from the sheriff's office speaking on the rights of drivers and passengers in traffic, search and seizure, and liability. A real estate expert spoke on tenants' rights and responsibilities, on contract, real estate loans, and calculations of loan interest. The assumption of the lesson, as introduced by Mr Guthrie, was that the students would soon be living on their own and that they would need to know defensive economic skills as well as positive planning. An insurance salesman gave a talk on beginning insurance planning early while rates are low and often locked in for many years thereafter. While the advice on whole life insurance as a major part of an investment portfolio might be open to question, the overall presentation was very practical. Another speaker talked of credit ratings.

These speakers strengthened Mr Guthrie's ties with the community (many were parents of students) and in turn provided the speakers with free advertising for their services. Unlike the Forest Hills and Freeburg teachers, who felt their low pay and adversarial relations with the administration connoted low community status and the need for low visibility, Mr Guthrie, like Mr Carrico, actively sought ties between the community and the schools, partly to link learning to the students' interests.

After "practical academics," Mr Guthrie's next favorite word was "synergistic." It guided his role in the department and his classroom assignments. Mr Guthrie believed that, if arranged properly, the whole could be greater than the sum of the parts. Working together, the faculty could build a far richer curriculum than would result from the total of the individual efforts of those same teachers. In the classroom, this translated into group projects and discussions. Especially in the science and economics of energy course, students were encourage to work together, even at the risk of some not working at all. He felt that if the weaker students worked along with the stronger ones, they would learn more than by working alone; he and Mr Erickson reserved the right to divide grades unequally if they saw differential effort. He felt that many educational innovations had failed because they had been fragmented, reforms of small pieces of schools rather than general "overhauls," as he advocated. When the innovations fail, he said, people blame the schools. "We need synergistic structures in schools for programming to succeed. We're unified within departments, but need more than that. One reason students have problems in school is that they can't see relationships." He chaired the committee to strengthen linkages among elementary and secondary schools, and he sought ways of linking social studies to English and other departments now that the science and social studies cooperative effort on energy had proven to be such a success.

The stack of handouts and notes for his lectures from Mr Guthrie's senior contemporary issues course was almost a foot tall. Each unit was first presented as a complete packet of handouts and activities, with additions coming as the topic progressed. Most of the readings were included in the printed handouts rather than in books. Some handouts were designed for future filing, such as insurance and mortgage schedules, sample contracts, tax information forms and the like. If there was a problem with the course, it was that students' job experiences were rarely brought into the discussion, even when installment contracts, consumer rights and employment laws were being discussed. In order to do everything in the limited time, Mr Guthrie left little to the students in the way of adding information.

An experiment in collaborative teaching

Mr Guthrie had been known in the region as a strong economics teacher and a standard bearer for improved economics information. When the Maizeville teachers, who were trying to add economics to their list of required courses, heard that Mr Guthrie had given up his economics class to team-teach a course on the science and economics of energy, they quizzed me on "Why on earth would he do that, Guthrie of all people?" The answer lay in his concern, shared with Mr Erickson, that the public was woefully unaware of energy issues, even as major policy questions demanded citizen literacy on the subject.

Mr Erickson provided the history of the course in an interview. Several years before, Mr Erickson had begun to share Mr Guthrie's concern that energy, when dealt with in science courses even as an extended unit, could not be understood since its use and sources are so dependent on political and social factors beyond the expertise of most scientists and science education materials. Mr Guthrie expressed a similar frustration in teaching the issue from a political and economic standpoint to students who had little factual knowledge about energy sources and uses. Over a couple of years, they talked of setting up a joint course to provide a more sensible approach. They worked over a summer roughing out an outline for their separate areas, then individually filling in their share of the information. They produced a lab-type text similar to the other science course manuals, with most readings, homework exercises, tables and charts bound into the manual. As with the unified science, the absence of a text designed to address their course goals dictated creating their own books.

In the beginning, the course was a one-semester course for high-achieving science and social studies students. The teachers' concern that all citizens be informed on energy issues led them to restructure the course in a way that could give average and even low-achieving students some success. In addition to this shift, the course underwent revisions each year, even each semester, though new editions of the manual were produced only annually. Constant updating and revisions kept the course up with current changes in energy research and policy; the teachers were never satisfied with the manual and had fun trying to figure out new explanatory models, gather latest energy figures and develop contacts with new sources of information.

The course began with preliminary explanations of economics concepts and with fundamentals on the nature of energy and energy resources. Each teacher taught his own area. Then the course proceeded to the economics of energy, in production and consumption. Energy alternatives were introduced, then energy was linked to quality of life. These units led to the culminating synergistic activity; students were to work in groups arriving at a formula for the energy use growth rate for the next 20-, 50- and 100-year periods. Based on this growth rate, the students were to work through complicated formulas to determine energy resources needed and their expected availability. Any short-falls were to require suggested alternative sources and uses of energy.

The 200-page manual began with a satire on gas consumption by Art Buchwald, but quickly moved into intimidating diagrams and mathematical formulas. One weakness of the course was that in their desire to have students understand the mathematics of doubling times, known and discoverable reserves of non-renewable sources and possible production from renewable energy resources, the teachers left little for examination of policy issues, political constituencies behind policy, or the shape of debate on the issues. The strength of the course was that many important concepts were included, from cost-push inflation and elasticity to the transformation efficiencies of various fuels. The manual was the student's to keep as a valuable reference; several graduates had written to praise its helpfulness in their college courses.

One of many student questions that went unanswered in the big

149

lecture hall format was about nuclear power. Many students and parents had strong reservations about the safety of nuclear power. The teachers said they were not pro-nuclear, but that nuclear power was essential as a bridge between the old patterns of dependence on fossil fuels and the yet-to-be-developed renewable sources of the future. They took the students through many calculations of the inadequacy of conservation and renewables to sustain "our way of life." They took students to tour a coal-fired electrical plant and investigated this alternative source of electricity, but advocated favoring nuclear power in the interim. When some parents complained (before I observed at this school) that the teachers invited in speakers who represented only the pro-nuclear power position of the region's electric utilities, the teachers responded by inviting the local anti-nuclear congressman. He was unable to keep his commitment. The teachers held the strong opinion that pro-nuclear speakers were speaking from *facts*, and that anti-nuclear speakers were speaking from *emotions*. They did not want emotions to enter into the discussion. They genuinely felt themselves to be open on the subject, but this one point hurt their credibility for some of the students interviewed, who volunteered their uneasiness.

Along with the question of the safety of nuclear power was one on "quality of life." The teachers based their projections of the inadequacies of conservation and renewables on maintaining the same "quality of life." They would state that the figures hold true "unless we are to drastically change our lifestyle." This question remained begged. It called for closer examination so that its abstractness might be made clearer to the students as their groups formed their end-of-year energy policy statements.

Aside from these two major student concerns, the course was considered very difficult but valuable. The year prior to the observations, the students had mailed their energy policy statements to their congressmen and received thanks from congressional staffs for sharing their concerns. Once students managed to conquer, alone or synergistically, the imposing mathematical exercises, they praised the comprehensiveness of the course. It definitely fulfilled Mr Guthrie's desire for practical academics.

**Problems at Nelson High**

In comparison with the other high schools, it would seem that the Nelson teachers had, and contributed to, a very positive learning–teaching environment. The adversarial component between teachers and administrators had not been a part of the school's history. On slim budgets, the school system had provided excellent materials and a workable building. Even though the starting and ending pay range at Nelson was slightly lower than in the nearest city schools, these teachers chose to work there because of its compatible philosophy. Several problems did come to light either as weaknesses in the present structure, or as future vulnerabilities.

The first is that, although the administrative structure generated much teacher effort, it had no means of discerning the impact of the curricula on students. This characteristic it shared with the other schools, though in lesser degree than Maizeville because of the greater concern of administrators for content, and less than Forest Hills, where sheer size of the school prevented much contact between administrators and students except in discipline matters. Despite their concern for students' practical learning, attention to instructional form, and thus student requirements and responses, was slighted in their planning. Part of this was due to the feeling within the department that all teaching styles are different; certainly Mr Hobbs would never have used Mr Lancaster's tests, nor would Mr Lancaster have used worksheets. More was required of students at Nelson than at the other schools, but there was no systematic attention to whether the needs of particular students rather than students in general were being met. Students voiced this concern in interviews.

Most of the teachers felt that the upper-ability students would find enough substance in the open-ended topics of the course to pursue them if interested; the teachers admitted that few students did. The weaker students were also potential losers in courses that taught everyone together. Mr Erickson described high and low groupings in science, with small group and tutorial work planned into both and immediate feedback on projects, but this plan was apparently the only program in the school designed to deal with the impact of instruction on students of various abilities. Many of the teachers were so enthusiastic about their courses that they focused on covering material with speed and thoroughness; this centralized information into the hands of the teacher in some of the ways that had occurred at Forest Hills. The difference was that Nelson High teachers placed few "walls" between their personal and classroom knowledge, nor did they want the students to have any such walls or to keep absolutely silent.

A second problem was the number of students working more than twenty to thirty hours per week.[2] The Distributive Education Club of America had been established to provide work experience for those students not expected to go to college. Many students who planned to go to college now used the program, allocating their elective credits to cooperative work that took them off-campus during some afternoon class periods. The new principal, having a vocational education background, found this a positive development. He said he approved of the work habits learned, the chance to experiment in different jobs, and the enhanced public relations in the community provided by hard-working students. One administrator voiced the sentiment, found at Freeburg and Maizeville among administrators, that jobs kept many students out of the halls and parking lots of the school and reduced supervision needs. The classroom teachers saw the matter differently. They saw students too sleepy to listen to lectures after working into the night cutting and packaging cheese at dairies or busing tables at restaurants. They saw students with little free time to read assignments, do extended projects or get together with other students as needed in the energy course project. They felt that students' and parents' priorities were inappropriate when students worked not to help support families or save for college but to buy stereos, cars and entertainment. These teachers had not reduced their assignments as much as teachers at the other schools, but they did feel hindered by the fact that many of these working students saw school as a place to rest until time for work.

A problem looming for the future was declining enrollments. Nelson Heights and Blackhawk were surrounded by the river and other townships. New housing development through urban sprawl would not be forthcoming to alleviate the declining school enrollments. Families who had settled in the area twenty and thirty years before now had "empty nests." The school district was committed to maintaining buildings, programs and as much staff as possible in anticipation of increasing enrollments as older people sold their property to younger families over the next two decades. In the interim, hard choices would have to be made. The real estate problem was underscored by a very energetic senior girl who had moved to Nelson Heights two years before. Her parents had been advised to buy a house in the area in order to have their children attend the schools. They had to stay in their former city for an extra year until a house fitting their needs could be found.

The declining enrollments posed several threats to the faculty. First, they introduced new uncertainties into a climate already unsettled by recent changes in the principalship and superintendency. The old superintendent had helped set up the school and knew its philosophy well; the new one was an unknown quantity, with a good reputation but rumored political ambitions. They feared his bottom line would be numbers and budgets rather than quality programs. The new principal had been committed to supporting the unified curricula but would be working with smaller and smaller budgets and so could not be expected to do everything the former principal had done. Neither man was feared, but the expectation that enrollments would soon drop beyond the point where natural staff attrition would take care of faculty reductions made teachers apprehensive and edgy.

The apprehension was especially understandable given the high levels of seniority among all the teachers. Most of the social studies teachers had been hired fifteen to twenty years before. None were near retirement age. After the few part-time teachers and the aide were let go, the only ones left would be teachers whose entire teaching careers had been built around the school, including unpaid summers. These teachers had accepted lower beginning salaries in order to participate in a program they could affirm, only to find that at the time they should have been able to see financial rewards for their long years of service they faced layoffs in an era of nationwide tight markets for social studies teachers. When rumors that merit would in some way determine lay-offs, one teacher wrote the board asking to know in advance what criteria would be used to determine "merit" so he could know. He received no reply. It is unlikely that at that time the administration had completely worked out those criteria and their relation to the union contracts and staffing needs.

Even with these present and future problems, Nelson High was a good place to teach and a good place to be a student. What was most interesting was the staff dissatisfaction with their courses. The first day I walked into Mr Guthrie's office to learn about the program, Mr Lancaster stuck his head through the doorway to say he wished they would deal with more international issues. Mr Hobbs spoke of wanting to develop a biographical history course, based on the lives of heroes and villains, philosophers and statesmen and others whose ideas had affected history. He too would like a course on international relations and comparative political systems. Mr Guthrie was dissatisfied that plans to publish his extensive work on economics curricula had so far been thwarted by bureaucratic procedures in the agency that helped underwrite the work; he was also always dissatisfied with the energy course, wanting to expand it from one to two semesters so that more explanation could be devoted to topics already included and more on economics could be added. He and Mr Lancaster were never satisfied with their contemporary issues courses, always looking for new materials and always designing new models of explanation. When not combined with problems of salaries outstripped by inflation and by threats of lay-offs, these frustrations kept the program vibrant and relevant: when seen in conjunction with these job survival issues, they pointed to some reduction of expectations about their careers and worth to their students.

The staff had dealt with large problems before, chiefly the creation from scratch of a set of impressive unified curricula out of slim resources and good intentions. It remained to be seen whether the new problems, which introduced tensions with students (and their jobs) and with administrators (over cutbacks) could be as creatively resolved. This school demonstrates so far the potential for structural mechanisms to overcome the tendencies of minimal effort on the part of staff when the commitment to the educative function of the school supercedes the goals of order.

# PART THREE
# Control and resistance

# 7
# Defensive teaching and classroom control[1]

From the four schools has emerged a picture of very uneven educational quality. That unevenness could not have been resolved by simply hiring "smarter" teachers. Many of the smartest, best-educated of these teachers felt that "really to teach" would be going *against* expectations at their school, not fulfilling them. The ideals they expressed for what their students should learn from their courses bore little resemblance to the simplistic "facts" dispensed in lectures and worksheets. The ideals implied open-ended, long-term learning, begun by broad-ranging, depth-seeking inquiry and discussion. Yet the content presented was often limited to brief, "right" answers, easily transmitted, easily answered, easily graded. The divergence implied by teachers' vision of "real learning" was contradicted by the uniformity of student behavior and lesson content typical of most class sessions. The teachers at the very first school demonstrated this contradiction between teaching goals and teaching style. They justified their over-simplified lessons as their ways of accommodating to a school where their only power came from the classroom. What the students saw as teacher strictness was for the teachers a complicated accommodation to changing power relations in the school, relations which over time had diminished teachers' voice in program and school policy. This accommodation has direct effects on classroom instruction.

Our image of the one-room schoolteacher, or the master of a Latin-grammar school, is of a teacher wielding the hickory stick to make students learn. Student discipline - sitting on hard benches, standing to recite, maintaining absolute silence unless spoken to - was instrumental to mastering the content. This study of four high schools reveals that today many teachers reverse those ends and means. They maintain discipline by the ways they present course

157

content. They choose to simplify content and reduce demands on students in return for classroom order and minimal student compliance on assignments. Feeling less authority than their Latin-grammar school counterpart, they teach "defensively," choosing methods of presentation and evaluation that they hope will make their workload more efficient and create as little student resistance as possible. These findings are interesting because they shed light on the daily processes by which schools mediate cultural knowledge to students. They are important because they demonstrate some of the specific dynamics that lie behind the much-publicized lowered expectations that students and teachers are bringing to the classroom. In addition, they are significant because the teachers who teach defensively do not fit any one ideological or demographic category, and they use these techniques of classroom control with students of all ability levels and perceived "differences". Defensive teaching was observed at each of these high schools. The variation in administrative structure affected the extent of the phenomenon but not its presence or absence. Administrative settings supportive of academics seemed to shift determinants to individual teacher characteristics; however, examples will show that even in these schools the tension with social control functions was strong enough to give teachers rationales for defensive instructional strategies.

## Concentric circles of curriculum analysis

When Dwayne Heubner (1970) described curriculum as "the accessibility of knowledge," he was making the point that the curriculum was not merely the content or curriculum guide, but the totality of the learning environment within which that content became accessible to students. Although he meant to call attention to many of the physical attributes of the educative setting, his conception of the curriculum as the means of making knowledge accessible has provided an apt phrase for shifting curriculum analysis away from formal definitions of course content and student achievement, toward the origins and nature of the content itself. The purpose of this study of school organization has been to trace the school knowledge to its sources in the institutional setting. The analysis has expanded upon previous classroom observation which focused on the processing of school knowledge: What kinds of knowledge do schools make accessible? How is school knowledge a product of the ways of knowing students encounter in school? At the institutional level, we may add: How is the treatment of school knowledge a factor of the way the school works, the way it is organized?

The original classroom study of social studies content (McNeil, 1977) found content tightly controlled by teachers, reduced to simplistic fragments, and treated with little regard for a reference to resources in the students' experiences or school's references. The teachers at that school, whose lectures provide many of the examples of defensive teaching to be discussed below, offered conscious reasons for wishing to control student access to information. Interviews with the teachers revealed that they had a much broader knowledge of history and the economy, both academically and experientially, than they admitted in class. Their stated goal of making sure students understood "how things work" was tempered by their expressed fear that students might find out about the injustices and inadequacies of their economic and political institutions. For those teachers, knowledge access – a goal consistent with the good reputation of their middle-class school and of their status in it – was countered by their deliberate selections of lecture topics that would distance the students from the content. *Their patterns of knowledge control were, according to their own statements in taped interviews, rooted in their desire for classroom control.* Their memories of the Vietnam war era made them wish to avoid topics on which the students were likely to disagree with their views or that would make the students "cynical" about American institutions. Administrative policies, which had redrawn the school's boundary to include more working-class families and which had done away with ability-group (IQ) tracking, had caused the teachers to feel that their school was not "as good as it used to be." The intangible rewards of teaching the "best" students in the "best" high school had been taken away, over their protests, and no incentives to deal with the new groups of students or newly heterogeneous classes had taken their place. Their expectations of their students and of their own ability to affect student learning skills had, in their minds, been progressively lowered over the recent past. They saw student ability levels as endpoints that limited what they could do in their classes, not as beginning points for teacher help and instruction.

Most important, they felt burdened by an administration that expected them to enforce rules of discipline, but that rarely backed them on that enforcement. As a result, they wanted to avoid as many inefficient exchanges as possible in order to get through the day. I have described their control of classroom knowledge as the "negotiation of efficiencies": they calculated how much of their personal knowledge of the economy and other aspects of the society under study to put at risk in the classroom, given the smallness of their financial rewards and professional incentives in relation to the potential for classroom disorder, dissent and conflict. The economics information they made available to their students, then, reflected not their level of training or interest in the subject, nor their particular political position on a topic, but their skill at maintaining classroom control. Ironically, their very attempt to minimize student cynicism by simplifying content and avoiding class discussion only heightened student disbelief of school knowledge and fostered in students greater disengagement from the learning process. Interviews with the students revealed how suspect they found school knowledge, especially if any teacher-supplied information was contradicted by an independent source. Just as the teachers masked their more complex personal knowledge of the topics because of their desire for classroom order and efficiency, the students appeared to acquiesce to the pattern of classroom knowledge, only silently to resist believing it (McNeil, 1981a).

Because the teachers attributed so much of their need for classroom efficiency to an administrative context that placed constraints without compensating supports (as in the addition of lower-income neighborhoods to the school's zone, or in de-tracking), the present study documented not only classroom treatment of content, but patterns of treatment which confirmed or varied from the calculation of efficiencies typical of the first teachers observed. As we have seen now from the four schools, the tension between social control and knowledge access is not limited to Forest Hills High. That tension is played out in different ways, resolved toward different ends, in the four schools. Whenever administrative personnel expend most of the staff's time, meetings and resources on discussions of hall order, discipline and numbers of course credits earned, teachers respond with overt but usually reluctant compliance on those goals, but reduce effort and aim for only minimal standards in their actual teaching. Students do not always understand where teacher motivations originate, nor even that the teachers know that the course is watered down or undemanding, but they do sense when the teachers take the work seriously. When students see minimal teaching, they respond with minimal classroom effort. (This is not the same as minimal learning; many students, like the teachers, are far more articulate and informed on a given topic than the classroom processes make admissible to the classroom.) *Much of the student apathy, and even occasional resistance, which administrators see as a motivation problem requiring more discipline procedures arises in these schools precisely because goals of order have already undermined the ability of staff to deal with educative goals.*

## Conceptions of school knowledge

By their universality and authority of mandatory attendance, schools legitimate certain cultural selections as "school knowledge." They further give legitimacy, by teaching methods and testing, to selected treatments of knowledge or ways of knowing. The dynamics within these four schools point to a need to understand how these selections we call "curriculum" and "learning" are related to the power structures internal to the institutions. Previous distinctions of high and low status knowledge implied control of schools by outside elites or correspondent economic factors. Classroom observations show us that external factors are intricately mediated through institutional forms and processes whose links to those external forces may be long hidden or forgotten. The rationalized structures of bureaucratic schooling have historical roots in attempts to emulate industrial powers of efficiency and roots in neutralizing old power networks through means of scientific management. Though on the surface public school knowledge seems to be in the service of a conservative ideology, it is currently being challenged or abandoned by elites as inadequate for international, high-tech competition. The bureaucratic forms which placed the "smooth running" of schools ahead of "literate" or "intellectual" education have failed to equip students with learning skills.

The current education reform reports place much of the blame for this failure on the recruiting and training of teachers. If we investigate course content closely, we see that even well-trained teachers are often unable to teach ideally in the face of the organizational systems controlling their workplace. By looking at the processing of content, rather than the outcomes of that processing as measured by student test performance, we can begin to see the factors at work in content selection, in validating ways of presenting or encountering information, and those factors beyond the classroom giving legitimacy to these processes. The processes are often not what their labels imply.

In making school knowledge itself the subject of inquiry, one goes against the long-standing tradition of social-studies curriculum research. A careful reading of the comprehensive survey of social-studies education research sponsored by the National Science Foundation and the Social Science Education Consortium (Wiley, 1977) reveals that most education researchers accept the course titles and educationist instructional jargon at face value. Every study cited in the sections on the "effectiveness" of social-studies instructional methods and materials left unexamined the assumption that schools exist to convey information, to increase learning, to increase achievements. Content and instructional method were discussed separately in the survey, reflecting their traditional theoretical separation in the ends–means conceptualization that underlies most education research. This attention to goal attainment ("effectiveness") omits two considerations. The first is the interrelation of instructional process and instructional content, irrespective of the effectiveness standard; that is, how the methods and forms of conveying knowledge affect the knowledge itself and, consequently, student perceptions of it. The second is the possibility that producing "effects" in terms of student learning or achievements might not be a primary goal of the classroom interaction. There was no analytical category for what might be left out of the information exchange. Our attention has been so focused on what teachers and curriculum planners want students to learn that we have no empirical precedent for looking at what teachers do not want them to learn, or at reasons for the limits that teachers impose.

While a research procedure for analyzing the inaccessibility of knowledge seems on the surface absurd, it should not, given the history of cultural biases in content selection and testing practices that has been brought to light by special-interest groups. Frances Fitzgerald (1979) and Jean Anyon (1979) have documented the selective omission of economic history unflattering to the myth of corporate and technological "progress" and free enterprise. Blacks, women's groups, hispanic-Americans and others have forced at least symbolic revisions of textbooks so that their contributions to American history will be acknowledged.

The remedy of the 1960s and early 1970s was to revise texts in order to try to "put in" whatever was being "left out." While this ameliorative approach was probably better than nothing, it left curriculum analysis largely at the planning level, the level of curriculum development, to the exclusion of such considerations as the institutional forces at work in those cultural selections and the impact of curricula on students. The distinctness of these three aspects of curricula as subjects of different professionals' research should not mask their interrelation in the real world of schools. Where school knowledge comes from is part and parcel of what it looks like, what values it embodies, what forms it takes and what impact it has on students.

Before demonstrating this interrelationship through examples selected from the observed courses, it will be helpful to ground these examples in the context of the broader question of the role the school serves in society. Although most curriculum developers would stand by their assumption that schools serve to increase achievements, we have the benefit of many insights to the contrary. Bowles and Gintis (1976), among others, have argued that the foremost role of the school is economic rather than educative, in the strictest sense. They claim the primary purpose of free public education in an industrial society is to sort students for positions of labor and management, and to stratify their access to knowledge to make them into docile and productive workers in an economy where they can expect to see the products of their labor appropriated into the profit structure of others. The structure of schooling into a credentialing system that supersedes instruction conforms to the individualized, alienating workplace with its external rewards. This view of the school as a tool that elites use to socialize the masses has different configurations in different societies. Bourdieu and Passeron (1977) have described the higher education system of France as a sophisticated system of stratified knowledge, wherein the high culture of aristocratic elites is promulgated as more worthy and more universal than the vernacular cultures of non-elites. "Real knowledge" and "true culture" are those historically characteristic of the aristocracy. Institutions of learning not only define what socially desirable knowledge is, but do so in ways that engender a "habitus," or disposition toward dominant values, that goes beyond holding specific pieces of information. The school serves to shape the consciousness of a nation by disposing individuals to define their world through the definitions of those in power.

Before World War II, British education accorded highest status to the cultural forms of the classical education of the gentleman class, and kept the technical knowledge of working people at lowest status.[2] This legacy persists in subtle forms; one's perceived job future, inferred from one's class background, helps determine which kinds of knowledge one has access to. By contrast, in the United States, where economic power has been more associated with corporate growth than with centuries of inherited wealth, technological language, especially in the sciences, has displaced the traditional Latin-school culture as high-status knowledge. Post-Sputnik investments in education were aimed originally at those students who showed, through standardized testing, aptitude for physics or higher mathematics, or who had proficiency in practical (non-literary) foreign language skills valued by the military and industrial complex. While valuing scientific inquiry among intellectual elites (to the point of applying scientific, or scientistic, modes of inquiry to almost every field of study), schools presented a very sanitized view of science to ordinary students in survey courses. There, science has been portrayed not as an arena of competing discoveries, but as an incremental series of progressing experiments whose results add up to "science."

This emerging critique of the social roles of school curricula forces us out of the habit of accepting the curricula as given, out of a research paradigm that manipulates all manner of instructional variables in search of the key to "effectiveness." However, this view of schools also seems to take too seriously the planning, or rational, component of school curricula. In talking about the role of school knowledge in cultural reproduction, writers frequently use terms that seem to imply that someone is deliberately pulling the strings of knowledge access, knowledge stratification and knowledge control: "The state encodes ..." or "The school stratifies." I have argued elsewhere (McNeil, 1981a) that both of the dominant models of curriculum theory – management and cultural reproduction – see the student as too passive, too acted upon, and that there is no interactive model for seeing whether the student is, in fact, resisting the processing of the school. Similarly, cultural reproduction models of curriculum analysis seem to accept too readily the implication of planning – that someone out there is stratifying school knowledge, that the interests vested in school knowledge necessarily reflect manipulation by elites in a way that can be explained as the direct exercise of power. In fact, schools' mediation of dominant culture can be far more subtle.

The interactive, contesting role of students' culture, especially that arising from the social location of their families, is one potential counter to the schools' role in cultural dominance (Connell *et al.*, 1982; Apple, 1982c). Another is the lag of school policy behind economic changes which affect the value of particular school credentials. The growing awareness among cultural theorists of factors influencing the role schools play in reinforcing only selected societal values is just beginning to be documented in studies of lived, in-use curricula.

At present, what cultural reproduction models conclusively give us is a view of the curriculum as problematic, as reflective of human interests. From this perspective, we are no longer bound by the pretense that school knowledge is the product of neutral, experimental inquiry, resulting in an objective selection of the information most conducive to "effective learning." We can begin to see that school knowledge, in some vague way, seems to correspond to the interests of powerful groups in the society. But it is dangerous to carry this model of correspondence too far, especially in the American setting. The French have had their academies and elite schools established by the aristocracy and the church, and the British have had their tradition of aristocratic and, later, nationally centralized schooling, but schooling in the United States is much more decentralized, much more chaotic. The mechanisms by which certain forms of knowledge are transmitted in schools, and others are omitted, necessarily have local as well as national characteristics.

Because they have been of fairly low status since the post-Sputnik promotion of science and mathematics, the social studies courses (sometimes called social science courses, in deference to technological trends) in most schools reflect little concern for national standardized tests or centralized curriculum planning. Authority for course titles usually rests with the state department of public instruction or local school boards, but the content of courses remains significantly at the discretion of the local school's individual teachers or social studies department. Social studies, then, is an interesting area in which to bring generalizations about the nature of school knowledge down to the level where selected knowledge about the society's institutions is encountered by the student. It is at the classroom level that we can best see the tension between making information accessible and making information inaccessible. By examining close up the ways the teachers offer and withhold information, we can test our generalization about the rationalities of curriculum planning, and the school's role in cultural reproduction, against the actual presentation of cultural selections.

## Knowledge forms as knowledge control

The examples of classroom knowledge cited here are drawn from US history classes observed in these four schools. The teachers were all middle-aged white men, except for one woman; all have at least a master's degree and many have additional university training beyond that. All have taught for at least ten years. We have seen that both the students and the teachers can be characterized by a wide range of political and philosophical values. Across these diversities, the techniques the teachers chose for controlling classroom behavior through approaches to course content were unexpectedly similar. After examining these techniques, we can better understand their relation to teacher and student diversities and to the role schools play in the dissemination of cultural knowledge and knowledge forms.

According to the teachers themselves, the techniques they used to convey course content to their students had to fulfill two goals: they had to give the information about American history and economics; and, at the same time, they had to impose firm limits on the complexity and topicality of class discussions, and on the efficiency of presentation. Most of the teachers resolved this tension by maintaining tight control over course content, eliminating almost all reading assignments or written work. Information related to the course came to students through lectures and teacher-selected films. As discussed in "Negotiating Classroom Knowledge" (McNeil, 1981a), students rarely spoke (as infrequently as twelve student comments all semester in one class of thirty juniors), and when they did it was to ask the teacher a question rather than discuss the topic with each other. Therefore, one may limit analysis to teacher comments and lectures and still gain a fairly full picture of the knowledge and, most importantly, the ways of knowing that the students encountered.

Educators usually see "lecture" as a negative term, to be contrasted with inquiry, discussion, or other more enlightened forms of instruction. "Lecture" can actually bring to mind a wide range of verbal activities, from the dull half-reading of a prepared text to brilliant discourse, within which the lecturer can argue, dramatize, compare, or question. Lectures themselves need not be a limitation on knowledge forms and content. With these particular teachers, however, lectures provided the best means toward the contradictory goals of giving the students information about the required subject in a way that maintained the teachers' professional role, while withholding from them ideas and information that might disrupt class efficiency. Within each lecture technique, we will see that control of knowledge really has as its objective the control of the students.

## Fragmentation

The simplest and probably most notorious lecture technique among social studies teachers is the reduction of any topic to fragments or disjointed pieces of information – lists. A list lets a teacher avoid having to elaborate or show linkages, and it keeps students, especially those weak at reading and writing, from having to express "learnings" in complete sentences or paragraphs. No one is called upon to synthesize or give a picture of interrelationships.

At all of these schools, fragmentation was most commonly used when the teacher considered the information vital to the students' knowledge. The list as a lecture device has the benefit of reducing all information to "facts," as though each term in the list represents a consensus among historians or the general public about an event, a personage or an issue. In fact, lists usually take the issue-ness out of issues by collapsing contradictory opinions into a single enumeration of fragments of the story.

Several examples will illustrate the transformation a segment of history undergoes when confined to a list. The characteristics of political parties, economic policies or major institutions, and the causes, results, or effects of various events are all likely to be presented as lists or as points in a formal outline. Almost every teacher observed in the four schools described labor history in

167

terms of the names of various unions and their founders or primary leaders. They printed on the blackboard lists of the "tools" or "weapons" labor and management had at their disposal during grievances (strike, lockout, injunction, and so on). The only exception was a seasoned labor leader, an organizer of teacher unions, who showed a film of the Triangle fire and told old stories about labor conditions. Otherwise, as Anyon (1978) notes, the conditions giving rise to the labor movement are almost never discussed, or even put into a list. In this instance, as in many others, the list is not an aid to remembering the details from a complicated study of a topic; it *is* the study of the topic. Suddenly, with little background, the course chronology arrives at industrialization; the teacher reads a list of new labor unions. The same strategy was used to convey information about the benefits of TVA ("soil conservation, an energy yardstick, advanced farming techniques"), without any background information about the energy needs or policies of the period. The names of New Deal agencies, again with little background information about the economic conditions and political compromises involved, is a favorite subject for lists.

The teachers at Forest Hills High were very articulate in explaining their view of their job and their rationale for these instructional techniques. They expressed the sentiment that their job as history teachers was to tell students the "true story" of American history. By presenting that story in fragments, they made efficient use of time, avoided arousing discussion, and presented information in a manner that facilitated quantifiable testing. When filled with lists, the course content appears to be rigorous and factual. It makes the teacher appear knowledgeable and gives students a sense of fairness in the grading; they know they have to memorize the lists. Lists and unelaborated terms reduce the uncertainty for both students and teachers. For this reason it is clearly the dominant mode of conveying information.

The effects of lists on students were twofold. Of all the strategies for controlling classroom knowledge, this one seemed to have the most pay-off for students. Depending on their abilities and diligence, they could turn the fragments of information in their notebooks into test points. Grades of B or C were easily earned because so little was expected in these classes; that softened the fact that the course was required for graduation.

But this fragmentation of information, without the opportunity for in-depth consideration of a topic, also carried within it a vulnerability of which the teachers seemed unaware. Interviews with the students revealed that their overt acquiescence to the lectures masked covert suspicions or rejection of much of the course content. One reason was that many of these students had had experiences (or had heard those of their parents) that contradicted teacher-supplied information. Many students mentioned that when the teacher presented as fact *one item* that the student believed to be untrue or misleading, the entire course became suspect for that student. Their information came from stories that their grandparents told, from their parents' professions or travels, from their own jobs, from television documentaries, or, occasionally, from books or newspapers. These students, whom the teachers dismissed as needing to have everything "spoon fed" to them, were silently comparing the classroom version of the "facts" with whatever other source was available to them. Any discrepancy discredited the teacher in their eyes. The brisk pace of the lectures and the consistency of the course format in preventing discussion also prevented elaboration of items in lists and prevented comparison with varied interpretations. No doubt such comparisons, if they had taken place, would not always have validated the students' personal information. In the absence of comparisons, the students' personal sources of information were more often credible to them. Thus the teachers successfully used fragments and lists to convey efficiently a vast number of facts and to limit discussion and disagreement by this appearance of factuality. The irony is that this technique created so much distance between the student and the content that it caused a backlash of the kind of cynicism the teachers were trying to avoid.

Mystification

Another treatment of information I have termed mystification. Teachers often tried to surround a controversial or complex topic with mystery in order to close off discussion of it. When the teachers mystified a topic, they made it appear very important but unknowable. When they mentioned the Federal Reserve or the gold standard or the International Monetary Fund, they asked students to copy the term into their notes. Then a comment would follow to the effect that students should know about this and remember the term for their next test, but that non-experts really could not go into depth on this subject. Sometimes this seemed to be a ruse to hide the teacher's lack of knowledge of the subject, as when one teacher said the students should write down that Nixon took us off the gold standard, but that he did not know what that meant and wasn't going to go into it with an "economics major" (referring to me, though I am not an economics major) present. This point had been on the transparency outline from which he lectured for years, so one doubts whether he had ever "gone into it" beyond this brief mention.

Capitalism, the importance of political parties, free enterprise, and progress are all aspects of our system that were mentioned with an aura of respect or reverence, then left as slogans. The intent seemed to be to have students internalize the affective component of the term so that their trust of the system would be enhanced. This attention to affiliative language best conforms to Bourdieu and Passeron's (1977) concept of creating "habitus" rather than mechanistic reproduction of the dominant culture. Surely this was the intent of the teachers. The woman teacher told me that she wished more than anything that students would appreciate their institutions, because the people who came before them had worked hard to create them, especially during the New Deal reforms. A male teacher at her school added, "You have to sell the system." Both attributed student cynicism toward business institutions and school rules to the partial information that students during the Vietnam war era had come across. This partial information had combined with student enthusiasm to make students disruptive in class, arrogant about their own opinions and generally hard to control. These two teachers reflected on their manner of presenting information and deliberately wove a story that reinforced simple themes and minimized differences.

The effect of mystification was that students did, for the most part, internalize some of the emotional quality of the term, while remaining unable to explain it. When asked to explain free enterprise, students would answer with affiliative language based on little factual knowledge: "It means you can own your own business without government controls," or "we have labor unions here but I don't know what they do." They seemed to know that the mystified term was meant to be comparative, showing the superiority of the US economic system, but they could not elaborate that system or the meaning of the term. For students suspicious of course content, and for some who were not suspicious but were frustrated that the course did not have more "meat" to it, this mystification created unease because they felt they should have a chance to have capitalism, or free enterprise, or fiscal and monetary policy, really explained to them until they understood it. Their common response sounded something like, "I hear that term every year, but I still don't know what it means."

Mystification also helped engender a client mentality; since students were not invited to pursue information on their own, to dig deeper into subjects that were mentioned and then closed off, they developed a feeling of dependence on externally supplied information. Frequently, when asked what they thought they should learn about a certain topic, the answer shifted to the third person: " 'They' never tell us," " 'They' should tell us" or "Pollution must not be a problem because *'they'* don't mention it anymore" (emphasis added), Since many of these same students felt they could not trust teacher supplied information, their "they" remained without antecedent.

Omission

The lecture strategy that produced the most suspicion, and the only one to which resistance was voiced in class, was omission. The students were less concerned about the omission of specific topics than about whole time periods omitted from the lecture. Several students did express concern that variant points of view were omitted from class, and most said they wished that students could discuss the topics that were mentioned. But their chief and almost unanimous concern was that their United States history courses dealing, according to the course title, with the most recent period of history, ended with Eisenhower or Kennedy. Especially at the first school observed, where the course was titled "Contemporary United States history," each teacher crammed the most recent twenty years, of the fifty or so to be covered by the course, into the last three to eight days of the semester.

There were several reasons for this. Most obvious was that to the teachers, events that had happened in their adulthood were "current events," even though to the students "current events" usually meant this year's happenings. The Vietnam war (which ended several years prior to the observation) got from zero to four and a half minutes' treatment in these three classes in the original ethnography. Current presidential campaigns and economic turmoil (inflation, unemployment, energy, near-bankrupt cities), which were of great interest to the students, were "lightweight" topics on which "historians do not yet agree," in the teachers' conception of the "story" of history. The teacher who lectured daily from transparencies did not want to relate current events to historical topics, because he preferred to use the same transparency outline year after year. He said that he spent the greater part of the course discussing the New Deal and the Depression because no one could hope to understand current situations without a thorough grounding in these periods, which so shaped our current institutions. Aside from this pedagogical reason, the teachers also stated emphatically that they intended never to return to the days of Vietnam and student rights protests, when students shouted teachers down and when class discussion thereby became "unbalanced."

One teacher said that he had cut out research papers because the weaker students could not think of a topic on their own, and although the brighter students had, during the antiwar movement, "written terrific papers ... they were *self-indoctrinated*." They learned something that contradicted the teacher's analysis of the events. This teacher told the class being observed that he was not going to discuss the Vietnam war (although his chronological coverage of American history had come to that period) because he had "heard Vietnam for the past ten years." He similarly dismissed poverty by saying that no one starves to death in this country; a black student tried to challenge this statement but had only intuition to go on and so was not believed. This teacher was a very friendly and caring person who usually tried to get students to realize how well-off Americans are compared to most other people. But one day he refused to accept a student's definition of "exploitation" as "rip-off." He said that the investment of American capital in other countries always had a beneficial effect on both the United States and the recipient economy. Again, a few students tried to object on the basis of news reports they had heard, but were unsuccessful, except that they did press the teacher to admit that United Fruit had given multinational corporations a "bad name." The concept of "exploitation" had come up in a one-day survey of

US policies toward Latin America. The framework of the course, built around lists of treaties, technical terms like exploitation, and similarly abbreviated facts, did not permit students or teacher to explore the emerging differences of interpretation. The students shrugged, wrote down the requisite terms, and resumed silence.

Omission also extended beyond current topics to include the controversial sides of topics that were mentioned. For example, no mention was made of protests against US entry into World War II, of people who disliked Roosevelt's New Deal policies or of people who disagreed with Truman's decision to bomb Hiroshima. Variation across region, ethnic group, social class, or gender was also notably absent. "We Americans ..." was usually the subject of any sentence describing an era or momentous event. Most of the students interviewed volunteered a concern that they felt was omitted from the course, whether it was a specific topic ("Why is so much money spent on the space program?") or a perspective ("What if your grandparents *liked* Huey Long?"). The girls were not too concerned that women were excluded from history, but the one black student, and many whites, wondered aloud why few issues related to blacks were included. Several noted the lack of mention of other countries or the comparison of American institutions or events with related ones in other countries. In short, the teachers actually stimulated interest in the contemporary period by omitting it, although omitting it allowed them to avoid dealing with it.

At Nelson High the teachers were less likely to omit current information. Nor did they totally shy away from controversial material. However, Nelson students did notice that "controversial" and "factual" have different meanings to different people. In a lesson on nuclear energy the teacher invited a spokesman from the utility company which does operate a nuclear power plant, because he could give the *facts* on the benefits or dangers of nuclear power. The teacher announced more than once that he would welcome a speaker *against* nuclear power if one could be found who was not "emotional." Factual speakers, with professional transparencies and industry films, are admissible to the classroom; emotional speakers are inappropriate for school. (Interestingly, the utility executive was very emotional. He brought out of his pocket a stone he said was processed radioactive waste; he held it to show his lack of fear and gave a very spirited defense of his company's investment in nuclear power.) Several students volunteered in interviews that they were not pleased to have their side of the issue dismissed as "emotional."

Any course involves selections. Omissions described by Anyon (1978) and Fitzgerald (1979) are those systematically characteristic of commercial textbook publishers. There were instances at each of these schools of a teacher's choosing not to deal with topic that was included in the text or in the school's resources or even in the course outline. While obvious constraints of time and student ability would account for some omissions any teacher makes, these teachers took pains to explain at some length the reasons for certain of their omissions. They wished to omit material, or perspectives on material, that would foster contradictory opinions and make students want to engage in discussion. Most teachers felt they could cover more material more efficiently if controversial topics were omitted. The pace of the lecture was critical to covering the course adequately. To maintain that pace, student talk had to be kept to a minimum.

Defensive simplification

The fourth strategy that will be mentioned here cuts across ideological lines and institutional contexts more than any of the others. Teachers use this strategy to circumvent what they perceive to be a lack of strong student interest, or as the weakness of student abilities. Rather than relying on that old standard, "motivation," the teachers will win the students' compliance on a lesson by promising that it will not be difficult and will not go into any depth.

While fragmentation, mystification and omission strategies may all be seen as efforts to simplify content, this last is distinguished by the term *defensive*. Unlike the old wielder of the hickory stick, the teacher announces the topic of study, which may sound very complicated, then apologizes for it and promises it will not demand much work. Examples might be supply and demand, or the industrialization–urbanization syndrome. Any real treatment of the topic would require time, comparison of varied interpretations, investigations of varied information resources and the effort of making repeated explanations or of offering distinct encounters with the topic (through small group discussion, film, research, reading, or whatever) until everyone in the class understood it at some reasonable level. Although the topic is formally listed in the course outline, and the teacher will present something about it for later use on a test, he or she may not intend for the students to go beyond this superficial treatment. Yet just announcing the topic makes students think they will have to do some work. The teacher gets them to cooperate without resisting by promising that, in fact, the study of this topic will require no commitment of effort, and little time, on their part. This strategy of making knowledge inaccessible makes twenty-plus years of research of "effectiveness" look incredibly naive. Equally naive was the research hypothesis that guided the classroom observations in search of the kinds of economics information made available in these classes. The specific topics became almost irrelevant when they were subjected to a defensive presentation.

Topics introduced "defensively" were less likely to be politically sensitive and controversial than those that were mystified. Rather, they tended to be topics that needed a great deal of unpacking to be grasped, topics not amenable to reduction to items in a list. Whereas the labor movement could be reduced to names, dates, famous strikes and weapons of labor–management dispute, fiscal and monetary policy could hardly be treated at all without explanation of the interrelationship of private- and public-sector economic decision-making, the concept of money supply and circulation, and other aspects such as public works programs, the tension between unemployment and inflation, and the nature of credit economies. Political trade-offs are a vital component, also. Sometimes such complicated topics were omitted altogether, although in an interview the teacher might say they were essential to a student's education. At other times, the teacher contrived a set of lists of factual terms that lay out key components of the topic. Yet other times, either because the topic was mentioned in a text or curriculum guide, or because a later unit built upon it, some treatment of the topic became unavoidable. When this became evident, the teacher very quickly followed the announcement of the topic with the caveat that "It won't be as bad as it sounds."

The simplification may take the form of a very brief sketch of the topic in the lecture, a worksheet with blanks to be filled in with fragments of fact, a filmstrip that reduces the topic to its simplest possible form, or a handout such as a one-page magazine article that talks around the topic without ever really explaining it. Most important is the ritual of seeming to deal with the topic. The

175

teacher makes a few remarks, the students groan, the activity (lecture, filmstrip, or whatever) proceeds and is briefly concluded, the teacher asks if there are any questions, and there are none.

The observations and interviews turned up several possible explanations behind this strategy of controlling students by simplifying the lessons. The first that teachers expressed is fatigue. Having reached middle-age or seen their paychecks long ago outstripped by inflation, the teachers said that they no longer felt the energy and drive to do whatever was necessary to make students understand. They felt that neither the support nor the financial reward was commensurate with the out-of-class time needed to prepare learning activities adequately, or to read and comment on the student essay tests or written assignments that a real treatment of such topics would require. The energy they recalled being willing to expend during their earlier days of teaching had dwindled now to minimal effort.

A second factor was the minimal effort students seemed willing to put forth. In two of the four schools, over half the juniors and seniors interviewed worked more than twenty hours per week in addition to going to school full time (McNeil, 1984). Other teachers noted that the 1960s enthusiasm for social studies courses had given way to high priorities for math and science in the 1970s and 1980s. Whatever school effort students were willing to spend, they saved for these courses, which they saw as more instrumental to job futures. There is no objective way to know if students observed were less willing to work at learning than were students of ten or twenty years ago, but teachers who had been around that long swore this was the case. One mentioned that he could no longer plan to center a class period around a completed homework assignment; many assignments would eventually trickle in, but not on time. Another mentioned that there seemed to be fewer "slow" students who learned by consistently pushing themselves to "overachieve" – in other words, to stretch beyond what is normally expected of them. Tired, bored and rushed to cover content, teachers and students met in a path of least resistance. Expected student resistance to taxing assignments was circumvented by making the assignments less taxing. Thus, again, the teachers maintained classroom control and control of information at the same time.

A third explanation teachers gave for simplifying content in order to gain student cooperation was the lack of a supportive administration. In comparing the four schools, the administrative context was analyzed for its effect on the ways teachers make knowledge and ways of knowing accessible to students. The basic finding was that there is a parallel between administrators' attempts to gain minimal compliance from teachers and teachers' settling for minimal compliance from students. In those schools where administrators devoted most of the schools' staff time and resources to maintaining order and to attending to such details as course credits, the administrators paid less attention to the academic quality of teaching. The content of the curriculum was clearly secondary to the maintenance of order. Teachers in these schools tended to expend minimal effort in the classroom; frequently this was deliberate and was explained by the teacher as retaliation for or reluctant accommodation to administrative pressure for precision in paperwork, extra hall monitoring, or extended meetings related to such matters as graduation requirements.

At Nelson, where the administration most supported the teaching function and gave most attention to the quality of instruction, teachers responded by demanding more of themselves in the presentation and preparation of lessons. They felt, and demonstrated, less of a wall between their personal knowledge and the "official" knowledge of the classroom. They developed entire courses, used original handouts and continually collected and re-designed materials. They used fewer lists and provided more extended descriptions, more opportunitities for student discussion, more varieties of learning experiences (including the willingness to bring speakers in from the community). Not even in this school, however, were teachers entirely free of the kind of "defensive simplification" that was prevalent at the other schools.

Mr Hobbs, a teacher whose classes were extremely rich in ideas and in materials he had collected or developed, explained that he did not have high expectations that the students would really deal with those ideas. Although he did require more reading than teachers at the first school observed, he had students answer questions on daily worksheets. He stated that he did not like the worksheets, but that he began using them after a year or two of teaching, when he discovered that students were not reading. He acknowledged that the worksheets did show that students had read, but did not necessarily mean they could discuss or integrate the ideas. He designed his own worksheets rather than rely on commercial ones;

they did therefore ask for more thought than possible on simple fill-in-the-blank sheets that often accompany textbooks. The work-sheet assignment allowed the teacher to deal with history in a way that kept his own interest because ideas were involved, but also in a way that let students know they were not responsible for more than the most basic components of the lesson. This same teacher was known for asking tough, analytical questions. He built his history courses around such themes as the relation of violence to human history and the obligation of the individual to the state. Yet he said that he had eliminated student research papers because "these students are too young to even ask a question, much less look for answers." Except for a few students, who in interviews talked about having wrestled with his "questions that catch you off guard," most of these questions became rhetorical, with the teacher and students knowing that the real grade was based on the work-sheet and tests.

## Variations and differences

Educators are accustomed to think in terms of student differences. Curriculum analysts speak of ideological differences among teach-ers. The examples of defensive teaching witnessed in these schools cut across differences in teachers' individual political and pedagog-ical philosophies and across formal definitions of variations in stu-dent ability. If we understand its pervasiveness in spite of expected variations and exceptions, we may better grasp what is at work when schools mediate social knowledge.

Most published educational research begins with the premise that differences in student ability and achievement are important and, in fact, lie at the heart of educational exchanges. This became clear to me as I presented these examples of knowledge simplification to various groups of researchers. Even those critical theorists most skeptical of formal educationist categories would ask, "What about the bright students? How was it different for weak students?" Our experiences with knowledge stratified by student achievement or social-class levels make the questions reasonable. But none of the observed teachers followed the truism by teaching to the brighter or upper-class students, or by watering down content only for the non-college-bound or lower-income student. The way these teach-ers dealt with student differences is much more complex and demonstrates how the contradictory goals inherent in institutional roles can be rationalized.

The teachers at all four schools talked about differences in student ability. Many mentioned that it was difficult to try to teach classes in which many students were "very bright" and other students "could not read." Only one teacher ever named specific students as belonging to either category, even though several were pressed in interviews to elaborate their distinctions. The teachers at Forest Hills felt that having to teach heterogeneous classes was a constraint, even a punishment. They felt that their ability to affect students' learning had diminished with the elimination of IQ-based tracking. Teachers at the other schools preferred the mixed-ability classes.

In both cases, teachers frequently made comments that demonstrated their knowledge of and consideration of traditional ability classifications for students. Yet the teaching strategies in their classes belied these differences. One teacher who had fairly weak students made his lectures simple and demanded no effort beyond answering a few questions each week in dittoed sheets. A teacher of an honors history class assigned roles for the students to play in a trial of Harry Truman for the Hiroshima bombings. He gave them no instructions on role-playing, did not check the extent of their background reading before the enactment, and interrupted the poor performances after only a few minutes and gradually resumed lecturing. Later he told me, "I knew they couldn't do it: I knew it would turn out like this." By abandoning the assignment instead of continuing it and giving the instructions the students needed to prepare properly, he in effect apologized for having expected something of them. It was easier for him to diffuse the expectations than to act on them.

His treatment of the honors students was very little different from the strategy of the teacher of a mixed-ability class who assigned only one book per semester and then accepted nominal book reports, some of which were openly copied from book jackets.

The most telling concern about student differences came from the teachers who had fought de-tracking. They were convinced that differences in student ability greatly affected student learning and called for vastly different teaching techniques. They fondly recalled being able to have panel discussions and research papers with the bright students, but had "spoon fed" the "masses" and had let the

179

lowest level of students read the morning paper with the football coach for their US history course. These same teachers applied their spoon-feeding techniques to all levels once the levels were mixed. Although the rationale of the school system had been further to democratize classrooms by eliminating tracking, making each individual the focus of instruction apart from group labels, the effect of de-tracking was that teachers treated all the individuals as they had formerly treated their "masses." They began to define all students as belonging in the middle-level categories, as having to have everything done for them. They saw these students as having to be controlled in behavior and learning. They structured the lessons accordingly.

The result was that they began to teach as though the differences were no longer there. Rather than teach to the brightest students, they simplified the content and assignments for everyone. To stratify assignments is time-consuming: it means dividing the class for discussion or directions occasionally; it means having to grade more than one kind of assignment; and it means adapting a standard grading code, set by the school, in a way that will fairly reflect the difficulty levels of the assignments. It is easier, say the teachers, not to have the bright students write papers. Writing papers calls for many procedural directions and much paper reading by the teacher. It also puts students into contact with resources that make them vulnerable to "self-indoctrination." If some of the students in the same class can barely read, the differential assignments will bring this to attention. When teachers are aware of the problem, they feel obligated to help these students find suitable reading material or help them learn how to read the regular text. If one ignores these differences, or structures the class in a way that hides them, one can remove oneself from the obligation of dealing with the inefficiencies these differences pose.

Thus these defensive teaching strategies do not deal with differences between students with the instructional stratification that one might expect. One of the purposes of the fragmentation was to reduce content to pieces that could be managed by students of many levels of ability. One of the purposes of systematically omitting current topics was to prevent the intrusion of verbal students' ideas into the pace of the lecture. One of the purposes of mystification was to avoid having to go into a whole series of presentations of a complex topic until everyone understood. The teachers who chafed at de-tracking were in a minority. All but two of the fourteen observed teachers preferred teaching mixed-ability classes. Teachers in both groups talked outside the classroom about differences between students, yet taught as though there were no differences. When asked which students' needs were not being met by their department's offerings, most felt that the weakest students were receiving some help from drop-out prevention programs and the like; one or two mentioned that the brightest students were probably bored, but that that "was inevitable." The others felt that if brighter students were not challenged, they should do something about it themselves: "They can always do more if they want to. Not many go that extra effort any more." In no school were any of the "defensive" teaching strategies limited to students of one ability group. In fact, according to their own explanations, teachers selected these strategies in order to deal with "all these different students."

Equally striking is the prevalence of these teaching strategies across differences in teacher ideology. My dialogue with Henry Giroux (McNeil, 1981b, 1981c) on the ability of teachers to foster emancipatory citizenship education through their resistance to technocratic rationale in schools centered on the failure of teacher practice to reflect teacher ideology (McNeil, (1981b). The selection of teaching strategies that maximize efficiencies and control of student behavior can be observed among teachers who otherwise would appear to have very different political values. Miss Langer taught American history as a chronology of presidents and congresses, and tended to reify the view that citizens must support whoever is in power, because history is made at the top. Her lists consisted of presidential plans and congressional enactments. Mr Schmidt frequently said that "We are all Progressives ..." and claimed ideological links to Jefferson, while making lists of Hamiltonian-like policies. Mr Seager was a labor organizer and teller of stories. He was clearly to the left of most of the other teachers observed; he assigned the reading of public-issues pamphlets designed to raise issues beyond the normal confines of consensus information, then turned them into seatwork by making students answer the questions at the end of the sections rather than discuss the issues, as the materials intended.[3] He himself loved political debate and had participated actively in state and national politics. He spoke openly with his students about the contrast between his own leftist leanings and the community's conservatism. Yet his treatment of course topics differed little from that of Miss Langer and her presidential lists or Mr Schmidt and his transparencies.

Miss Langer reduced content to fragments but never apologized for assignments. One teacher who innovated consumer-economics courses and was well-versed on consumer rights and regulatory policies presented even these issues close to the lives of students in list form and made assignments without expecting any real interest or commitment from the students. Mr Lancaster, the most intellectual of the teachers observed, was determined to stretch the minds of students. He said that he deliberately used difficult words to force students to learn them, and required students to watch *Washington Week in Review* and difficult films on such topics as futurology. Yet he permitted students to carry on conversations during class, accepted the briefest of outlines as an "independent project," and in general demanded little of students. His pleasure came from his own intense involvement with the subject without the expectation of much student reciprocity; in the classes observed, he got little.

One last example serves to demonstrate the power of simplification strategies to obscure differences among teachers and reduce content to its most trivial, least controversial level. Mr Lennon at Freeburg described himself as a Marxist and at other times as a social democrat. He was as politically different from the man with the transparency lectures as could be expected within a range of high-school teachers. Mr Lennon would have *liked* his students to understand the very inequities and injustices of capitalist economies that the teachers at the first school wished to hide from their students. He would have liked his students to see the validity of some aspects of Marxian analysis of their economic system and to see that people may have honest disagreements about economic goals and political means. On the surface, the content of his lectures appeared somewhat radical. Yet, when seen in the context of its method of presentation, it mirrored the defensive simplifications of the more conservative teachers. While he was much less likely to mystify a subject deliberately, Mr Lennon lectured in a very casual, low-key way, making minimal assignments in an apologetic tone, and expecting little student involvement in the topic. He told me that by the time the students become juniors and seniors they are "adults" and should learn on their own. He contradicted this by not requiring them to work on their own, and in fact did not even require them to listen attentively to his lectures. He occasionally presented reading material that contained two opposing perspectives on an issue, but he had little means of checking whether students read or understood the differences. His motivations were very different from those of the teachers reacting against de-tracking and Vietnam war era protests. He was one of the protestors. His reactions within his school were against what he saw as capricious and unsupportive administrators who overemphasized rules rather than instruction and faculty support. He openly admitted that he had lowered the standards of his own efforts in recent years and was unwilling to exert effort on preparations or paper grading or forcing student compliance with demanding assignments. Points in his lectures that could have earned him censure in the 1950s came across as just another boring set of social studies facts to his students. Their test scores were very low, and a constant hum of side chatter accompanied each lecture. He was liked for his rapport with students and his willingness to discuss the headlines at the beginning of class. But once the lecture started, his ideas became "social studies" and were taken less seriously.[4]

Variation across school structures was not as marked as might be expected. Examples of defensive teaching occurred at all four schools. The particular defensive techniques did vary according to the presence or lack of administrative support. One key variation was the degree of involvement of the teachers' or students' personal knowledge of the subject. At Forest Hills and Freeburg, schools with least supportive administration, the walls between public (classroom) and private information seemed more rigid. There was much less attempt to bring students into the learning process. Even teachers with rich personal stores of information limited classroom treatment to a far simpler presentation, creating efficiencies not otherwise provided by the administrative setting.

At Nelson, with strong support from the principal, and at Maizeville, where a strong department chairman supported academics, use of defensive teaching strategies varied more by personality than by building. Nevertheless, at Maizeville one teacher expressed an unwillingness to prepare complex learning activities or lectures in light of lack of administrative support. The teachers at Nelson did not exclude controversial or contemporary material so much as teachers did at the other schools, but they did tend to combine assertive, non-defensive lectures with meakness and qualifiers in making assignments. Their defensiveness, where it existed, was visible in the disproportionate load carried by teachers rather than students in preparing for class. While this point may seem unfair in comparison to very light assignments, if any, at Freeburg and Forest Hills, it is mentioned because it varies so from the otherwise self-confident, productive lesson presentations made by these teachers. In lectures and in passing out gathered or teacher-composed materials, they were far from defensive. Only in their demands on students did they consistently follow a less demanding path.

## Institutional goals and personal knowledge

One must not draw from this study that all teachers deny students access to information critical to their functioning in society, or that all teachers use the techniques outlined here under the guise of lecturing just to limit student access to information. We have seen that when teachers do wish to control knowledge access, they often do so consciously. Their chief criteria for selecting strategies of knowledge control seem to be based on maintaining their own authority and efficiencies. The desire to control knowledge is as much a desire for classroom control as for selective distribution of information. This finding is crucial for our understanding of the ways schools legitimate certain kinds of information and de-legitimate others. An appreciation of processes and rationale of legitimation, and the legitimation of processes or ways of knowing, is central to any understanding of the role of the school in transmitting fairly narrow selections from the infinite range of human knowledge.

Although cultural reproduction is generally discussed on a societal level, as the product of a complex of systemic forces, the mediation of cultural forms in these schools is highly conditioned by the individual's attempt to deal with institutional constraints. The constraints are not the same in each school. The philosophical values the individual brings to the classroom are not in all cases the same. Yet the strategies for instruction are quite similar: *control students by making school work easy*. The result is content that neither the teachers nor the students take very seriously. It is frequently distinct from their personal knowledge.

This has two important implications for our understanding of the nature of secondary schools. First, their role in reproducing dominant cultural forms is far more complex than any direct correspondence theory would capture. Second, the resulting "official knowledge" is often too impersonal to be appropriated, but its effects are nevertheless damaging.

## De-skilling and teachers

In every case, these teachers can be said to have resisted the dominant technological forms of knowledge in their conceptualization of social studies curricula. Two of the teachers participated in a strike in which one issue was the imposition of teaching-by-objectives standards for teacher evaluation. None of the teachers taught to prepare for standardized tests, or valued technical knowledge above narrative, intuitive, experiential warrants for knowledge claims. None had adopted a social science model of history, although materials for doing so were available in their school systems and professional associations. With two exceptions, their theories of politics and historiography admitted conflict and rejected simplistic consensus. They were not stratifying students for the labor force, nor deliberately reinforcing racial or class inequities. Neither the state nor the business community intruded directly into the treatment or, for the most part, the selection of course topics. *From their personal values alone, it would seem that these teachers are not "reproducing" technological culture.*

Yet their instructional strategies embodied the very values they wished to avoid in teaching-by-objective models. In accommodating to institutional priorities for order and efficiency, the teachers demonstrated the very technocratic values that they did not respect in administrators and on which they placed much of the blame for the need for efficiency. By reducing course content to its most manageable and measurable fragments, the teachers were splitting the learning process into means and ends and reinforcing a concern for extrinsic rewards. The strategies of classroom control have their basis in the reward system of the institution (teacher pay and student credentials, as examples) and the power structure of the institution (the hierarchy that makes teachers responsible for control of students). The societal factors shaping quiescence, discretion and autonomy within the institutions are real but are not direct manipulations of school processes. What the data show is that theories of the social role of schools must be grounded in the processes within schools that disseminate selected societal values to the students.

At the elementary level, it can be argued that external forces have more directly shaped curricula by de-skilling teachers through the adoption of "teacher-proof" materials. Packaged materials, produced by commercial publishers, adopted by state and local school systems under the direction of experts such as child psychologists and reading specialists, have the purpose of reducing teacher discretion and variation. The "teacher-proof" materials contain pre-tests, instructional techniques, sets of content reduced to measurable items, and post-tests for mastery. All the teacher need do is to follow the directions; no decisions, background, experience or personal knowledge is necessary (Apple, 1982c).

Secondary teachers at the observed schools had resisted such pre-packaged materials. They saw themselves as professionals, and, as such, responsible for course content and evaluation. So far, no outside experts or political pressures had attempted to insulate their students from their discretion through pre-packaged materials. Yet these teachers were participating, and many of them willingly, in their own de-skilling. Their assessment of their effectiveness or even survival within the institution had led them to split their personal knowledge from their classroom teaching in much the same way as pre-packaged materials divorce elementary teachers' ideas from instruction and evaluation. The secondary teachers expressed disrespect for administrators who saw only needs for hall order or completed paperwork. They felt frustration when faculty meetings month after month focused on graduation requirements and credit course content. They resented having to do hall duty during their planning periods, as though "planning lessons" were nothing more than a coffee break. They felt alienated from institutional goals that subordinated teaching and learning to institutional maintenance.

Yet, within their classrooms they reinforced these goals of order with the justification that doing so was the only way they could protect themselves from the institutional pressures. They felt no encouragement to deal with differences in ability, so they structured lessons that obscured these differences. They got no reward for holding discussions, but felt sanctions for not "covering the material," so they minimized discussion in the interest of speeding up the lecture pace. Each one of the simplification strategies for gaining student compliance could be seen as the participation by high school teachers in their own de-skilling. The gaps between what they are doing and what they could be doing were not the perceptions of an outside observer but are the teachers' own views expressed in interviews as they discussed their personal ideas of what students ought to learn and what the subject is really all about. Their entrapment in the institutional reward structure could be seen as an excuse for lazy teaching, or as the most potent of the school's ways of reproducing technological culture. Even the teachers who least supported that culture resorted to instructional strategies aimed at the kind of minimal standards and desire for order that they rejected at the administrative level. Their personal ideologies were not enough to counter this de-skilling.

If the de-skilling of secondary teachers is more participatory, it is also more *individualized* than the de-skilling of elementary teachers. The development of "scientific" curricula which took from elementary teachers the planning, instructing and grading functions helped to de-skill a huge number of the professionals within a short period. We have seen that secondary teachers as a group held on to their professional roles of developing and evaluating courses. While their profession did not immediately feel the de-skilling of competency-based or teacher-proof curriculum packaging, individuals within the profession were adopting classroom practices which would help bring about their own de-skilling, separating personal command of a subject from classroom treatment of it. Because this de-professionalizing, or de-skilling, seemed to be occurring on an individual basis, there may be more optimism for reversing this pattern once it is better understood.

One interpretation for the imposed de-skilling of elementary teachers as a professional group, while secondary teachers traditionally retained greater curricular autonomy, is that elementary teaching is seen as "women's work." As such it has been more susceptible to external, managerial controls, similar to those imposed on secretaries as word-processing has divorced their technical skills from personal expertise (Apple, 1985). Secondary teachers, especially in social studies, are more likely to be men. Men teachers may have been seen more as professionals rather than as semi-skilled labor, thus more protected from de-skilling imposed through pre-packaged curricula and similar controls. This explan-

187

ation is not entirely adequate to explain the slowness by which high school curricula have been subject to pre-packaging. One better explanation may be the power of job markets and, even more, of university entrance requirements to influence high school course offerings and to keep them from being reducible to packaging.

The gender issue is significant, however, as one of many factors affecting teachers' professional roles. In these schools the teachers with outside jobs (especially entrepreneurial ones) or positions of community leadership tended to resist de-skilling more than those teachers whose primary identity in the community was "just a teacher." Since the non-school life of most women teachers was centered on child-care and family chores rather than civic leadership or entrepreneurial income, they were less buffered from this de-skilling tendency than the men teachers whose non-school life centered on jobs or visible community service.

## De-skilling and students

The teachers' splitting of their personal knowledge from the institutional in attempts to gain minimal compliance may be seen as a kind of de-skilling of students as well. Yet the data also point to the danger of carrying this conclusion too far and deducing social-control effects from social-control processes. In a separate discussion (McNeil, 1981a), I have elaborated the forms of student resistance that have only been mentioned here. What is clear is that where knowledge control is used as a form of classroom control, alienation increases for all participants, further reinforcing patterns of control. Resistance to forms of control does not mean that students are escaping the effects of the way information is processed. One real effect of the alienation students feel toward school-supplied information is the opportunity cost of rejecting much course content without having any sense of how to find (or generate or evaluate) credible information on their own. The teachers seem fairly successful in placing a distance between the students' own questions and concerns and the course content. This seems to make the students withdraw into their own personal information (their "real" knowledge) so that it will not become contaminated by school-supplied knowledge.[5]

The supreme example of teachers' promoting the split between personal knowledge (their own as well as the students') and classroom knowledge occurred in a class on contemporary social problems. This popular elective took a social-psychological approach to the selection and discussion of social issues such as death and dying, theories of personality, the family, and so on. The teacher, Mr Hansen, used many lists, despite the discussable nature of the topics, so that a topic such as theories of personality, for example, might include a few handouts and lists of Freudian concepts.

During the unit on death and dying, the teacher handed out a lengthy questionnaire on attitudes toward death. Such ostensibly impersonal questions as "When did you first become aware of death?" were followed by more personal inquiries about one's views on the life after death, killing for moral reasons, dying for a purpose, and so on. One set of questions asked whether a student had ever considered suicide, and if so by what means, and with what degree of actual success. On the way out of class, I asked if the teacher had designed the questionnaire and whether he had ever had any qualms about asking about suicide in such graphic terms (such as checking off preferences for different methods). He answered that he got the questionnaire "from somewhere." At first he had had second thoughts about the suicide section until he "checked with a psychologist," who told him it is impossible to put ideas of suicide into another person's head and that people come to this act on their own.

Then Mr Hansen said, "Maybe you wondered what I was doing at the door during class. It was about this boy that sits in this seat [he points]. I was checking with the counselor because of his past background." He went on to say that except for this one course the boy was confined to a mental hospital for attempting suicide about three months before. The teacher had "checked with" the school guidance counselor who in turn had "checked with" the boy's psychologist. It was determined that the boy was indeed a high risk for future suicide attempts but that "it was okay for him to sit in on this." The students would exchange questionnaires, which would bear no names, and count the responses checked for each question. That this boy would, if answering honestly, have been the only student to check "attempted suicide, with high probability of success" was less important than his presence for the "covering of the material." (If he had answered untruthfully he could have been subjected to added strain, because many in the class knew of his suicide attempt.) "Learning the content" was not

189

confused with relating to it, even at the risk of a boy's life. The discussion placed the topic on the usual casual level; the field trip for the unit was a trip to a funeral home.

In addition to exacerbating the split between personal and institutional knowledge, knowledge control that was not successfully resisted by students had the effect of individualizing classroom interaction. The individualization of rewards and sanctions in schools, in terms of credits and failures earned, is fairly widely understood. What the control strategies in the observed classes accomplished, beyond the power of the credentialing system, was to make resistance more private. As students acquiesced to controlled patterns of classroom interaction (or non-interaction), their resistance to the resulting content became silent and hidden (knowable to the researcher only through interviews). Because there was no discussion or exchanges of papers (except to mark each other's answers on multiple-choice tests), students tended to feel isolated in their alienation from the content. There was no mechanism for collective response. Occasionally they would grumble together about the tests or about the boredom of the transparencies, or protest with a groan the announcement of a difficult-sounding topic (before the teacher backed off from it). But the teachers had successfully prevented the kind of collective resistance that a few of them recalled being challenged by during the anti-war movement. The vulnerabilities within the patterns of control – including widespread student cynicism toward oversimplifications, student rejection of facts that contradicted their own information, and teacher alienation at having to apologize for assignments in order to get students to cooperate – remained too hidden to be seen as emancipatory possibilities. So long as they are hidden from participants, the cycle of alienation and control will presumably persist. So long as they are hidden from researchers, these patterns of control will be seen as the inevitable result of schooling in a capitalist society. As we have seen, however, domination is not mechanistically inevitable, but highly responsive to institutional variability. And with teachers, domination in the classroom may also be interpreted as resistance to their own alienation and lack of control within the larger institution. These many layers of control and resistance must be examined if our theories of cultural reproduction are to be founded in reality, are to help us understand the complex effects of schooling, and are to be instruments of social change.

# 8
# Economies of learning[1]

Adults who visit high-school classrooms are often struck by the dullness of the lessons. Those who visit systematically note the overwhelming prevalence of boring content, dull presentations and bored but patient students (Goodlad, 1983). We have seen that the dull presentations are not caused merely by poor teacher preparation or teacher burnout, but by deliberate, often articulated, decisions teachers have made to control the students by controlling the content. The effects of these controlling mechanisms on the content and on the students themselves provide additional keys to understanding what appears to be low instructional quality.

Defensive, controlling teaching does more than make content boring; it transforms the subject content from "real world" knowledge into "school knowledge," an artificial set of facts and generalizations whose credibility lies no longer in its authenticity as a cultural selection but in its instrumental value in meeting the obligations teachers and students have within the institution of schooling. The potential richness of such content as historical events, and their interpretations and the conflicts inherent in economic systems, are flattened into the lists, slogans and mystifications that defensive presentations comprise.

As the course content is transformed into "school knowledge," there is little incentive for the student to become involved in that content. It is there to be mastered, traded for a grade and, as some students have said, deliberately forgotten afterward. When school knowledge is so divorced from the lively cultural content of societal experience, students receive it, but do not understand where it comes from, nor how, nor why, it became a part of school requirements. Defensive teaching, then, also transforms the role of the student. Instead of being expected to master skills and content

191

until they are their own to understand and apply, students are expected to be participants in an exchange of information entirely remote from their experience except that of going through school requirements. In the case where the knowledge is seen as having only instrumental value, we can liken the role of student to that of *client*.

Clients of bureaucracies are in a role of dependence, needing a service. To obtain a service, the client gives evidence of meeting a requirement of the bureaucracy. To obtain unemployment benefits, for example, a person must submit proof of job loss and proof of current job search. Original, creative, elaborated applications for jobless benefits receive no more attention, and no more compensation, than those with the minimum basic information. In much the same way, defensive teaching at its worst reduces the role of the student to that of a client. School knowledge becomes the medium of exchange, the evidence of eligibility for benefits, in this case a diploma. The client role for students is especially evident when the course content is to be covered but not taken seriously.

Not all defensive teaching takes the student role to this extreme. Where content *is* to be taken seriously, learned, even believed, but where students are still passive receivers rather than participants, their role may be more like that of *consumer*. They do not work with the teacher producing (or organizing or evaluating) the course content, but they are to see more information in it than if it were only instrumental rather than substantive. The metaphor of consumer of school knowledge is not entirely apt, as there is little actual market freedom whereby students may select within the course what to study, but they are consumers in being receivers and users. And they do have choices as to the level of mastery they wish to attain and, more important (according to student interviews), the degree to which they find the content credible, that is, worth remembering after the test.

The nature of defensive teaching is to transform the role of the student into client or consumer rather than active learner. What is interesting in these social studies classes is that the political and economic content processed through defensive teaching confirmed the message conveyed by the nature of instruction; the economy, like the classroom, works best when students/clients/consumers are passive recipients of its benefits rather than active participants. The implication of defensive teaching strategies is that if students do not disrupt the pace of lectures or question the authority or expertise of the teacher, the teacher will not place many demands on the student working for the course credit. The parallel implication for social studies instruction is that we should trust the system, trust the experts and learn only a little to get by; we are receivers of public policy, not shapers of it. By following the processing of social studies content through defensive teaching strategies to the resulting school knowledge and client roles for students, we can see the messages of instructional method and content merge; the hidden curriculum becomes the overt curriculum.

Within the tension between educative goals and control goals in public schools, social studies curriculum has rested on the rhetoric of educative goals in the name of democracy – education for democratic participation. Although content analyses of social studies texts have shown social studies, especially history, to be very selective in defining whose history American history really is (Anyon, 1978, Fitzgerald, 1979), the ideal of the discipline has been "citizenship" education. Interestingly, those teachers who talked at all about the purpose of their course in this sample articulated that ideal frequently and fervently. They saw in the teaching of history and economics a mission, a chance to make students aware of their governmental and economic systems so that they could be good citizens, so could make wise choices. The teachers most likely to teach as though students were merely clients tended to define good choices as those that showed appreciation for our institutions. The teachers who wanted students to inquire, to study, to learn varied opinions, but whose instructional methods did not match their content goals, were more likely to treat students as consumers of knowledge rather than as mere institutional clients. Also, those in intrusive or remote administrative settings were more likely to reduce the student role to that of client than were those teachers in a supportive environment. These are rough sketches of the dynamics involved, not typologies. None of the teachers, as we have said (with the one possible exception) taught defensively all the time; none was consistent in keeping students in client roles or consumer roles all semester. Instead, as purposes shifted, teachers would accommodate to the particular strategies which helped them maintain authority over content and efficiency over classroom processes. By examining the general patterns of client and consumer roles for students, then considering some variations from these patterns, we can better understand how the tension between controlling students and educating them can result in unintended consequences for the course content and for the student.

## Classroom clients

Although the transformation of student role ultimately involves the reward system of the school as a whole, the calculation of benefits most typically takes place within the reward structure of the particular classroom. The final pay-off is the course credit, but the immediate determinants of compliance are the demands and rewards the particular teacher lays out. The teacher whose instructional methods most clearly reduced course content to a component of bureaucratic exchange was Mr Schmidt, who lectured each day from outlines printed on transparencies. The exchange was simple; each day he went through several transparencies in the course outline, reading them to the class with or without slight elaborations of fact, or standing aside while students silently copied. This teaching strategy relied mainly on lists. Very complex historical events and economic issues on the course outline that portended an interesting, informative course, were transformed by Mr Schmidt's outline into items in lists, into headings and sub-headings of outlines. The outline gave consistency to chaotic events, economistic jargon to potentially controversial or personal issues, and eliminated the potential for debate or even question. The strategy for controlling content was the outline and list; the strategy for controlling students was the notebook. To keep students listening (and attending class), Mr Schmidt gave only open-notebook tests. Students who had copied the outline verbatim could answer the test questions, which had to have verbatim agreement with the outline.

The content took the guise of official, consensus history. Labor history became, abstracted from the lives of workers and managers, the list of "labor's tools" and "management's weapons" against each other. There was no implication that anyone in the class might be, now or later, a worker or manager (many were workers). History, and especially economics, took the form of "policies," and policy implied Washington. Most students took notes; few made high grades on the tests because answers could not deviate from the transparency. This was one of the first classes where students began in interviews, without being asked, to question the credibility

194

of the course content. Interestingly, they did not do so in class. They learned right away that this man's outlines were "student-neutral"; that is, they were prepared many years before and allowed no consideration of the needs or abilities of a particular student or class. When asked in interviews if they had ever studied "poverty," no one in this class related that word to the six-weeks' unit on the Great Depression, Mr Schmidt's favorite unit. He saw it as the basis for understanding the New Deal and all subsequent American policy. The students saw it as a section of an outline they needed to have in their notes. If they did not connect poverty to the New Deal, they could be forgiven since that unit was also a series of lists, mostly of New Deal agencies by their names and acronyms. Students interested in history had to talk with their parents, or so they reported. Others sat very quietly, taking what notes they could, and venturing fewer comments or questions than in any other class observed. Having seen one or two classmates offer personal observations or ask questions about events, only to be rebuffed, the students quickly decided to copy, answer short-answer tests, but not internalize the content. Mr Schmidt's lesson, that the system is to be trusted because of all the fine institutions created during the New Deal, was lost on his students because they did not feel they could trust the course content without some discussion and variant opinions. He transformed their classroom role to client in a simple exchange, but did not succeed in having them agree with his lesson. Ironically, he probably was more successful in contributing to their self-perception as clients since in interviews they were the students who most often shifted answers to unidentified "they's," when asked their opinion about policy issues. These students had no sense that they could find out what they needed to know; they hoped another "they" would tell them after they finished school.

No other teacher so effectively kept students in a client role all semester. Miss Langer, however, did rely on students' calculations of exchange to maintain the orderly pace in her class. Since her ideal of "real" participating students was a mere memory in the absence of ability group tracking, Miss Langer wanted a tight rein on the "masses" she felt herself to be spoon feeding. She controlled the content with very organized chronologies of history based on presidential administrations. The message she gave, in her teaching and in the extended interviews, was that the teacher was

the source of "the story" of American history. Questions or volunteered opinions merited negative "class participation" grades in
her class for slowing up the pace she needed to maintain to cover
the material. That material emphasized the need for stability in
American institutions and, like Mr Schmidt's, was focused on
top-down policies that shaped those institutions. Her uncritical
chronology of presidential administrations and their degree of success with legislative programs implied trust for whomever is in
power; again, there was no implication that any of these students
would be in policymaking positions (a reversal of the ethos prevailing in her top track classes, according to a former student from
those years).

Both Miss Langer and Mr Schmidt taught at Forest Hills, where
the administration was perceived as remote and unsupportive. Another teacher who reduced students to a client role taught at Freeburg, where the administration's erratic policies kept the school in
a state of siege. While he was less affected by those policies than
the other teachers, Mr Jackson did keep his students in a client
role, where a simple exchange between simplified content and
course credit prevailed. In his case, he was reacting less against
administrative structures than from his own lack of expertise in the
subject. His world studies course raced around the globe; his own
knowledge of many of these countries was barely more than
that of his students. To have them ask questions would have been
embarrassing to this teacher aspiring to be an administrator. For
him, then, the client role for students helped sustain his authority
over content. He presented most of the countries first on a map,
then in lists. Place names, customs, leaders and products had an
exotic ring that carried an authority all their own, though quite
often Mr Jackson would make a comment about the strangeness
or quaintness of a foreign custom. In this sweeping survey, students
picked up the message that one does not need more than superficial
knowledge about these other countries; the US is the "best" and
able to deal with all the diversity and conflict. Our customs are
normal; "theirs" are strange. The passivity of world citizens in this
class matches the passivity necessary for US citizens, and for classroom behavior, in the Langer and Schmidt classes. It is interesting
to note that the three teachers who felt most optimistic and unre-
flective about US governmental and economic systems, and who in
personal classroom style were assertive rather than defensive,

nevertheless relied on simple lists and facts to keep their students in line and to keep them from questioning the "system."

## Classroom consumers

Most of the teachers observed used a combination of teaching styles and strategies. Some taught defensively only when they felt threatened by a particular administrative policy (de-tracking), by a certain group of students; or by lack of confidence with the course material or more open instructional methods. The teachers who kept students in the role of consumer of teacher-supplied knowledge tended to be those who wanted to present rich content but who were reacting against administrative conditions by reducing their own workload (and thus student assignments) or those who had not resolved the tension between their own genuine goals for equipping students and the need they felt to be the source of all content and classroom control.

Mr Carrico vacillated between opening up instruction to make demands on students to invite their discussion and controlling the content himself. He was known as an excellent economics teacher who had developed original metaphors and models for explaining difficult concepts. A part of his history course involved having students read paired readings of opposing viewpoints; they interviewed senior citizens about the Depression; they had to write critiques of books they had read. He challenged them to answer questions and often presented difficult material having no specific right answer. At other times he was so dogmatic that students were afraid to disagree with him. On factual matters they were willing to answer questions, but on matters of opinion they felt ill-equipped to match his clever retorts. Through this mixture of teaching strategies he gave equivocal messages about their own role, both in the economy and in class. Several students expressed, again without being asked, a fear of challenging him, or even of asking a question. He took this to mean, much as Miss Langer had after de-tracking, that students could not think analytically enough to rely on their opinion rather than his.

After several students said they were uncomfortable with his analyses, two categories of "resisters" seemed to emerge: those who did not know enough to decide whether his interpretations were right; and those who were beginning to have experiences of their own which added to their understanding of topics being covered in the course. The former group usually had something to say (in interviews) about *waiting*. Unsure of the authority on which the teacher spoke, but unable to ask questions in class that showed this uncertainty, they were memorizing his presentations for tests but bracketing them as credible knowledge until "later." This unwillingness to appropriate school-supplied knowledge, even from a well-respected teacher (many respected his views on economics because he was thought to be wealthy), got them playing the exchange game, not so differently from the "clients" in the more controlled classes.

One girl serves as an example of a student whose experiences outside class determined the credibility of course content for her. A very thoughtful girl, Kathy had taken a job volunteering at a residential hospital for severely retarded and handicapped children. Her compassion for the children had led her to get to know something about their families. In her interview she said that she liked Mr Carrico's course very much, but she was unsure how much to trust the course content. He was a strong advocate of nuclear power. She had discovered that many of the retarded children she cared for had parents who worked as X-ray technicians or radiologists. She was beginning to make a connection between environmental risks and their human costs. She did not feel expert, and so never mentioned this in class in discussions of energy, technology or other topics which might have prompted her to voice her concern. But she did know that information she learned on her own weighed in her personal career choices and concerns. In class, however, she played along as consumer of teacher-supplied content.

Mr Carrico, as strong chair, was in control of his department's resources and taught with confidence in his style and command of subject. Where his controlling of content came partly from that confidence and relative autonomy, Mr Reznick and Mr Lennon at Freeburg taught defensively in response to a more erratic and controlling administrative setting. Both had goals of really instructing students in the complexities of economic realities. Mr Reznick specialized in consumer economics and Mr Lennon, in his history class as well as in his economics class, focused more on economic theories, events and policies on a societal level. Both were well-informed; neither was provided with adequate teaching materials.

Mr Reznick's book was simplistic and out-of-date. Mr Lennon was always waiting for the overdue copies of his text.

Their books were not their only handicaps at Freeburg. The overall climate of the school was so geared toward behavior controls that serious academics were absent in all but a few classes. So, with the addition of short attention spans and low student expectations, both teachers were working against the odds of anything of educational significance happening at the school. In addition, both of these teachers felt unrewarded for going to the trouble of assignments which were meaningful to the students but time-consuming to grade. A part of their decision to keep students in a consumer role, depending on teacher-supplied content, was shaped by these two factors.

Mr Reznick was thoroughly interested in economic issues. He gave interesting and timely presentations on advertising, including the deceptiveness and psychology used in marketing techniques with which the students were very familiar. He invited a series of guest speakers on such topics as energy conservation, auctions, insurance and other matters about which he knew his students would soon be making decisions. He demanded a tremendous amount of himself in presenting material. He was unable to demand so much from students. One reason seemed to stem, ironically, from his desire that they learn as much as possible. Most of his students were those who were not academically strong enough to take the more theoretical economics course. His was the last chance for those not going to college to learn at school how to manage their money, understand community resources and regulatory laws available to protect them, and understand in detail how to make choices rather than be victimized in the market. For him to demand extremely difficult reading or writing assignments would cause him to lose a good many of his students, some because of weak ability and others because of attitude. The overall feeling of doing the least possible to get by was so prevalent at this school that a teacher trying to give meaningful assignments was working against an enormous inertial from the beginning. One of Mr Reznick's solutions was to give an independent project, allowing a broad range of choices. These included reading and reporting on a book related to the course; creating consumer "alert" posters; producing a film, slide show or photographic essay related to the course; visiting a consumer-related agency to interview persons responsible for poli-

199

cies affecting consumers; monitoring meetings or hearings such as a small claims court or the insurance commission. In addition, there were two very simple assignment choices: read and summarize ten magazine articles appropriate to the course; or read and summarize clippings on consumer topics. The most frequent choice was to collect and read newspaper or magazine articles or to do none of the assignments, even though that option meant failing the course.

Mr Lennon, dealing with even more complex and theoretical issues, kept students in a consumer role quite against his own choice. He would have preferred to take a lively political and intellectual interest in the course. He tried to present diverse opinions that would engage students' attention. On rare occasions he succeeded. The rest of the time, his students remained very passive; his lack of demanding assignments and his tendency to back away from requiring student effort in discussion or preparation for class placed students in a passive role. His course is worth looking at more closely because of the interplay between what he would have considered "real teaching" and the tendency to let students disengage in order to reduce work for himself.

Mr Lennon was, at rare times, a wonderful lecturer. His defensive teaching was all the more regrettable because, among all the teachers, he had the most engaging style when he was actually teaching. The gap between his engaging the students and his letting them "consume" course content came between the official content of the course and his extended asides. Interestingly, it was during his asides that he did his best and most effective teaching. In lectures on the "official" lesson, he rambled, simplified, made lists and asked few questions of students; in response, students read novels, wrote letters and carried on conversations while he talked. He assigned reading, but only a few seemed to read the material or master what they read. Embittered over years of frozen pay rates and increasingly controlling administrative policies for teachers and students, Mr Lennon decided that assigning written work to students meant more work for him than he was being paid to do. This, plus the long wait for a class set of texts, made him depend on lecturing more than on student involvement with the content. His lively accounts of historical events, his unorthodox (for this community) political interpretations, and his rich supply of anecdotes (many of them personal) should have made him one of the best teachers observed. Because many of his presentations were defensive simplifications, to the students this all came through (as we have mentioned in first describing him) as "social studies" – official school knowledge with little relevance to themselves.

Although he demanded little of students, his openness and sense of humor did invite questions at times, and his lack of walls between his personal knowledge and the classroom version of economics gave rich possibilities to his teaching. Sometimes these were realized. In discussing the Taft-Hartley Act, Mr Lennon could have done what the other teachers did in listing the four or five major provisions and at least two times in history when policy was changed because of this law. Instead, he introduced the topic, then told about being a college student hired to work on a form-setting crew for construction. He told about not having enough money to pay the union dues and having it loaned to him by another worker so he could work to support his wife and baby. When he explained the difference between union and closed shop, a boy asked, "Is it true that when Republicans are in [power], there are fewer strikes because the president puts them down?" Mr Lennon explained the difference between using injunctions and using the threat of injunctions and other powers to close strikes. The boy proceeded with other questions: "Are they ever used against teachers?" and later, "Are strikes ever called against unions, by their own employees?"

Mr Lennon answered with examples from the organization that managed a local union trust and from a neighboring school system. He took these as serious questions, intended to elicit information, and he answered them both with "textbook" answers and personal information. He explained that in the case of the school system the arbitrator of the dispute said that "this isn't what the contract means even though it says it." The boy got a lesson in the politics and uncertainties of contract law. The exchange in its substance is not remarkable. What *is* so remarkable is that after hundreds of hours of observing in social studies classrooms, there are so few such exchanges to report. (Less remarkable is that only a few students in the class were paying attention.) Far more often, the student questions were held privately, perhaps coming out in interviews, if the student was thinking along with the lesson at all.

In Mr Lennon's class, students were more involved and he was more solicitous of their involvement in the unofficial content of the course – the treatment of current events at the beginning of class, the reminiscences, the digressions. Testable material took on a different tone for both student and teacher and implied different roles from their livelier interchanges. The union example is one of the few exceptions where the "official" content engaged student response to the degree that the unofficial content did.

Even in Mr Lennon's best teaching moments there were rarely more than a handful of students engaged in discussing and thinking along with him. This was typical of the classes observed. It gave the impression that the students had nothing to offer, no ideas of their own. One lesson transcript contains the names of a number of students who volunteered answers to a question. It led to what was noted in the transcript margins as a "real teaching moment." It shows that students do have things on their minds, despite their apparent passivity:

Mr Lennon: Take thirty to sixty seconds and think of a reform you would like to make in American society and why.
(The answers came quickly and spiritedly.)
Tim: Murders should have the same punishment as the crime. Shoot the one who shoots someone.
Mr Lennon: How would that help American society?
Tim: Cut down on crime.
Mike: Stop tearing up all the wildlife, building big houses, etc.
Mr Lennon: That would help the environment ...
Bill: Restrictions on foreign cars.
Mr Lennon: To help the US economy?
Lynn: Come back to me.
Dick: Uh ...
Ricky: Get rid of the Susan B. Anthony dollar. I confuse it with quarters.
Tim: They don't use it much.
Lucy: Dress up like whales and dolphins and club the Japanese and Russians. Let them feel what it's like. God put them [whales and dolphins] here ...
Luann: End busing. [There was no busing in this school except to bring rural children to town schools.]
Sally: Bring trains back.
Mindy: Reduce taxes for hunters. They pay for wildlife management.
Dick: [Still does not have an answer.]

Lucy: Spend more money to research colonizing the moon. We're overpopulating the world.

Tim: Build space cities with skyscrapers. No blacks. A cleaner environment.

Mr Lennon: *Which ones of these might the Progressives have been in favor of?* [emphasis added]

The previous day's discussion of the Progressives had followed a rather standard lecture pattern, with some lists (Progressive Party concerns, participating sectors of the population, their reform policies), some extended descriptions, a few students taking notes and others paying scant attention. To apply that "dispensed" information, Mr Lennon had started this day's lesson with the concerns of the students, affirming that they too could think, could reason ("tell why"), and could relate academic content to current social problems.

This was not a remarkable demonstration of innovative teaching nor of especially informed or carefully planned instruction. It is actually a fairly straightforward discussion technique, to begin with the concerns of the participants. What is remarkable is that among the classes observed, such a session, even if only for a few minutes, involving a number of students and having no walls between their "real" knowledge and school content was rare. The lesson went on a few more minutes with a sustained level of interaction. The students had mostly questions, lacking enough background reading to contribute information, but they did ask questions that made Progressivism make sense to them: "Were they liberal or conservative?" "Would they like the railroads?" The teacher's answers were brief and only partially helpful but in answering their questions he was more likely to get his own questions answered: "Did they have a position on integration/segregation?" and "Would they favor or oppose busing?' "What is [was] their approach to people and people's problems?" The lesson quickly moved on to a few facts about Theodore Roosevelt and Woodrow Wilson, lapsing back into a consumer role for students. But while it lasted, it showed the potential, even at the school with the most intrusive administrative policies and the least professional-feeling teachers, to go beyond a model of passive consuming for students.

For the teachers at the school whose administration supported academic efforts, the role of students as consumers was prompted by a different set of dynamics. We have said that at Nelson High the teachers demanded more of themselves and of each other and they were much more comfortable with student involvement. Their emphasis on practical academics assumed that students would be active in their communities, would be making purchases, choosing jobs, voting in elections and in general participating in life as active adults. The consumer economics unit, the futures unit, the study of the Constitution and Bill of Rights all proceeded as though they mattered to real life experience. The quality of materials, many of them designed by the teachers; the level of teacher intellect and commitment; the expectations teachers held for students – all point to the power of school organization to help overcome the inertia described in the other schools and in most of our high schools.

What was not fully developed was a role for the students that matched, or even came close to, the role of the teacher in the teaching–learning exchange. In Mr Lancaster's class, he was content to let students opt for a consumer role because he saw his goal as stretching their minds, whether they wanted it or not. He saw himself as the chief resource in building their vocabulary, introducing them to important ideas and shapes of ideas and in testing them in ways that made them think rather than repeat facts. He rarely had them with him, but saw any progress as more than would have come with traditional teaching.

Both in class and in interviews, he specifically disavowed a link between a receptor–consumer role in class and one's future place in the economy. He wanted to sharpen and challenge their imaginations because, as he said over and over, "I have this great fear that we will back into the future." He wanted them to be aware of choices and of the ramifications of choices so that they would participate in shaping their personal futures as well as that of the society and of the planet. He did not see a contradiction between their passive, even resistant, classroom posture and the message he wanted to get across in the content.

Mr Hobbs had students in active roles at times and at other times worked with them as consumers of the knowledge that he supplied through lecture, personally prepared readings or a text. He much preferred to have students discuss and think but was having to bring them along slowly because the issues of the course, including the rights of the individual versus those of the state, were

204

new to them. They were not accustomed to teaching which had no definite right answer, and they were not accustomed to arriving at a consensus as a class only to have the teacher raise another tough question. Like Mr Lancaster, Mr Hobbs wanted students to be active in their lives, especially in ethical and policy choices, and so did not want the classroom consumer role to carry over beyond the classroom. His role was in building a base for more complex thought.

One teacher who got the advantage of this building of ideas was Mr Guthrie, who had the same students three years later in his science and economics of energy course. This course demonstrates more than any other the way teachers can manipulate choices in the roles they want students to take and in the mesh between content and instructional modes. The purpose of the science and economics of energy course was to de-mystify *energy*, including both the science of energy resource discovery and distribution and the economics of energy consumption and conservation. The course was outlined in such a way that students were given the tools to analyze energy resource and consumption data for themselves so that they could make personal decisions and participate in policy decisions which made wise use of energy resources. The emphasis was very much on equipping students, on enabling them, both in the classroom treatment of the information and in their future application of the knowledge gained. *De-mystify* is the appropriate term for the approach the teachers took in gathering material and producing the curriculum for this course. They drew on printed material from coal, electric power and gas industries, from regulatory agencies, from governmental bodies involved in energy and from scientific and commercial data-gathering sources such as the American Petroleum Institute and the National Geographic Society. The lab manual they wrote for the course made clear the active role students were to take as they worked through graphs, formulas, intricate technical language and charts. Students learned to calculate reserves, compare btu conversion potentials from energy sources and estimate doubling times of depletion or consumption. None of the exercises was just-for-school busy work. The data were real, the issues were real and the processes learned were those used by chemists, market analysts, physicists, engineers and refiners who work with energy. The scientific portion of the course was heavily dependent on student involvement and encouraged group work to complete the difficult calculations and charting. No evidence of artificially simplified or mystified content was evident.

The same cannot be said of the political, social and economic aspects of the discussion of energy use. The teachers felt strongly that they were, as they put it, "pro-energy," not advocating one form over another. However, this meant that they endorsed nuclear power at least as an alternative in the interim between declining non-renewable hydrocarbon resources and the technology adequate for dependence on renewable forms such as solar and geothermal. They were not against conservation but led students through elaborate calculations which demonstrated the inadequacy of conservation to compensate for more than a few percentage points in the gap between declining reserves and increased energy use as more of the world industrialized. The economics of energy sections were based on the premise of maintaining "our way of life as we know it." This phrase occurred over and over. In this regulatory- and conservation-oriented state, many families and businesses were actively converting to energy-saving technologies and conservation techniques, from household insulation to industrial reclamation. It would have been essential in the course to specify whether "our way of life" indicated this new push for conservation, the old wasteful ways, or something different that encompassed the broad society or was narrowed to specific family differences. A few student questions attempted to break through this slogan but were met only with affirmations of being "pro-energy" in all its forms.

The economics of energy portion of the course involved mystification at two levels. The first was at the level of slogans such as the one above. The other was to keep the presentation of economic aspects very close to that of a traditional economics course which introduces students to such technical vocabulary as utility, value, price, discretionary spending and cost of living. These definitions were stipulated or explained in relation to energy but were not brought down to the level of family or societal decisions about energy production and use.

The teachers were attempting to keep this part of the course uncontroversial and unemotional, even though they mentioned throughout the course that energy was a highly controversial topic because it was so central to the economy and to people's lives. They invited speakers to represent utility companies but did not invite speakers who criticized nuclear power because they defined these as "emotional" and not factual. Students did not question this priority in class but confined most of their classroom questions to clarifying technical terms and calculations. In interviews, however, they expressed frustration at not being able to hear and discuss the *issues* surrounding energy. They were well aware that the course placed them in two contradictory roles. They were without exception grateful to be introduced to the vocabulary and technicalities of energy and often shared these with their parents. The bracketing of the "emotional" side of energy frustrated them and blunted the credibility of that side of the course. The teachers, sincerely attempting to enable students to be participants and producers rather than passive consumers and clients, would have been surprised to find that students felt this suspicion of the credibility of the course. Their own frustrations centered more on the lack of time for the extensive amount of content they wanted to deal with; they wanted a two-semester course, partly to allow for more student participation. It is likely, given their commitment to enabling students, that more time could have been what was needed for them to open up the political and economic aspects of energy for student consideration.

**De-skilling and the role of students**

The reform reports criticize ritualized teaching because it seems to reflect teachers' lack of subject-matter expertise, it ignores what we know about the psychology of learning and the need for supportive learning environments, and because these two incompetencies together bolster the case that we are not attracting the "best" people into teaching. The implication is that bored students will be less committed to learning and therefore will not learn as much as they should.

The case studies presented here point up basic fallacies in this logic. The first is that in looking at *how much* is learned, we fail to look at the nature of *what* is learned. And the focus on "how much" ignores the impact of such instruction on those who do "achieve" within ritualized patterns of teaching and learning. The ways of knowing into which they are initiated helps set students' expectations of themselves as people who can learn, ask questions, contribute new answers, or who must be dependent on others to tell them what they need to know.

The defensive teaching shows that the participation by teachers in their own de-skilling has equally serious consequences for the content and students in their classes. Simplified, mystified content becomes so artificial that it loses its credibility of substance and retains only whatever value it has in the exchange student effort for course grade or graduation credit.

The role of students in such a setting is more complex. If content is taken seriously but "spoon fed" to them, we say they are in the role of consumers of classroom knowledge, receiving (with some degree of choice) but not participating. If the content has been truncated in its meanings by reduction to lists or mystified slogans, then the content has only instrumental value for the students. As clients of a credentialing bureaucracy, they exchange minimum participation for a standard credit. The content of the exchange becomes only incidental. If it is a topic that interests them and arouses frustration for its lack of adequate treatment in class, then they may become cynical or skeptical about that course content or school knowledge in general.

We cannot say that students are being de-skilled without some conceptual notion of child development and the acquisition and discovery of skills that progress through the child's education. But we may say that these teachers, when they reduce students to client roles or even to consumer roles, are helping to de-skill the *role* of the student. They are separating the organic processes of learning from the process of institutional exchange. The links between individual and craft are prevented from developing, at least in a school setting.

This has been especially noticeable in these social studies classes, where the rhetoric of the discipline and of interviewed teachers is that of educating students for democratic participation. The message of the social studies content in the most controlling of these classes is that the system can be trusted, it does not need to be questioned, it does not need our active involvement. The classroom rewards for passive student roles have confirmed the value of acquiescence. A de-contextualized assessment of social studies content may reveal boring lectures, shallow survey texts and disengaged students. By placing these elements in their organizational context, we see that the overt behaviors are symptoms of imbedded patterns of control, not merely failures within patterns of educational efforts.

# 9
# Contradictions of control

Teachers reducing content to rituals of lists, apologizing for assignments; students quietly engaging in minimum efforts for a course credit, doing the least to get by in school; defensive teaching, and its transformation of cultural content into "school knowledge" – it all brings us back to the Gryphon of Alice's wonderland: "That's the reason they are called lessons, because they lessen from day to day."

The lessening of educational quality is now the center of intense public debate, sparked by several extensive studies of American schools – Goodlad (1983); the Carnegie Foundation (Boyer, 1983); Sizer (1984); and the US Department of Education (*A Nation at Risk*, 1983). Because these studies investigated the broad nationwide pattern of school problems, they were unable to focus in detail on the internal conflict between administrative control goals and education goals in public schools. Yet all these studies assume that schools are supposed to educate, not just control students. All these studies stress that our schools are in trouble because of the declining quality of instruction.

Tragically, policymakers are reacting to these studies by passing knee-jerk reforms that are imposing even more controls on teachers. The reforms standardize curriculum, increase teacher paperwork and proliferate ever more testing of both teachers and students. Easy to implement, these reforms originate with top-down management, further divesting teachers (and sometimes even local school administrators) of the power to make decisions about their courses and students. They threaten to push the de-skilling of educators even beyond what we have witnessed in the schools in the preceding chapters. These reforms are completely insensitive to the need to balance education and control goals in public schools. As a result, the reforms only heighten the contradictions of control and worsen the cycle of defensive teaching and student apathy. The result is more than the ironic effect of lowering the potential for meaningful teaching and learning rather than improving educational quality.[1] The failure to address the contradictions inherent in the organizational tensions in our schools may create even greater contradictions between school knowledge and the knowledge students need about their world. As the internal contradictions foster greater external contradictions, the legitimacy of schools, and thus the public's willingness to invest in possibilities of school improvement, may be seriously undermined.

It is at this point that intensive case studies can be helpful in going beyond the broader reports. On the one hand, it is heartening to see that data gathered in the small sample of schools in this book are consistent with the generalized pattern of flattened content, mediocre instructional methods and disengaged students depicted in the nationwide samples. On the other hand, this smaller set of case studies has offered an opportunity to unpackage the many relationships often hidden at the bottom levels of school bureaucracy.

The teacher-level perspective is so important because it is at that level that the contradictions of the social control purposes and the educative purposes of schools are resolved. The teachers are supposed to juggle subject matter, student skills, and at the same time student behavior and the technicalities of grades, attendance and course credits. We have often ignored this basic truth, because we have thought of education and control functions of schools as somewhat insulated or "loosely coupled" activities. After all, the divided nature of our high schools relegated business matters to administrators and academic pursuits to teachers.

The case studies in this book, however, demonstrate that this is not the reality of school organization. The control goals center on aggregates of students and routinized procedures for dealing with them. The educational goals imply unpredictable outcomes among students who as individuals vary in abilities, interests and development. The teachers are at the juncture of these two purposes. In the historical period when large-scale high schools were created, the administrative structure took this management–worker split in order to justify to external constituents (taxpayers, industrialists, management consultants) the efficiency of public schools. That efficiency was a requisite for legitimacy. As it evolved, these control structures became convenient mechanisms for imposing ever more credentialing and testing requirements upon students, even though the administrator and teacher remained formally separate in their day-to-day activities.

The case studies in this book offer a window into the effects of these controls when they are not kept in balance with the educational purposes of schools. The examples of poor teaching among the teachers described in the case study schools are the result of a vicious cycle that cannot be simply explained as poor teacher preparation or even faulty hiring criteria. Instead, what might on the surface appear to be untrained teaching was in fact the active response of some of the best teachers observed as they confronted the organization which rewarded their ability to control students more than their ability "really to teach." Their defensive teaching was no accident, nor a factor of simple burn-out. It was an accommodation to a complex organization which embodied conflicting goals and gave powerless teachers the responsibility of resolving the conflicts.

## Administrative context and patterns of adaptation

The four case studies were deliberately chosen to analyze variations in the degree to which administrators directly involved with curriculum and teaching. Forest Hills showed an apparently distant relationship not supportive of quality instruction. At Freeburg High, the administration became very involved – primarily, however, to keep students "in their place." At Maizeville High, the administration was also preoccupied with student control, but a "strong chair" operated to buffer the teachers. To the degree that chairman supported educational goals, the teachers benefited, but to the extent the chairman had supported the principal's concern for controlling student behavior, the result could have been as bad as at Freeburg High. Only in Nelson High did the administration actively provide *incentives* for quality teaching. The dramatic variation – even at the individual high school level – illustrates how important the administrative context can be for shaping the quality of instruction. Likewise, the variations show the fragility of the potential for improvement, especially if new management-oriented reforms sustain the tendency of school organization to emphasize social control goals.

211

Forest Hills High is probably most typical of American high schools, with its administrative remoteness from teaching activities. This remoteness does not mean that administrative priorities had little effect on curriculum, or on students' learning. The patterns of defensive teaching were first observed at this school. Teachers at this school were most articulate in attributing their choices of instructional method and their view of a consensus curriculum to their need to establish authority in a school where teacher views had little effect on school policy. They stated, without being asked, that their own knowledge of the subject was broader than what they permitted in class presentations, but that imperatives to preserve efficiency in a school with few supports for teacher effort made them limit content and discussions of it by students. They believed their model of teaching to be the only choice within the constraints imposed by school administrators to keep the school smooth-running and the content aimed at graduation requirements. In helping everybody pass, and letting no one dominate class discussion, they set an evenness which protected their own efforts, even while it contradicted their stated hopes that the course content could help students understand their country and its institutions.

Does the Forest Hills example lead to the conclusion that administrators should be more involved in educational aspects of the school? Two of our schools have shown that closeness which is merely intrusive rather than supportive can also be detrimental to teachers' willingness to open their store of knowledge to students. At Freeburg High, the administration was preoccupied with student behavior problems. This set up a climate which drained off teacher energies in patrolling duties while inadvertently promoting student resistance to these behavior controls. That student resistance not only grew into new discipline problems but also carried over into student attitudes toward classes. Students became very apathetic about academics because they saw the staff giving too little attention to it. Monitoring students took precedence over teaching them. To gain student compliance with even minimal assignments, teachers had to make class "pleasant," or at least tolerable, rather than demanding. Far from breaking the cycle of lowered expectations, the preoccupation with school "discipline" only worsened it.

The organization at Maizeville High shows that a strong-chair arrangement can temper somewhat an administration's preoccupation with student control, but even then teachers tended to back off from difficult assignments or complex lectures. Having a strong chair helped keep the staff from being overwhelmed by administrative concern for students who were tardy or skipping class. It gave not only an organizational basis for teachers' exercise of professional judgment (that of the chair himself and that which he helped solicit and implement from some of the others in the department), but helped overcome the privatized modes of resistance at the other schools. Here, rather than resist by controlling their students (thereby hurting both the students and their own potential for classroom efficacy in classes where students were in turn resisting), they could collectively act to shape at least some of the factors governing their teaching. As we have seen, they rarely took advantage of this latitude in opening content up to their students in ways that demanded student involvement as well as compliance. That one teacher in particular forfeited this leverage except to use the abundant resources to create seatwork and passive film-viewing demonstrates the inadequacy of this model to compensate fully for a context of low academic priorities. In addition, if the chair had not taken full advantage of his discretionary powers (and chairs in some department ments did not), there would be no administrative pressure to make instructional improvements.

The one school that stands out against the cycle of defensive teaching is Nelson High. Here teachers were rewarded (though with slim resources and more moral support than personal gain) for building curricula which brought their personal store of knowledge to the students, which affirmed their professional judgments about their subject fields and their students.

Nelson High's environment was not dramatically different from the environments of the other schools in this study. It too carried the legacy of divergent purposes. However, in this case the tension between control and education was resolved in favor of educational priorities. The order-keeping, course credits and credentials, the external accountability, were still present, but they did not overwhelm attention to teaching and learning. This school demonstrated both the possibilities and fragility of attempts to overcome the inertia of defensive teaching. This structure was not created internally by teacher resistance. Rather, when the school was established, the community, in reaction to more bureaucratized schools in neighboring communities, insisted the school be organized so as

213

to support its teachers in curriculum-building and its students in active learning. Teachers were involved in planning the building and the curriculum sequence; the program and very modest school building were planned to maximize teacher effectiveness. A simple example is the construction of department libraries and offices adjoining the main library; another is the insistence on hiring only those teachers willing to work collectively and to create curricula. The personnel policies and job divisions among administrators and teachers differed in few other ways from those at other schools; the difference is that they followed rather than preceded curricular priorities. One can easily imagine how quickly the teaching at Nelson High could be crushed by legislatively imposed standardized curricula which would further de-skill teachers, and even more artificial testing of students, which would only trivialize their encounters with school knowledge.[2]

**Control and legitimacy**

Critics may point out that the real problems with our schools do not lie in the control systems, but in low teacher salaries, poorly trained teachers, very real discipline problems including violence in some schools, and broader societal tensions which make the controls necessary. Indeed, the point of this analysis is not to suggest that a mere change in "administrative context" will reform American public schools. This study fundamentally points to the contribution of administrative structures to the cycle of defensive teaching and student disengagement which cannot be broken by resources or teacher training alone. The reason many highly qualified persons do not enter the teaching profession is that they see no way really to teach in a setting where their professional role is constantly devalued and diverted. One reason discipline is such a problem in many schools is that students are bored by course content which is so divorced from their real world that it seems not worth their efforts. For legislatures simply to raise teacher salaries and then justify this to the public by imposing more management controls is to miss the pervasive reality of defensive teaching and the increased de-skilling of teachers which this kind of solution promotes.

We are clearly at a watershed, a critical moment, in the history of American public schooling. Management models imposed in an earlier historical period have outlived their usefulness. The value of the high school credential in the marketplace, a value which once provided an incentive for students passively to accept boring curriculum content, is rendered problematic by changing economic realities. The contested legacy of our public schools has brought students, teachers and administrators to a negotiated bargain in the classroom which benefits none of these groups.

That contested legacy began with a management structure devised to legitimate the extension of secondary schooling to masses of students. That structure, designed first to socialize immigrants into American culture and to process workers into new industrial jobs, was built on top of an older legacy of educating for democratic citizenship. Once designed to extend educational opportunity, it now has the contradictory effect of contributing to the eroding of educational quality.

This central contradiction has led, as we have seen in these case studies, to a further contradiction which threatens the legitimacy of the very public schools the management model was created to guarantee; that is, the contradiction between the knowledge processed in schooling and that which teachers and students experience in their non-school lives and which comprises their broader cultural heritage. The tendency of teachers and students within this organizational context to bracket their personal knowledge in the exchange of information reducible to minimal classroom exchanges heightens the feelings of both that schooling is a ritual rather than an education. The curricular reforms of the 1960s attempted to redress the gap between school knowledge and the knowledge of subject field professionals, bringing school math and physics, for example, into closer correlation with the substance of those fields as practiced by mathematicians and physicists. Those reforms, where successful, had to deal both with the substance and forms of content as it was developed into curricula for schools.

To close the gap between personal knowledge and school knowledge, it will not be enough to add "more" information to content. The very relations within classroom and within schools will have to be transformed. For schools to be places where students have access to knowledge about their world, they will have to be places where student engagement in learning is merited by the course content and the forms of instruction. For that content and those instructional forms to emerge, we will need not only educated and

215

trained teachers. We will need organizational environments in which teachers do not have to teach *against* the reward structures and organizational priorities of their schools in order to overcome the controlling policies which encourage, even reward, them to participate in their own de-skilling. Those reward structures, as they now stand, represent attempts to legitimate secondary schooling in a time period that has long past. For schooling to be meaningful for students today, legitimate for their investment of energy as well as legitimate as a societal institution, it must take on organizational forms and internal reward structures which affirm the potential of students to learn in a complex world. Reversing ends and means, we need to reclaim the Jeffersonian legacy and legitimate school practice by what students need to know to empower them to function as citizens.

# Notes

## Chapter 1    School structure and classroom knowledge

1  Collins, R. (1979), *The Credential Society: An Historical Sociology of Education and Stratification.* See the statistics of the changing populations of secondary schools and other data related to the growing roles of schools in credentialing workers.

2  Wrigley, J. (1982), *Class Politics and Public Schools, Chicago 1900–1950.* The wealth of primary source material in this book documents beyond question the attempts to structure schools for working-class children in order to produce the attitudes necessary for a docile labor force as well as the limited skills. This quote is from Chapter 4, "Centralization versus democracy in the schools."

3  Weick, K. (1976), "Educational organizations as loosely coupled systems," *Administrative Science Quarterly.* The split between school management and the domain of teachers has developed into a loosely-coupled system, in the terminology of Weick, an organization where professionals work almost independently of each other in separate domains. This split distinguishes American secondary schools from their European (and some American private) school counterparts, in which the headmaster is in fact the head teacher. Although Horace Mann is said to have thought of himself as an educational statesman, the rise of the administrator, modeled after a business executive, attending to cost accounting, attendance and the procedural and disciplinary controls in schools, shifted school leadership away from academic leadership and toward a non-academic set of tasks. The content, instruction and evaluation of students were left to teachers. As we will see in the first high school observed for this study, the apparent split between school administrators and teachers masked a more intrusive role for administrators into the instructional domain than would have been anticipated by the tradition which has developed between the two professions. They have their separate educational programs and separate preparation for their jobs, separate journals, separate languages and theories of school practice and separate systems for evaluating their performance. While many school administrators have

217

been classroom teachers, the explicit content of their professional
preparation divorces most of them from curricular or instructional
concerns and replaces academic background with skills related to
management of school facilities, budget accounting, school law,
management of personnel and disciplinary controls of students.
4 Tyler, R. (1949), *Basic Principles of Curriculum Instruction*. This slim
volume establishes a recipe or formula for curriculum "planning"
which separates ends from means and focuses evaluation on
outcomes (proximity to "ends") rather than on processes or open-
ended or variant experiences in learning.
5 McNeil, K. (1978), "Understanding organization power: building on
the Weberian legacy" is a key theoretical source on this issue. See
also Selznick, P. (1949), *TVA and the Grass Roots: a Study in the
Sociology of Formal Organization*, Berkeley, University of California
Press.
6 Bourdieu, P. and Passeron, J. C. (1977), *Reproduction: In Education,
Society and Culture*. In this analysis of cultural reproduction in
France is demonstrated the means the upper classes, in this case in
specific traditional class formations, arrange institutions they control
in order to have those institutions appropriate their elite values and
definitions of reality as the official high culture of the society. One
intent is to create, whether direct socialization takes place, a
"habitus" or frame of mind which affirms the authority of the high
status culture. The work of Whitty and others has analyzed the role
of universities in reinforcing cultural stratification and reproduction.
In industrial societies with inherited class systems, technological
knowledge has had to contest its rise to high status knowledge; in the
US technological and scientific knowledge has enjoyed high status
since the beginnings of the republic.
7 Apple, M. W., (1982), *Education and Power*. See especially his
discussion beginning on page 42 of the differences between school's
role in knowledge distribution and knowledge production.
8 Apple, M. W. (1982c), *Education and Power*; Arnot M. and Whitty,
G. (1982). As used by both of these authors, *transformation* is used to
indicate the overcoming of institutional controls by counter-
hegemonies. In their use of the concept, resistance *transforms* the
impact of controls, including knowledge controls. This usage seems
too limited, since the transformation of culture in schools can have a
number of origins. For that reason, I am using the term here to
indicate the way the institutional controls themselves transform
culture in mediating it to students.
9 Valli, L. (1983), "Becoming clerical workers: business education and
the culture of femininity." This is an analysis of the forms of
resistance used by working-class girls to school tasks they found
meaningless (and related to meaningless job futures).
10 Hogan, D. (1982), "Education and class formation: the peculiarities
of the Americans." This analysis of the role of education and class
formation is both analytical and historical and offers important

insights into the role of schools in engendering productive and
counter-productive resistance.

## Chapter 2   Structure and choice

1 McNeil, L. (1977), "Economic dimensions of social studies curricula:
curriculum as institutionalized knowledge"; McNeil, L.,
*Contradictions of Control: a Report to the National Institute of
Education*, Chapter 2, Washington, DC; McNeil, L., "Critical theory
and ethnography in curriculum analysis," Symposium on Uses of
Ethnography to Extend Theory, Annual Meetings of American
Educational Research Association, New Orleans, 1984. The
application of ethnographic methods to the study of curricular
content (rather than "social relations" in classrooms) was original
with the first reference. For further details about the gathering and
annotating of ethnographically derived data, see the second reference.
See the third reference for a discussion of the appropriateness of
ethnographic methods for critical educational scholarship. The
research reported herein included at least one full semester's
classroom observation in selected teachers' social studies classes.
Lectures were noted nearly verbatim; course materials were analyzed,
as were classroom patterns of interaction. Teachers gave information
through informal conversations over the course of one semester and
in tape-recorded, semi-structural interviews. Administrators who had
direct or indirect, formal or informal authority over subject fields,
teachers' evaluation or curriculum development were similarly
interviewed. The formal organizational hierarchy, the informal
organizational authority patterns and the locus of decision-making
were all the subject of documentary, interview and observational
scrutiny. Data for each school include the student populations, the
neighborhood and overall school climate, both at the time of
observations and, where possible, historically.
2 These high schools are located in one state in the American midwest.
The names used here for the schools, towns, teachers, students and
administrators are all pseudonyms. Descriptive details of individuals
or schools have occasionally been altered to protect anonymity. The
slight factual variations in descriptions preserve the spirit of what was
observed but hopefully prevent identification. The purpose of the
research was not to single out teachers or schools but to raise
analytical questions and refine the conceptualizations we have of
school processes.
3 No state policy dictated differential programs for categories of
students. A growing movement for programs for gifted children and
similar innovations for reading disabilities or other special needs
arose from university programs, federal funding possibilities or local
initiatives across the state. District choice was the basis for tracked or
heterogeneous groupings.

4 For further analysis of the de-skilling of teachers, see Chapter 7, and Apple, M. W. (1982c), *Education and Power*.
5 Table N2.1 (figures compiled by the state department of public instruction for one of the years of observation) shows several striking similarities and differences. The schools are quite similar in ethnic ratios and numbers of students going on to college; three are similar in size. They vary in per pupil expenditures. At the time of observations, no standard test scores for students were available for comparison across the four schools. Figures for enrollment of each high school and per pupil expenditures for each district were supplied by the statistical division of the state department of public instruction. Racial percentages were derived from a survey research instrument on student employment among junior or senior students at each school. The same database was the source for percentages of students expressing the intention of attending a 4-year college or a 2-year or technical college.

Table N2.1 *Comparisons of the four schools*

| School | Size | Districts' per pupil ($) | % to 4-yr college | % to 2-yr or tech. college | % of non-anglo students |
|--------|------|--------------------------|-------------------|----------------------------|-------------------------|
| Forest Hills | 2,280 | $2,702 | 57.3 | 39.2 | 7.2 |
| Maizeville | 1,050 | $2,644 | 34.7 | 73.9 | 1.5 |
| Nelson | 940 | $2,688 | 36.9 | 55.7 | 1.6 |
| Freeburg | 1,260 | $2,474 | 34.3 | 46.2 | 1.8 |

6 McNeil, L. (1977), "Economic dimensions of social studies curricula."
7 McNeil, L. (1981a), "Negotiating classroom knowledge: beyond achievement and socialization." This work elaborates the students' responses to tightly controlled classroom knowledge. McNeil, L. (1977), "Economic dimensions of social studies curricula." This documents research methodology and original findings.
8 The study which surveyed teachers, students and administrators during this important transitional period cannot be cited without compromising the anonymity of the school and its staff. The author is indebted to that researcher for the timeliness of his investigation. The appropriateness of the study, and the active role its data on student and teacher attitudes played in the public debates, however, is questionable given the potential divisiveness some of the questions might have inspired. Examples include such inquiries as "Do you think the students coming in from (school X) will have better grades (or more family income or better attendance) than the students from your class?"
9 Callahan, R. (1962), *Education and the Cult of Efficiency*; Wrigley, J. (1982), *Class Politics and Public Schools: Chicago 1900-1950*. The general history of aligning school administration with industrial management is the subject of the Callahan book. For political and

social class ramifications of these alignments in a particular city, see
the Wrigley book.

10 McNeil, L. (1984), "Lowering expectations: student employment and
its impact on curriculum," A survey of student employment in these
same schools, this work asked not only kinds of job, rates of pay and
length of employment but also reasons for working, perceived
conflicts with demands of school work, and methods of balancing
school and job.

## Chapter 3    Forest Hills High School

1 The names of the school, the teachers and students and some names
of courses are all changed to preserve the anonymity of the
participants.
2 McNeil, L. (1977), "Economic dimensions of social studies curricula:
curriculum as institutionalized knowledge." The details of instruction,
including extended transcripts of daily lectures and excerpts of
teacher and student interview transcripts, are found in this doctoral
dissertation, which also gives a detailed account of the ethnographic
methods and interview questions by which data were collected.
3 The Joint Council on Economics Education is a group of business,
university and government professionals, as well as social studies
teachers, whose organization promotes and creates curricula on
economics, provides workshops for teachers on economics topics,
administers tests to school districts requesting them to assess students'
knowledge of the economy and of economics terminology. Each state
has an affiliate organization to the national organization. The
primary assumption of the Joint Council is that economics is seldom
taught well because social studies (and other) teachers usually have
little background in the subject (thus the workshops) and have
inadequate resources to use in teaching economics.
4 McNeil, (1984), "Lowering expectations: student employment and its
impact on classroom knowledge." As a footnote to the comparative
research on school administration and its impact on classroom
knowledge, a survey was conducted to determine the extent and
nature of students' employment during school terms and to elicit
from students information about conflicts they felt between demands
of jobs and school work. Their reasons for working and the trade-offs
they felt they made between academic work and jobs are included in
the report of this research.

## Chapter 4    Freeburg High School

1 McNeil, L. (1984), "Lowering expectations: student employment and
its impact on classroom knowledge."

*Notes*

2 "Bulletin on graduation requirements," (related) State Department of Public Instruction, September, 1977.
3 Educational specialist thesis written by a teacher at Freeburg in 1980–1; the citation in full would divulge the identity of the teacher and school.

### Chapter 6  Nelson High School

1 Those teachers whose non-school time included business or community involvement tended to feel and seize more autonomy in their teaching. This pattern gave evidence of a gender-based dichotomy, especially since the non-school lives of most women teachers encountered during the research centered around family and household responsibilities. This relationship of teacher gender to de-skilling is further disclosed in Chapter 7, herein.
2 The analysis of student work is found in Linda M. McNeil "Lowering expectations: student employment and its impact on curriculum" (1984), Report 84–1, Madison, Wisconsin, Center for Education Research.

### Chapter 7  Defensive teaching and classroom control

1 A slightly different version of this chapter appears as Chapter 5 in Apple, Michael W. and Weis, Lois (eds) (1983), *Ideology and Practice in Schooling*, Philadelphia, Temple University Press.
2 Conversation with Geoffrey Whitty, Madison, Wisconsin, December, 1979.
3 See the *Public Issues* pamphlets series written by Donald Oliver and Fred M. Newmann, and published by Xerox.
4 A return visit to the school several semesters after the observation found Mr Lennon's students hard at work on an assignment. He had grown impatient with his *laissez-faire* methods for teaching economics theories and had begun to demand more of students, especially written work.
5 McNeil, L., "Structuring excellence: the potential for district-level intervention," research on magnet high schools, funded by National Institute of Education, 1983–6. The role of gender in the different degrees and processes of de-skilling any elementary and secondary teachers needs more direct, systematic investigation with a sample of teachers that includes more women.

### Chapter 8  Economies of learning

1 A slightly different version of this chapter was presented under the title "Client and consumer roles: the message of social studies

222

methods and content," Symposium on Locating Knowledge Across
the Curriculum, Annual Meetings of the American Educational
Research Association, Chicago, April 1985.

## Chapter 9   Contradictions of control

1 The teachers observed for this study worked prior to the imposition
of recently legislated controls, and in fact were in schools where, even
now, legislated controls over curriculum and testing of students are
not influential as compared to such legislation in many other states.
For a discussion of teachers working in a district whose centralized
controls became a model for state-level legislation of content and
evaluation procedures, see McNeil, L. M. (1985), "Teacher culture
and the irony of school reform."

2 My more recent research centers on the effects of district-level
interventions in curricula, with magnet schools as exemplars of
attempts to merge administrative and teacher efforts constructively in
order to improve students' access to knowledge in schools; that work
is funded by the National Institute of Education (US); reports are
forthcoming. In those schools, teachers supported by management to
specialize and build on their professional expertise for students
grouped by ability or academic speciality are confronted by
contradictory management directives to standardize. The
standardizations are meant to improve educational quality across
aggregates of students and schools; ironically, they undercut
initiatives of the best teachers, in their attempt to bring up the quality
of the worst teaching.

# Bibliography

Anyon, J. (1978), "Elementary social studies textbooks and legitimating knowledge," *Theory and Research in Social Education* VI, vol. 3, pp. 40–55.

Anyon, J. (1979), "Education, social 'structure' and the power of individuals," *Theory and Research in Social Education* VII, vol. 1.

Apple, M. W. (1980), "Social structure, ideology and curriculum," unpublished paper, University of Wisconsin, Madison.

Apple, M. W. (1982a), "Reproduction and contradiction in education," in Apple, M. W. (ed.), *Cultural and Economic Reproduction in Education: Essays on Class, Ideology and the State*, Boston and London, Routledge & Kegan Paul.

Apple, M. W. (1982b), "Curricular form and the logic of technical control," in Apple, M. W., (ed.), *Cultural and Economic Reproduction in Education: Essays on Class, Ideology and the State*, Boston and London, Routledge & Kegan Paul.

Apple, M. W. (1982c), *Education and Power*, Boston and London, Routledge & Kegan Paul.

Apple, M. W. (1979), *Ideology and Curriculum*, Boston and London, Routledge & Kegan Paul.

Apple, M. W. (1985), "Teaching and 'women's work': a comparative historical and ideological analysis," *Teachers College Record*, vol. 86, no. 3, pp. 455–74.

Arnot, M. and Whitty, G. (1982), "From reproduction to transformation: recent radical perspectives on the curriculum from the USA," *British Journal of Sociology of Education*, vol. 3, no. 1, March.

Bernstein, B. (1977), *Class, Codes and Control, Volume 3, Towards a Theory of Educational Transmissions*, London and Boston, Routledge & Kegan Paul.

Bossert, S. T. (1979), *Tasks and Social Relationships in Classrooms: A Study of Instructional Organization and Its Consequences*, ASA Rose Monograph Series, New York, Cambridge University Press.

Bourdieu, P. and Passeron, J. C. (1977), *Reproduction: In Education, Society and Culture*, London, Sage Publications.

Bowles, S. and Gintis, H. (1976), *Schooling in Capitalist America*, New York, Basic Books.

Boyer, E. (1983), *High School: A Report on Secondary Education in America*, The Carnegie Foundation, New York and London, Harper & Row.
Callahan, R. (1962), *Education and the Cult of Efficiency*, Chicago, University of Chicago Press.
Collins, R. (1979), *The Credential Society: An Historic Sociology of Education and Stratification*, New York, Academic Press.
Connell, R. W., Ashenden, D. J., Kessler, S. and Dowsett, G. W. (1982), *Making the Difference: Schools, Families, and Social Division*, London and Sydney, George Allen & Unwin.
Corwin, R. (1970), *Militant Professionalism: A Study of Organizational Conflict in High Schools*, New York, Appleton-Century-Crofts.
Cusick, P. (1973), *Inside High School: The Student's World*, New York, Holt, Rinehart & Winston.
Cusick, P. (1983), *The Egalitarian Ideal and the American High School: Studies of Three High Schools*, New York, Longman Inc.
Delamont, S. and Hamilton, D. (1976), "Classroom research: a critique and a new approach," in Stubbs, M. and Delamont, S. (eds), *Explorations in Classroom Observation*, London, John Wiley & Sons.
English, F. W. (1979), "Management practice as a key to curriculum leadership," *Educational Leadership*, March, pp. 408-9.
Everhart, R. B. (1980), *The In-Between Years: Student Life in a Junior High School*, University of California, Santa Barbara.
Fitzgerald, F. (1979), *America Revised*, Boston, Atlantic, Little-Brown.
Floden, R. E., Porter, A. C., Schmidt, W. H., Freeman, D. J. and Schwille, J. R. (1980), "Responses to curriculum pressures: a policy-capturing study of teacher decision about content," Institute for Research on Teaching, Michigan State University, East Lansing, Research Series #74.
Flude, M. and Ahier, J. (eds) (1974), *Educability, Schools and Ideology*, New York, Halsted Press, John Wiley & Sons.
Freire, P. (1971), *Pedagogy of the Oppressed*, New York, Herder & Herder.
Furlong, V. (1976), "Interaction sets in the classroom: toward a study of pupil knowledge," Hammersley, M. and Woods, P. (eds), *The Process of Schooling*, London, Open University Press, Routledge & Kegan Paul.
Giroux, H. A. (1979), "Schooling and the culture of positivism: notes on the death of history," *Educational Theory*, vol. 29, no. 4, pp. 263-84.
Giroux, H. A. (1980), "Critical theory and rationality in citizenship education," *Curriculum Inquiry*, vol. 10, no. 4, pp. 329-66.
Glaser, B. and Strauss, A. L. (1967), *The Discovery of Grounded Theory: Strategies for Qualitative Research*, Chicago, Aldine Press.
Goodlad, J. (1983), *A Place Called School*, New York, McGraw-Hill.
Gorz, A. (1977), "Technical intelligence and the capitalist division of labor," in Young, M. and Whitty, G. (eds), *State, Society and Schooling*, Sussex, Falmer Press.

225

*Bibliography*

Greene, M. (1978), *Landscapes of Learning*, New York, Teachers College Press.
Habermas, J. (1971), *Knowledge and Human Interests*, Boston, Beacon Press.
Habermas, J. (1973), *Legitimation Crisis*, Boston, Beacon Press.
Hammersley, M. (1977), *The Social Location of Teacher Perspectives*, Milton Keynes, Open University Press.
Harty, S. (1979), *Hucksters in the Classroom*, Center for the Study of Responsive Law, Washington, DC.
Hogan, D. (1982) "Education and class formation: the peculiarities of the Americans," in Apple, M. W. (ed.), *Cultural and Economic Reproduction in Education: Essays on Class, Ideology and the State*, London, Routledge & Kegan Paul.
Huebner, D. (1970), "Curriculum as the accessibility of knowledge," paper given at Curriculum Theory Group, March 2, Minneapolis, Minnesota.
Ignatovich, F. R., Cusick, P. and Ray, J. E. (1979), "Value belief patterns of teachers and those administrators engaged in attempts to influence teaching," Institute for Research on Teaching, Michigan State University, East Lansing, Research Series #43.
Jackson, P. (1971), *Life in Classrooms*, New York, Holt, Rinehart & Winston.
Karabel, J. and Halsey, A. H. (1977), *Power and Ideology in Education*, London, Oxford Press.
Katz, M. B. (1968), *The Irony of Early School Reform*, Boston, Beacon Press.
Keddie, N. (1971), "Classroom knowledge," in Young, M. F. D. (ed.), *Knowledge and Control*, London, Collier Macmillan.
King, N. R. (1976), "The hidden curriculum and socialization of kindergarten children," unpublished thesis, University of Wisconsin-Madison.
Kirkendall, R. S. (1975), "The status of history in the schools," *Journal of American History*, September, pp. 557–8.
Larkin, R. W. (1979), *Suburban Youth in Cultural Crisis*, New York and Oxford, Oxford University Press.
Lightfoot, S. L. (1983), *The Good High School*, New York, Basic Books.
Lipsitz, J. (1984), *Successful Schools for Young Adolescents*, New Brunswick, Transaction Books.
Lortie, D. (1975), *Schoolteacher*, Chicago, University of Chicago Press.
MacDonald, M. (1977), *The Curriculum and Cultural Reproduction*, Milton Keynes, Open University Press.
McNeil, K. E. (1978), "Understanding organizational power: building on the Weberian legacy," *Administrative Science Quarterly*, March.
McNeil, L. M. (1977), "Economic dimensions of social studies curricula: curriculum as institutionalized knowledge," unpublished dissertation, University of Wisconsin-Madison, revised for publication as *Making Knowledge Inaccessible*.
McNeil, L. M. (1981a), "Negotiating classroom knowledge: beyond

achievement and socialization," *Journal of Curriculum Studies*, vol. 13, no. 4.

McNeil, L. M. (1981b), "On the possibility of teachers as the source of emancipatory pedagogy," *Curriculum Inquiry*, vol. 11, no. 3, pp. 205–10.

McNeil, L. M. (1981c), "Response to Henry Giroux's 'Pedagogy, pessimism and the politics of conformity'," *Curriculum Inquiry*, vol. 11, no. 4, pp. 393–4.

McNeil, L. M. (1983), "Defensive teaching and classroom control," in Apple, M. W. and Weis, L. (eds), *Ideology and Practice in Schooling*, Philadelphia, Temple University Press.

McNeil, L. M. (1984), "Lowering expectations: student employment and its impact on curriculum," Center for Education Research, University of Wisconsin, Madison, Report 84–1.

McNeil, L. M. (1985), "Teacher culture and the irony of school reform," in Altbach, P., Kelly, G., and Weis, L. (eds), *Perspectives on Excellence*, Buffalo, Prometheus Books.

McPherson, G. (1972), *Small Town Teacher*, Cambridge, Mass., Harvard University Press.

March, J. and Olsen, J. P. (1976), *Ambiguity and Choice in Organizations*, Universities-forlaget, Bergen, Norway.

Mehan, H. (1979), *Learning Lessons*, Cambridge, Mass., Harvard University Press.

Metz, M. H. (1978), *Classrooms and Corridors: the Crisis of Authority in Desegregated Secondary Schools*, Berkeley, University of California Press.

Meyer, J. W. and Rowan, B. (1978), "The structure of educational organizations," in Meyer, M. *et al.* (eds), *Environments and Organizations*, San Francisco, Jossey Bass, pp. 78–109.

National Commission on Excellence in Education (1983), *A Nation at Risk*, Washington, DC, US Department of Education, US Government Printing Office.

Oliver, D. and Newmann, F. M. (1967–73), *Public Issues*, Columbus, Xerox Corporation.

Ollman, B. (1972), *Alienation: Marx's Conception of Man in Capitalist Society*, Cambridge, Cambridge University Press.

Popkewitz, T. S., Tabachnik, B. R. and Wehlage, G. (1980), *School Reform and Institutional Life: A Case Study in Individually Guided Instruction*, Wisconsin Research and Development Center for Student Diversity and Schooling, Madison, Wisconsin, September.

Porter, A. C. *et al.* (1978), "Impact on what? The importance of content covered," Institute for Research on Teaching, Michigan State University, East Lansing, Research Series #2.

Porter, A. C., Schwille, J. R. *et al.* (1979), "Teacher autonomy and the control of content taught," Institute for Research on Teaching, Michigan State University, East Lansing, Research Series #4.

Rist, R. (1978), *The Invisible Children: School Integration in American Society*, Cambridge, Mass., Harvard University Press.

Rothschild, E. (1981), "Reagan and the real America," *New York Review of Books*, vol. XXVIII, no. 2, February 15, 12ff.

Rutter, M. *et al.* (1979), *Fifteen Thousand Hours: Secondary Schools and Their Effects on Children*, Cambridge, Mass., Harvard University Press.

Sarason, S. (1971), *The Culture of the School and the Problem of Change*, Boston, Allyn & Bacon.

Schlechty, P. (1976), *Teaching and Social Behavior: Toward an Organizational Theory of Instruction*, Boston, Allyn & Bacon.

Schwille, J., Porter, A. *et al.* (1979), "Factors influencing teachers' decisions about what to teach: sociological perspectives," Institute for Research on Teaching, Michigan State University, East Lansing, Research Series #26.

Sharp, R. and Green, A. (1975), *Education and Social Control*, London and Boston, Routledge & Kegan Paul.

Shaver, J. P. (1979), "Political and economic socialization in elementary school social studies textbooks: a reaction," *Theory and Research in Social Education*, vol. VII, no. 1.

Shaver, J. P., Davis, O. L., Jr and Helburn, S. W. (1978), *An Interpretive Report on the Status of Pre-College Social Studies Education Based on Three NSF-funded Studies*, report to the National Science Foundation, National Council for the Social Studies, Washington, DC.

Sizer, T. (1984), *Horace's Compromise: the Dilemma of the American High School*, New York, Houghton Mifflin.

Spring, J. (1972), *Education and the Rise of the Corporate State*, Boston, Beacon Press.

Swidler, A. (1979), *Organization Without Authority*, Cambridge, Mass., Harvard University Press.

Tapper, T. (1976), *Political Education and Stability: Elite Responses to Political Conflict*, London, John Wiley & Sons.

Tapper, T. and Salter, B. (1979), "Political education in Britain and the US: comparative lessons," *Teaching Politics*, London and Beverly Hills, Sage Publications, vol. 8, pp. 223–37.

Taylor, S. (1980), "School experience and student perspectives: a study of some effects of secondary school organizations," *Educational Review*, vol. 32, no. 1.

Tyler, R. (1949), *Basic Principles of Curriculum and Instruction*, Chicago, University of Chicago Press.

Valli, L. (1983), "Becoming clerical workers: business education and the culture of femininity," in Apple, M. and Weis, L. (eds) *Ideology and Practice in Schooling*, Philadelphia, Temple University Press.

Vavrus, M. J. (1979), "The relationship of teacher alienation to school workplace characteristics and career stages of teachers," Institute for Research on Teaching, Michigan State University, East Lansing, Research Series #36.

Warwick, D. (1974), "Ideologies, integration and conflicts of meaning," in Flude, M. and Ahier, J. (eds), *Educability, Schools and Ideology*, New York, Halstead Press, John Wiley & Sons, pp. 86–111.

Webb, K. (1979), "Classroom interaction and political education," *Teaching Politics*, London and Beverly Hills, Sage Publications, vol. 8, pp. 221–32.

Weick, K. (1976), "Educational organizations as loosely coupled systems," *Administrative Science Quarterly*, March, pp. 1–19.

Whitty, G. (1976), "Studying society for social change or for social control?" in Whitty, G. and Young, M. (eds), *Explorations in the Politics of School Knowledge*, Driffield, England, Nafferton Books.

Wiley, K. B. (1977), *The Status of Pre-College Science, Mathematics and Social Science Education: 1955–75. Volume 3: Social Science Education*, Social Science Education Consortium, National Science Foundation, Boulder, Colorado.

Willis, P. (1977), *Learning to Labour*, Farnborough, Saxon House.

Wolcott, H. F. (1973), *The Man in the Principal's Office*, New York, Holt, Rinehart & Winston.

Wolcott, H. F. (1977), *Teachers vs Technocrats*, Center for Educational Policy and Management, University of Oregon, Eugene.

Woods, P. (1979), *The Divided School*, London and Boston, Routledge & Kegan Paul.

Wrigley, J. (1982), *Class Politics and Public Schools: Chicago 1900–1950*, New Brunswick, Rutgers University Press.

# Index

230

Forest Hills, 31, 44, 86-7; at Freeburg, 39-40, 43-4; and innovation, 116; at Maizeville, 49-52; at Nelson, 136-7; and teacher rewards, 51-2, 86; and teacher sanction, 52; *see also* school administration
principals: and control goals, 93; general, 81
Progressives: general, 73, 181, 203; Progressive party, 203

reform movement (1980s), xvii, 3, 9, 209, 215, 223
Republicans, 201

school administration: administrative context of school knowledge, 80-3, 93-5; administrative structure, 31-4, 38-45, 48-54, 55-9, 63; distance from instruction, 22; involvement with instruction, 22; management objectives, 33
school knowledge: and bureaucratic structures, 161; and critical scholarship, 12; fragmentation of, 167-9; mystification of, 169-70; and omission, 171-4; and school structure, xi-xiii, 3-18 (*see also* curriculum); simplification of, 174-80; and transformation of cultural context (*see also* transformation of culture), *see also* credibility
school management: general, xvii; scientific management of, 6; *see also* school administration
school organization, history of, xii, xx, 67
Sharp and Green, 74
Sizer, Theodore, 209
social class: distribution of knowledge, the, 163-4; general, 78
social control: as behavior control, 45, 124, 166; correspondence of school practice to elite, 5-7; as credentialing, 8, 45, 215; and history of high school organization,

8, 15; and school knowledge, 176-7, 188, 193; in schools, xviii; and the social efficiency movement, 4-7, 215; in tension with educational purposes, 45, 209-13; *see also* school structure and order
social efficiency: and education in Chicago, 6; and education and role of superintendent, 32; and education and social class, 6, 7; and school organization, 5-7
Social Science Education Consortium, 162
social studies curriculum: as elective, 96; energy, study of, 205-6; general, 168; Gilded Age, 127-8; history (Civil War), 52 (*see also* economics curriculum and US history curriculum); history (Good Neighbor Policy), 72; history (New Deal), 172; history (Viet Nam), 171-2; literature (Erik Erikson's Eight Stages of Man), 107; literature (*Grapes of Wrath*, the), 72; *see also* contemporary social issues curriculum, women's studies, world history curriculum, US history curriculum, economics curriculum
social studies: and faculty gender, 26; general, xix; instructional resources, 130; status of, 165; teaching, 70; teaching and coaches, 83; teaching curriculum, 72-3, 168; teaching strategies, 177; *see also* economics curriculum and world history curriculum
socialization, xviii, xx, 5, 15, 73
Sputnik, 164
Stone, I. F., 140
stratification in labor force, xvix
students: and administrators' views on, 53; as clients, 78, 171, 192-7, 205; as consumers of school knowledge, 129, 197, 207; deskilling of, 207; differences, 74-5,